Dear Reader:

The book you are about to read is the latest bestseller from the St. Martin's True Crime Library, the imprint *The New York Times* calls "the leader in true crime!" Each month, we offer you a fascinating account of the latest, most sensational crime that has captured the national attention. St. Martin's is the publisher of bestselling true crime author and crime journalist Kieran Crowley, who explores the dark, deadly links between a prominent Manhattan surgeon and the disappearance of his wife fifteen years earlier in THE SURGEON'S WIFE. Suzy Spencer's BREAKING POINT guides readers through the tortuous twists and turns in the case of Andrea Yates, the Houston mother who drowned her five young children in the family's bathtub. In Edgar Award-nominated DARK DREAMS, legendary FBI profiler Roy Hazelwood and bestselling crime author Stephen G. Michaud shine light on the inner workings of America's most violent and depraved murderers. In the book you now hold, THE OFFICER'S WIFE, veteran true crime author Michael Fleeman recounts a story of a devoted wife who betrayed her husband and evaded the law for months, letting her lover stay in jail for the crime she orchestrated.

St. Martin's True Crime Library gives you the stories behind the headlines. Our authors take you right to the scene of the crime and into the minds of the most notorious murderers to show you what really makes them tick. St. Martin's True Crime Library paperbacks are better than the most terrifying thriller, because it's all true! The next time you want a crackling good read, make sure it's got the St. Martin's True Crime Library logo on the spine—you'll be up all night!

Charles E. Spicer, Jr.
Executive Editor, St. Martin's True Crime Library

ST. MARTIN'S TRUE CRIME LIBRARY TITLES
BY MICHAEL FLEEMAN

Laci

"If I Die..."

The Stranger in My Bed

Over the Edge

Deadly Mistress

The Officer's Wife

Killer Bodies

Seduced by Evil

THE OFFICER'S WIFE

A True Story of Unspeakable Betrayal and Cold-Blooded Murder

MICHAEL FLEEMAN

St. Martin's Paperbacks

THE OFFICER'S WIFE

Cover photos of Officer Theer courtesy *Fayetteville Observer* / Polaris. Photo of Michelle Theer courtesy AP/Wide World Photos.

For information address St. Martin's Press, 175 Fifth Avenue, New York, NY 10010.

ISBN: 0-312-99259-9
EAN: 80312-99259-0

Printed in the United States of America

St. Martin's Paperbacks edition / July 2006

St. Martin's Paperbacks are published by St. Martin's Press, 175 Fifth Avenue, New York, NY 10010.

10 9 8 7 6

1

She could be anybody she wanted to be. Fantasy and reality were intertwined like lovers. Time and date had no meaning. She could go anywhere, set any limit. She didn't even have to be a she. A few keystrokes, and suddenly she was no longer lost and numb.

"Sexy brunette seeks rendezvous man," she typed. "Attractive, intelligent, very sensual professional seeks regular activity partner two to three times a week for long, hot, passionate encounters."

She gave her vital statistics: age 28, white, agnostic, college educated, employed full-time and a resident of Fayetteville, with interests in dancing, dining, movies, music, photography, theater and travel.

"Looking for emotionally stable, very attractive, physically fit, intellectually stimulating, fun-loving man who is not going bald, 25 to 35, Caucasian, D/D free"—drug and disease free—"Over six feet tall," she wrote, using online shorthand. "Must live or work in Fayetteville. Please do not write if you live in R/D"—Raleigh/Durham.

"I turn heads," she continued. "If you do too and meet all the above requirements, let's meet for coffee and see what happens next. Will only respond to inquiries that are interesting and stimulating. Will not reply to messages such as 'tell me what you're looking for' or to anyone with crude screen names. Discretion is a must."

Sometimes she went by Susan, other times Cheryl. Her computer screen name was marriedbrunette.

No sooner did she send out her ad than the replies flooded her inbox, the sexual laws of supply and demand in action. She knew intimately this world of lonely men, and even lonelier women. She'd grown up in this world. She'd married into it, endured it, loathed it. Now she'd found a way to exploit it.

"Hello, my name is Brian," one man wrote back in a reply that was typical.

> I'm also married and would like to find someone for discreet encounters on a regular basis. I do meet all your requirements that you stated in your ad. I'm not much over six feet tall so I don't know how much you care about that. I do have all of my thick hair and I have all my teeth, too. Laugh. Does that count for bonus points? Laugh.

Apologetic in his pitch, Brian braced himself for rejection even as he courted her. "I do have a hard time believing any man in Fayetteville being able to turn a woman's head," he wrote, and it was true. This was a military town.

> I'm good looking but that may be excessive for me to say. Women here in Fayetteville don't exactly have a hard time getting a man's attention, much less a good-looking woman. I don't want to waste your time so I'm being upfront and honest. I would like to hear from you and possibly meet some time. I know you probably have a lot of responses so you can be very selective. If by chance we meet, I believe we could have a

> good time b/c I'm very likeable. Thanks for your time.
> Take care,
> Brian.

She did get a lot of responses. "Hi, Cheryl," wrote Catman_NC, the NC standing for North Carolina.

> I saw your ad and wanted to respond. I am a single white male, 31, five foot 10, 170 pounds with brown hair and blue eyes. I live in Fayetteville, North Carolina. I am also very nice, honest, discreet, clean, drug and disease free. I would love to talk with you. I think that I meet all of your qualifications except for one, since I am not over six foot. Anyway, if you are still interested, please respond back. I think that you could have some good times together. Hope to hear from you soon.

"You sound great," wrote another man, whose screen name was Chillslave, an appropriate monicker.

> Now, I don't know if any this will appeal to you or not, but let me tell you about myself. I'm 35 years of age, SWM, attractive, I've modeled, athletic, I've played college sports, intelligent, multi-degreed, professional, employed and funny.
>
> I do have one flaw, however. I'm sexually submissive.
>
> I simply adore to submit to an attractive woman and to lick, massage and smell her feet, suck her toes and orally satisfy her pussy and perform other services as she orders. I thought I'd tell you this up front since I don't want any problems with sexual compatibility.
>
> I don't know if you were into having a good looking guy under your command. For all I know you

> have one now. But I know sometimes women like to sort of have things their own way and get guys to do things for them. Plus, men have often used women as slaves historically or even today sometimes. So I thought you might want to turn the tables and put a good-looking guy in his place.
>
> I'm pretty normal otherwise, but sexually I'm submissive and it's kind of hard to approach women in bars, etc., and explain this to them face-to-face. So that's why I'm using the Internet.
>
> If this interests you, please reply. If this doesn't interest you or if you're totally repulsed, I understand. I know you don't expect this kind of mail in your box and I sincerely apologize if this has offended you in any way.
>
> Submissively, David.

She would receive a lot of this kind of email—the line between outgoing and outrageous blurry in cyberspace.

"You sound like a very beautiful and interesting person. I'm a captain in the Air Force. You probably hear us fly over your house," he wrote. "I have a passion for life," he continued, "and love great conversation, holding hands, cuddling and long passionate kisses. Unfortunately, I have a void in my life where passion is concerned. I'm personally in a dead relationship that is going nowhere."

She knew all about Air Force captains and the planes they flew. It wasn't the roar of the engines she heard. It was the months of silence that followed.

She read on.

"Hello," wrote a man giving the name Tim, "I also live in Fayetteville. Have you seen my pictures anywhere on the net? Well, I hope to hear from you soon."

This was more like it. Out of the clouds, down to a place she craved.

Randyclimbs described himself as six-foot-one, brown hair, blue eyes with 205 pounds of athletic build:

> I have an incredibly busy schedule and don't get out much. I figured meeting somebody this way might be easier than going to a bar and competing over women with military guys. My job is currently what keeps me so busy. I have about two months of nonstop work and sometimes just have the energy to put into the above scenario. I am in the medical services field and am completing a portion of studies for my field. So I have told you a little. What about you? What is your real name and what do you do? Obviously we met through the personals, so does that mean you are going out for personal satisfaction and gratitude with no regrets? Please explain. I am intrigued.

Years later, a psychiatrist would attribute her fascination with online couplings to loneliness, depression, low self-esteem and anxiety—the emotional wreckage from a bad marriage and a jarring life change. She tried in vain to medicate the pain away. Where Xanax and Ambien failed, she hoped the Internet would succeed.

Had it stopped there, with a provocative personal ad and sexually charged banter with eager and anonymous men, it could have been written off as kinky fun, escapism that was arguably harmless enough as long as her husband didn't come home from the skies and find out.

But she took it a step further.

2

Sergeant Ralph Clinkscales got the call at home at 11:30 p.m. He dressed quickly and warmly for a long December night. It was eight days before Christmas. Temperatures hovered around freezing. Frost covered roofs and windows.

The drive to the crime scene took fifteen minutes. He pulled his car into a parking lot at 2500 Raeford Road, where already the business of murder investigation was under way. Emergency vehicles filled the parking lot: police cruisers from the Fayetteville Police Department, a fire truck and a paramedic vehicle. Temporary floodlights cast an eerie glow. Officers and medics huddled against the cold. Yellow crime-scene tape marked off a large section of the pavement leading up to the rear of a two-story office building. At the foot of an outdoor stairwell was the only non-official car in the lot: a burgundy Ford Explorer.

Near the front passenger-side tire of the SUV lay a body on the pavement in a large pool of blood.

It was not unusual for Clinkscales to get such a late-night call. Murder came frequently to Fayetteville, North Carolina. It was called Fayette Nam back in the 1970s, the last stop for thousands of Fort Bragg soldiers before the jungles of Southeast Asia. The town gave the boys what they thought they needed: strip clubs, bars and easy access to drugs. Three decades of renewal projects and master plans, and the dynamics are the same: Base town blues. In North Carolina, Fayetteville usually ranks at the bad ends of the charts: highest in crime, lowest in employment.

As University of North Carolina anthropologist Catherine Lutz noted in her book *Homefront*, Fayetteville, as a neighbor of the 160,000-acre Fort Bragg Army post, "is both a city of cosmopolitan substance and humane striving, and the dumping ground for the problems of the American century of war and empire, the corner of the American house where the wounds of war have pierced most deeply and are most visible."

All too often the darkest of those corners looks like it did this night: a floodlight-bathed parking lot with a body on the pavement.

But what was odd about this crime scene, Detective Clinkscales reflected as he got out of his car, was that this wasn't one of those parts of town that gave Fayetteville its bad rap. This was in the good area, away from the line of strip clubs outside town, located across the street from the Highland Country Club. Judges, business people and military personnel at the rank of captain and above had homes nearby. The parking lot by day was filled with the upscale cars of the professionals who worked in the two-story buildings in the complex. Crime came here infrequently, if at all. Only the occasional panhandler wandered by—and even that wouldn't be a problem on a night as cold as this.

Clinkscales walked up to the crime scene and received a briefing.

The 911 call had been made at 10:57 p.m. from a Video Hut movie rental store about 200 yards away on Raeford. Store manager Chondra Fuzie and manager trainee Joyce Smith were in the back office waiting out the final minutes of a very slow night. It was December 17, 2000, a Sunday. If anyone came at all, they would be returning a video from the weekend.

The employees happened to look at a security monitor

from the cameras trained inside the store. That's when they saw the image of a woman leaning across the rental counter.

"Is anyone in here?" she yelled.

The employees came out of the office. They saw an attractive brown-haired woman dressed for a holiday party: short skirt, black tights and a colorful Christmas sweater decorated with stars and Santas.

The woman wore no shoes.

Blood covered her face and hands.

She panted and spoke in loud bursts. She was so upset that the employees struggled to understand her. She was saying something about needing to call 911.

Joyce Smith dialed the emergency number on a cordless phone, spoke to the operator, and handed the receiver to the woman. Between gasps, she said in a high-pitched voice that her husband had been shot outside a building down the street at 2500 Raeford Road and she needed help immediately.

The woman gave the phone back and darted out of the store in her stocking feet just as Mitchell Nance arrived to return videos he had rented for the weekend. He asked the employees about the woman who'd swept by him. They told him that she had called police to report that her husband had been shot at 2500 Raeford. Nance knew the address. His accountant had an office there.

Nance drove down Raeford a couple of blocks and pulled into the back parking lot, empty except for one car, a red Ford Explorer, parked under a street lamp near a two-story office building. Next to the vehicle was a sobbing woman kneeling over a man lying at the foot of an outdoor stairwell.

Surrounding the man was a pool of blood that flowed down to the front tire of the Explorer several feet away.

Nance got out of his car and went up to the woman, asking if she was all right. She told him she was. But the man was badly wounded. Blood soaked his head. He didn't seem to be breathing. Nance checked the man's pulse. He had none.

Nance asked the woman what had happened.

"Someone has shot my husband," she said.

Nance told the woman he was going to seek help. Just as he started to dial his cell phone, he saw the emergency vehicles arrive in response to the 911 call, first a fire truck, then two Fayetteville Police Department cruisers, then a paramedic truck, then more police cars.

Among those first to arrive was Officer Michael Allen Reid, who had been on routine Sunday night patrol for the Fayetteville Police Department when he got a radio call of a reported shooting. He raced to 2500 Raeford Road, getting there within three minutes, at shortly before 11 p.m. Just behind him came paramedics.

In the parking lot behind the building, he saw a woman cradling the head of a man lying in blood. When Reid got out of his car he could hear the woman talking to the man.

"It's OK, honey, it's going to be all right," she was saying.

The man's face was pale and he didn't seem to be breathing.

Reid pulled the woman away as a firefighter and two paramedics approached.

"Let them help him," he said.

The rescue people cut away the man's clothes—light dress shirt and dark slacks—and found wounds to his chest, buttock, left leg and head, which gushed blood. The man's heart had stopped and he wasn't breathing. They attempted to resuscitate, but it was hopeless. He had lost too much blood.

Officer Reid led the woman away from the bloodied man and asked her what had happened.

She told him that she'd gone into her office on the second floor of the building while her husband waited out in the Explorer. While in her office, she'd heard loud noises outside. She knew they hadn't come from a car backfiring, because they were several pops in a row. It had to be gunfire. She came outside, and, from the top of the stairs, saw her husband on the ground.

Reid asked if the woman had seen anybody in the area. She said she wasn't sure, but might have seen some movement out of the corner of her eye.

"If you did see anyone," Reid asked her, "which way did they go?"

She pointed to a low hedge at the back of the building.

"Through the bushes," she said.

On the other side of the bushes was Raeford Road, deserted at this hour and, beyond that the country club and golf course, dark.

Up walked another police officer, Jennifer Sylvester, who had arrived shortly after Reid and the paramedics. Sylvester had also been on patrol when she got a radio call before 11 p.m. to respond to a 911 call at a Video Hut store. The employees there directed Sylvester down the street to the office building.

"Just take her over to the patrol car," Reid told Sylvester. "Stay with her."

Sylvester noted that the woman, now crying, had on a sweater and no shoes in the frigid night. Sylvester placed her in the heated patrol car. When the woman settled down, Sylvester continued the questioning.

The woman said her name was Michelle Theer and that she worked in that building. The man on the ground was her husband, Frank Martin "Marty" Theer, an Air Force captain who piloted planes out of Pope Air Force Base, adjacent to the northern border of Fort Bragg.

Michelle repeated her account: that she had been in her second-floor corner office to get something when she heard the series of shots outside. She rushed out of the building through the side door at the top of the stairwell and saw Marty at the foot of the stairs. Michelle said she'd tried to get back in the building to call for help, but the metal door had locked behind her and she couldn't get in—in her haste she had left her keys on her desk and was now locked out.

Michelle said she'd run down the street to the Video Hut store to call for help, somehow losing her dress shoes along the way. After speaking to the 911 operator from the video store, she had returned to her husband. That was when Nance had shown up, followed by Reid, the paramedics and Officer Sylvester.

Sylvester watched the woman closely to see if she was in shock and needed medical care. Michelle was upset, but didn't appear to require hospitalization. This was confirmed when one of the paramedics checked her, finding her blood pressure and pulse both normal despite the night's traumatic event. The officer had Michelle stay in the patrol car for now.

Outside, Reid radioed for a supervisor to oversee what was now clearly a homicide investigation. As he spoke, another patrol car pulled into the parking lot. Reid shooed it away because it was getting too close to the body.

The car was driven by Officer Kurt Richter and his trainee, both of the K-9 unit. In the back was their police dog, a German shepherd named Whiskey.

Like Sylvester, these officers also had initially responded to the Video Hut and were directed to the parking lot. Richter parked farther away and he and the trainee helped Reid secure the scene, setting up the yellow tape, keeping other police cars and medics away.

That completed, the K-9 officer went to Sylvester's patrol car and spoke with Michelle Theer to see if she had seen anything or anybody whom Officer Richter could put his dog on.

Michelle was still crying off and on, but was not hysterical. She seemed to understand Richter and could answer his questions clearly. She repeated the story about hearing the shots and going outside the office to see her husband on the ground and a possible flash of activity out of the corner of her eye. She told Richter she thought that what she'd seen was someone running across the grass by the hedges in the direction of Raeford Road.

By now it was 11:18 p.m., about twenty minutes after the 911 call. Richter led Whiskey to the break in the hedges where Michelle thought she might have first seen something. The bushes were about three feet high and three feet wide, just east of the building, about four feet from the man's body. It was the perfect place for a shooter to hide and the best place to start with the dog.

Whiskey searched for the recent smell left behind by a person, an odor that to a dog is as distinctive as a fingerprint. Whiskey immediately picked up a scent. Richter knew it wasn't from one of the police officers in the area, because the dog didn't go toward any of them. Instead, Whiskey followed the scent partly around the office building to where no officers had yet gone, then trotted over to an adjacent office building and sniffed around some bushes. Suddenly, he cut across the grass toward Raeford Road.

Now scampering so fast that Richter struggled to keep up, Whiskey crossed the four lanes of Raeford and went into the parking lot of the Highland Country Club. The dog followed the scent around to the side of the country club building, seemed to lose it, then picked it up again behind the building on a sidewalk that ran alongside a fairway.

Whiskey led Richter about a third of the way down the fairway, then went across the grass and into a paved cul-de-sac. It was a construction site on Longleaf Drive, a third of a mile from the body. Richter was winded from the nineteen-minute run in the cold night. Whiskey nosed around the street. The scent ended, as if somebody had gotten in a car next to the golf course and driven away.

As Whiskey was searching the golf course, other police officers were pouring into the crime scene. One investigator, who had arrived while the paramedics were still working on the victim, and Reid and Richter were securing the crime scene, interviewed Mitchell Nance, the video store customer. Nance said he hadn't seen anything else at the scene—nobody running through bushes—just a distraught woman and a man in a pool of blood. Also interviewed were the two employees, who recounted how, about a half-hour earlier, the woman with blood on her face and hands had come in needing to call 911. Police then canvassed the neighborhood.

One resident, Jacquelyn McBride, said she was on her sofa watching television at 10:50 p.m. when she'd heard three gunshots. The noise had sent her dog into a barking fit. She said it had sounded like the shots were coming from the rear of her house; the parking lot of the office building is about fifty yards away.

McBride calmed down her dog, then looked out her bathroom window in the direction from which the shots had come. In the office parking lot, she saw a burgundy car—the Theers' Explorer—and a silver SUV. A man in a plaid shirt had a cell phone to his ear and was walking around the silver car. That turned out to be Mitchell Nance.

The McBrides' next-door neighbors, John and Amy Corner, had also heard shots. They'd counted three at first, followed by a pause during which John had walked to his back door to look outside. He then heard what he'd thought was a fourth shot that had sounded louder than the previous ones.

Ramsey Lewis, whose home was located on McBain Drive, twenty-five yards away from the crime scene, with only a chain-link fence separating the properties, said he'd been home sick with the flu, lying on his living room sofa watching "some kind of rap video thing" on VH1 when he'd heard a series of gunshots, so loud he could feel the vibrations in his chest.

"Man, somebody is getting killed," he'd told his fiancée.

Lewis believed the shooter seemed to fire deliberately:

Bang!, pause, bang! pause, bang! a longer pause, bang!—four shots he could recall.

Back in Officer Sylvester's patrol car, yet another Fayetteville PD investigator, Jeffrey Huston, spoke with Michelle Theer.

It was up to him to make the official notification.

He looked at her and said the paramedics had done everything they could.

Her husband was dead.

At first, she had no reaction. Her face went blank. Then she cried for ten straight minutes.

When she recovered, Huston asked her yet again what had happened. For the fourth time, she repeated her account of hearing the gunshots and finding her husband at the foot of the stairs, though now she added some details: she said that when she'd gone down the stairs to check on her husband, he was still alive, breathing, but not talking. She also said that she had first gone to the building next door to call for help, but nobody was there. She'd then gone to a gas station on the corner, but it was closed for the night. That's when she'd run to the Video Hut.

Michelle Theer then agreed to comply with a simple test. A crime-scene technician placed sticky tape on her hands, front and back. The tapes would be sent off to the state crime lab to determine whether Michelle's hands contained any gunshot residue.

This brought Sergeant Ralph Clinkscales up to speed. He now knew all there was to know about the murder of the man at the foot of the stairwell, and of the police work that had been done prior to his arrival. The investigation would be his from now on.

Clinkscales walked over to the body. The victim was a

young man, no doubt handsome in life, trim, with an athletic build, chiseled face, brown hair cut Air Force regulation short. He lay on his back, his head turned to the right, his eyes closed, with that slightly dumb look so often seen in those killed suddenly. His arms were flailed out on the pavement, though they had likely been moved into that position by the paramedics. The man had been dressed for a holiday party. He had on a gray dress shirt, dark slacks, dress shoes, a Christmas tie and bright red suspenders covered in sequins. The pants and shirt had been ripped by the paramedics.

He lay at the base of a metal staircase that rose about fourteen feet above him to the back door of the two-story office building. This was the rear of the building, which spanned to the right, with a row of top-floor windows overlooking the parking lot. It would have been dark when he was shot, but not pitch black. There was a street light nearby and a light over the door at the top of the stairs.

Putting on latex gloves, Clinkscales began examining the body. One bullet had traveled through the left forearm and into the chest. Another had struck the right lower back. A third had hit the right buttock and a fourth had entered the left thigh. These four wounds were deceptively small—tiny red spots—and had caused very little external bleeding. But Clinkscales knew the damage inside the body could be severe.

The wound causing the external blood loss was a shot to the back of the head behind the left ear, with the bullet exiting out the top of the head. A reddish rash had formed around the wound, the sign of gunpowder burn. This was a point-blank execution-style shot.

Near the victim's body were two brass casings from a 9mm Luger—a common semiautomatic pistol. The three other casings from the other wounds couldn't be found—either they were hidden somewhere in the darkness, or the shooter had picked them up.

With his gloved hand, Clinkscales reached into the back pocket of the man's dress slacks and pulled out a wallet. The North Carolina driver's license showed that the man was in fact Frank Martin Theer, age 31, of Fayetteville. This, combined with the wife's statements, would be sufficient to confirm identity.

Clinkscales also found a pilot's license that certified Captain Theer to fly single- and multi-engine planes by instrument. Another card showed he had passed a motorcycle safety course. In addition, there were a Pope Air Force Base fitness card, a Delta Airlines frequent flyer card, a card with a list of work phone numbers at Pope, a library card, a credit card and a photograph of an elderly couple.

There was also cash: $66, in three twenties, a five and a one. Not a fortune, but people had been killed for less. Also, in one of the front pockets was a set of keys, including what appeared to be the ignition key and electronic door key to the pricey Ford Explorer parked just feet away. Whoever had done this hadn't taken Frank Theer's money or SUV.

Also in the wallet was a receipt from a Quick Stop gas station. It showed a purchase of 15.107 gallons of unleaded at $1.359 a gallon, for a total sale of $20.53. The gas was purchased at the pump on the Visa card of Michelle Theer.

The time of the transaction was 10:42 p.m.—just fifteen minutes before Michelle had called 911.

Finally, tucked amid the other cards was this little printed note:

To The Love of My Life:

You were my knight in shining armor right from the very start. One look at your leather jacket, and STUD, you stole my heart! All these years together, you've made all my dreams come true. You're my one and only Zoomie and I'll never stop loving you. Wher-

ever your silver wings take you: Saudi, Iceland or Kuwait, I'll be home waiting for you, never losing faith.

Leaving the body, Clinkscales walked up the metal staircase, finding what appeared to be tiny blood drops at the upper steps. On the landing, he found what looked like the red sequins from the suspenders. A hole on the side of the building just above the doorframe appeared to have come from a bullet.

Clinkscales theorized that a shooter at the base of the stairs had fired up on Marty Theer while he was at the top of the stairwell, then kept shooting at him as he'd stumbled down. When Marty was on the ground, the assailant had fired the final, coup de grâce to the head.

Clinkscales snapped off the latex gloves.

It was time to talk to the widow.

3

She still sat in the passenger seat of Officer Sylvester's cruiser. Although the employees at the video store had said she had blood on her hands and face, Clinkscales never made note of any blood on Michelle Theer. How—or whether—she'd cleaned off the blood would remain unanswered for the life of the case.

As he got in the patrol car with her, Clinkscales wanted to treat the woman gently, hoping to build a rapport and take her slowly through her story. He introduced himself as the lead investigator on her husband's murder case and told her he wanted to ask her a few questions, encouraging her to take "baby steps," and not feel like she needed to tell him everything at once.

"Can you tell me what happened here?" Clinkscales asked.

The evening had begun with Christmas dinner, she said. That's why they were dressed so festively, she in the sweater with stars and Santas, her husband with the sequined suspenders and holiday tie. She and Marty—a pilot assigned to the 2nd Airlift Squadron at Pope—had met another couple, Heidi Mougey and her boyfriend, Dominique Ryan Peterson, in the office parking lot earlier that evening. Marty had then driven the four in the Explorer to the Fox and Hound restaurant in Raleigh, about an hour away. At the restaurant, they'd met with Michelle's boss, Thomas Harbin, and his wife. Michelle worked as a psychologist in the Harbin & Associates practice in the building; she also taught college psychology part-time. Heidi was the office manager.

After the dinner, the Theers and Heidi and her boyfriend had driven back to the office parking lot, arriving around 10:30 p.m. Heidi and Dominique had picked up their car, a blue Trans Am—the only car in the lot at that hour—and driven away. The Theers then left for home, stopping for gas at the nearby Quick Stop.

It was while they were at the gas station that Michelle remembered she had left reference books in her office that she would need the next day, Monday, for the class she taught. After gassing up the Explorer, they'd driven back to her office, and Michelle had gone upstairs while Marty stayed in the car. She had been in her office less than four minutes, finding her books and getting ready to leave, when she'd heard the series of gunshots. She didn't know how many, except that it was more than two.

She'd run to the door and looked down the stairs, seeing

her husband on the ground. She ran down the stairs as the door locked behind her. Her husband was still breathing, but not responsive.

She didn't know why Marty had left the car. She speculated that he had gone up the stairs because he was tired of waiting for her and may have needed to use the bathroom. He had drunk a lot of iced tea at the restaurant that night and "had a small bladder," she said.

After finding her wounded husband, she'd run out of the parking lot, about thirty-five yards away, and tried to flag down a passing car on Raeford, but it wouldn't stop. She then ran another two hundred yards to the Video Hut down the street to call 911. When she'd returned to her husband, he was no longer breathing.

Carefully, Clinkscales asked Michelle more delicate questions. Although not a suspect, Michelle was the last person to have been with her husband before his murder—and so far the only witness.

He asked whether she owned a gun or had recently fired one. She said no to both questions.

He then asked about her relationship with her husband. Michelle told Clinkscales that the couple had been married for ten years—they were high school sweethearts, both originally from Colorado—and had no children. They'd lived for the last year in an upper-middle-class subdivision about twenty minutes away, transplanted from Florida because of her husband's work at Pope Air Force Base. She had no relatives in the area; her mother lived in Colorado, her father in Louisiana. Marty's mother also lived in Colorado.

This was a common arrangement in Fayetteville, the husband stationed at the base, the wife following him there, leaving home and family behind. It could be stressful for even the most stable couples. Clinkscales asked whether there had been any troubles in the marriage. Michelle acknowledged that they had recently hit a rough patch and had attended couples counseling that previous summer.

She had no idea who would want to kill her husband.

Up until now, Michelle had alternately been crying and calm, and answered all the questions without coercion.

But near the end, Clinkscales saw her demeanor change. It started when her husband's wing commander, Colonel Paul Montgomery, and his wife, also named Michelle—a friend of Michelle Theer's—arrived at the crime scene. There are differing accounts of what happened after this. According to police, the couple gave a police captain a note asking to speak with Michelle, who was still in the patrol car talking to Clinkscales.

When handed the note, according to police, Michelle read it and threw it on the floor, saying, "Fuck them, they've never been there before for us." The captain was "dumfounded," he would later say. He looked at her face. She was shedding no tears and had 'almost . . . like a cold look." He didn't know what to say to her and was embarrassed by the situation.

According to Michelle, she had never been given the note and didn't know her friends were there. It was a mix-up that would grate on her for years.

In any event, it was a long night for her—and getting longer. At 1:25 a.m., after Michelle was interviewed by the detective, she was taken at her request to a nearby Servco gas station for a bathroom break. Officer Sylvester watched her the entire time. When she returned, an ambulance took away Marty's body. Michelle wasn't allowed out of the patrol car.

After her interview with Clinkscales, Michelle gave police permission to search the Explorer and her office, signing a consent form. A building maintenance man was tracked down to open the locked metal door.

Inside the building, Clinkscales and other investigators

found Michelle's meticulously clean and organized office. On the corner of her neat desk sat two reference books; on top of them were her keys, just as she had said. The wastebasket was empty save for a single candy wrapper. Nearby was a bowl of candy. In the bathroom, the water in the toilet was yellow.

Theorizing that neither Marty nor the killer had ever entered the building—that all the activity had taken place outside at and around the stairwell—Clinkscales found no reason to dust for fingerprints.

Back outside, Clinkscales inspected the Explorer. The dust on the hood appeared disturbed, so crime-scene technician Carrie Sonnen was called over to look for fingerprints. She found nothing, and Clinkscales concluded that the hood dust had been caused by the medics putting their gear there.

Clinkscales opened the car and found Michelle's purse and cell phone in the back tucked under the driver's seat. He decided against dusting the inside for prints. It was a cursory search of the car. He didn't seize or even look inside a gym bag in the back, two more decisions for which he'd be criticized.

As Clinkscales went about his work, Sonnen documented and collected the evidence. It was Sonnen who had checked Michelle's hands for gunshot residue earlier in the evening. She now performed the same test on the hands of the dead Marty Theer. Using a kit produced by the North Carolina State Bureau of Investigation, Sonnen placed sticky tape strips on the backs and palms of his hands, wet the tape with a Q-tip dipped in nitric solucid acid, then sealed the tapes in tubes. She filled out the labels asking for the name of the person from whom the sample had been taken, and the date and time. The kit would then be sent to the state for analysis.

After taking Polaroid pictures of the body as it had been left by the paramedics, Sonnen sketched the crime scene before photographing and collecting evidence. She collected the two 9mm Luger Winchester shell casings near the body, flecks of red sequins at the stop of the stairs, a tiny bloodstain on the right side of the second step from the top of the staircase, another bloodstain from the right side of the next step down and a blood sample from the pool near Marty's head.

Sonnen next photographed the contents of Marty's wallet, his keys and a Mitsubishi cell phone from Bell South found in the car.

Farther from the body, in the adjacent parking lot, she found a pair of size 9 high-heel shoes with silver buckles that had blood on the soles—the shoes that Michelle said she'd lost while running to the video store.

Sonnen returned to the crime scene and photographed the bottoms of Michelle's feet, in the torn stockings. She then took full-figure photos of Michelle. Michelle was cooperative, as she had been all evening, putting up no resistance to being photographed.

It was by now 3:20 a.m. the next day, Monday, December 18. The picture shows a grim and tired Michelle Theer, still in her Santa sweater and stocking feet.

At 3:30 a.m., Sonnen collected another bloodstain—this one on the seventh step from the top—that she had missed during the first search. She then picked up three cigarette butts and a crumpled cigarette pack found in the grass to the right of the building behind a fence.

With dawn approaching, the crime scene had been completely processed, in Clinkscales' opinion. As a health precaution, the blood was washed away by a fire hose; people would be coming to work later that morning to start the week.

Michelle was told she was allowed to go home—though she was informed that detectives would likely want to question her further.

Clinkscales later said he had offered to have a police officer take her, but Michelle insisted on driving herself. She was no longer crying and Clinkscales felt it was safe to let her drive. Before leaving, Michelle went into her office to get her keys, walking up the soaking steps, sprayed clean of her husband's blood, then returned to the Explorer. She drove to her home on English Saddle Drive, escorted by police cars.

When she got into the house, one of the female police officers asked her to take off her clothes so they could be examined at the crime lab. Michelle ignored the officer and immediately called her mother, Ann Forcier, in Colorado, from the kitchen phone to tell her that Marty had been murdered. She asked her mother to contact her father in New Orleans—her parents were divorced—as well as Marty's mother, who also lived in Colorado. She called friends, but they were all out of town for the holidays. She was able to reach her boss, Tom Harbin, who said he would come right down.

When she hung up, she stripped away her clothes and gave them to the officer. The garments were logged into evidence: red sleeveless turtleneck, size large; tan underwire bra; pair of black hose, size B; black decorative Classic brand sweater with red trim and six stars and six Santas on the front, size medium; one red, white and black plaid belt; size-five button-down miniskirt; and a size-six pair of lavender thong underwear.

As she handed over the clothes, Michelle told the officer she never wanted to see them again. It was now about 6 a.m. The confusion over whether she'd wanted to speak with the Montgomerys had been worked out, and her friend Michelle Montgomery was with her at the house, while Paul Montgomery headed to the airport to pick up relatives of Michelle's and Marty's who were rushing to Fayetteville from out of state.

Michelle Theer had been awake for nearly twenty-four hours. Exhausted but unable to sleep, she popped a sedative and a sleeping pill and finally drifted off.

4

The computer would save her secrets, tucked in obscure places. The delete key and trash bin gave only a false sense of security; they would prove a weak match against advanced retrieval software that found bits and pieces of her clandestine life.

And so it would one day be known that on an October day in 1999, just hours after she had sent that personal ad out on the Internet—"Sexy brunette seeks rendezvous man"—and gotten dozens of replies, from the apologetic to the weird, that one of those replies had intrigued her.

The man had given his name as Rob and used the provocative email address of Luvmachin4u. In his response, Rob told marriedbrunette that he not only possessed the requisite looks—tall and athletic with a full head of hair—but also a self-confidence nearing cockiness that she found desirable. Computer records showed that she had promptly responded to Rob and his promise of "hours-long sex marathons through all positions."

The actual text of her message wouldn't be found, but her intentions were clear from his replies to her notes.

"Hello, thanks for your reply," wrote Rob.

> Yes, I live in the Fayetteville area, Cumberland County. Also have a home at Lake Gaston that I commute to and from. Want to take a day and visit the lake? Well, I think you'll be very pleased with your choice and pleased if you want to meet. I've got to say, not in a cocky way, but I'm a cool, fun, great guy

> that you can have lots of fun and excitement with in many ways. I'd love to have coffee, dinner, something any time. You have nothing to lose. Talk to you LATA. Have a great weekend,
>
> Rob

From his next message, it was clear that her enthusiasm was growing.

"Hi, what's your name?" he asked.

> I like you, a woman that works fast. Don't want to waste time. I can dig it. Yes, love to meet you tomorrow at 1:30 p.m., give and take ten minutes. Tell me where if you have a preference. If not, let's say somewhere on Fort Bragg Boulevard would be feasible.
>
> Can't wait to prove my description. Love to see if you can put fire in my hot body. Also, I've got a nice F150 Ford truck short bed, dark blue, looks black, bigger tires than stock. The electric module went bad this morning, can't repair it 'til Monday. Maybe it was meant to be, so we could connect today. I will get transportation to meet. No problems with that.

He provided his pager number and reminded her to "always enter your area code."

> Hope to hear from you today. If you have time, tell me some things you like.
>
> C-ya,
>
> Rob.

It was here that the electronic trail ended, and it would never be known whether the married brunette had dialed the love machine's pager. The computer hid the rest of the email exchanges between her and Rob, if there were any more. But what was known was that she hadn't limited her online activities to mere flirtations.

She would fall for one of her online suitors, a man named Mike who apparently worked as a firefighter, as evidenced by his email handle: "firenguts."

"Hello, Mike, so nice to hear from you," she had written, this time her messages preserved and retrieved. For this communication she used the pseudonym Susan and the email address lookn4unow.

> I just started looking for fun and adventure and you sound like my kind of guy. I just may have a fire you can put out (I bet you hear that all the time). I'm trying to avoid clichés in the future.
>
> I'm a very discreet MWF, 29, brunette, five-foot-five, attractive, intelligent, looking for someone to push all the right buttons. I have to be up front: Physical attraction is key. Sounds like we have a good match.
>
> The other question is: Will we be hot and heavy for each other? I don't have a number for you to call me at just yet. I have to meet you and make sure you are not a psycho, stalker or serial killer.
>
> I'd love to hear from you. The sooner the better. When are you free? I'm self-employed so my schedule is very flexible. Let me know.

Although the text of Mike's response was lost, he seemed equally intrigued by Susan—he called her "interesting"—but he was also concerned about meeting because he was married.

"Yes, we are on the same wavelength again about being very discreet," she replied to Mike.

> I decided to look for a married man for just that reason. Single men are too unpredictable and have nothing to lose. I sound interesting? I have to wonder what caught

> your attention. I'd love to meet you tomorrow afternoon. Are you staying up all night? Sleeping during the day tomorrow?
>
> I'd like to meet you soon so we can see if this is going to happen. I'm going to [be] running around tomorrow afternoon over by the mall and wonder if you are available.
>
> Susan.

Here, again, the computer trail went cold, and it would be unknown whether "Susan" had found Roy the next day at the mall. Either way, the computer continued to reveal evidence of online connections and hints of real-life liaisons through the fall and early winter of 1999, as she sank deeper and deeper into Internet love.

One of the men would one day come forward to tell his story.

In December of 1999, using the screen name "Six8_01," he visited Yahoo.com's Personals page. For the last two months, he had been separated from his wife of nine years. She'd moved out and he'd stayed in the house in Sanford, a forty-five-minute drive northwest of Fayetteville. He was trolling the ads for a single woman who "sounds interesting" and "hopefully something local" when he came upon the ad from a woman with the user name "lookn4unow."

He'd sent her a message and she'd replied, telling him her name was Susan. For about a week they'd exchanged emails—he couldn't remember if they'd spoken by phone. Finally, they arranged to meet face to face in the Barnes & Noble bookstore's coffee shop in Fayetteville on a Friday or Saturday night.

Neither one knew what the other looked like; no pictures had been exchanged. He hadn't even known for certain if "lookn4unow" was really a woman or a man.

So that he would recognize her, she told him she would be wearing business attire and seated by herself. He gave only the most general description, telling her he was tall. This was his escape plan. He would check her out privately, and if she wasn't attractive, he'd leave.

At about 8 p.m., he went to the coffee shop. There weren't many customers. She was easy to spot, sitting by herself in a business suit, a vision out of her personal ad. She was in fact brunette, fit and attractive with warm brown eyes.

He walked up to her and introduced himself, giving her his real name, Charles McLendon.

She then introduced herself.

For the first time, she gave him her real name.

5

While Michelle Theer was in a drug-induced sleep in her home the morning after her husband's murder, Detective Ralph Clinkscales plowed ahead with the investigation. It was now 8:30 a.m. on Monday, December 18, 2000, and Clinkscales had been working all night. He had already inspected the crime scene, looked quickly inside Michelle's office and the couple's car—finding nothing of great interest in either—and taken the statement from Michelle. As was his practice, he had not tape-recorded anything she'd said. He'd taken notes and would put together a report.

The murder had been committed about nine hours earlier, and police had no idea who had killed Marty Theer or why. There was no sign of robbery. His wife said he'd had no enemies she knew of. There were no fingerprints at the scene. The police dog's search suggested only that somebody had gone from somewhere near the crime scene and across the street to the golf course, but that could have happened a day or two before the murder. The new widow, Michelle Theer, remained a person of great interest—those closest to a murder victim always are. That fact that she was the last person to have seen her husband alive made her more interesting.

At about 7 a.m. the morning after the murder, Michelle's boss, Thomas Harbin, made himself available for an interview with Clinkscales. The detective met with the psychologist in Harbin's office. Joining them was a second investigator, Mike Murphy, who would help Clinkscales with the early interviews.

The detectives began by asking Harbin to review the events of the previous night, and he gave the same account as Michelle Theer. Harbin and his wife had had a Christmas dinner with the other two couples—the Theers and Heidi and her boyfriend, Dominique—at the Fox and Hound restaurant in Raleigh from about 7 to 9 p.m. Harbin said it was one of three or four times he had socialized with Michelle. He described his relationship to her as being something more than just an employer; he was also her friend. Michelle, he said, had been working in his office for more than a year, since September 1999. Her husband was an Air Force pilot, flying C-130 transport planes, but that was about all he knew about the murdered Marty Theer.

Harbin did know, however, that the Theers' marriage had had problems. Michelle had confided to him that over the previous summer she'd suspected that Marty had been having an affair with a woman in Florida, where the Theers had lived before moving to North Carolina. Michelle also told him that the couple had clashed over the subject of children: Marty had wanted them, but Michelle had not.

In July or August 2000, the tensions had grown so bad that Michelle separated from Marty for about two months, Harbin told the investigators. At Harbin's recommendation, the couple attended marriage counseling with a Dr. Kenneth Kastleman, a Chapel Hill–based therapist who had an office in Fayetteville.

Intrigued that Michelle's relationship with her boss was more than just professional, the detectives asked Harbin if he knew the names of any of Michelle's other friends. Harbin said Michelle had mentioned one close friend, a man named Rafael, also a psychologist, who had gone to school with her. As far as Harbin knew, Rafael worked at a counseling center at Appalachian State University in Boone, in the northwest corner of North Carolina near the Tennessee border. But, he said, it would be difficult to find Rafael. He was scheduled to leave the country the next day for a trip to Venezuela.

This piqued the detectives' interest: a second male friend of Michelle's, only this one was headed for South America within hours of the murder.

But what Harbin said next would prove even more interesting. Harbin said that Michelle and Marty Theer's marital problems ran deeper than her suspicions about his fidelity or a dispute over children. Michelle had told him that a month earlier, in November, she had had an affair with a man named John.

Harbin didn't know John's last name, but said he believed he was a soldier at Fort Bragg.

Harbin knew something else about this John.

He was in the Special Forces, trained as a sniper.

6

As it turned out, Dr. Thomas Harbin wasn't the only one who knew about John. After interviewing the psychologist, Clinkscales and Murphy interviewed the other members of the Christmas dinner party, Heidi Mougey, the office manager, and her boyfriend, Dominique Ryan Peterson.

These interviews also were conducted early that Monday morning in Harbin's office, with Clinkscales talking to Heidi, and Murphy handling Dominique. Although interviewed separately, they provided similar accounts of the evening, corroborating the statements from Michelle and her boss. Heidi and Dominique said they'd arrived in Dominic's car at the Harbin & Associates parking lot around 5 p.m., and waited about fifteen minutes until the Theers showed up. The women introduced the men to each other; Marty and Dominique had not yet met. Marty then drove the four in the Explorer to the Fox and Hound. The Theers seemed happy and relaxed. At one point during the drive they'd held hands, Heidi and Dominique said.

They'd arrived at the Fox and Hound at about 6:15 p.m., dashed into the restaurant from the cold, and gone to a table next to the bar for a couple of drinks while waiting for Dr. Harbin and his wife. Michelle and Heidi went to the bathroom. Marty didn't drink any alcohol, explaining that he had to fly the next day. When the Harbins arrived about twenty or thirty minutes later, a little before 7 p.m., the party of six was seated for dinner.

Dominique Peterson didn't recall anything eventful during dinner. The group had ordered a bottle of wine, which Marty again passed on. People talked comfortably. Nobody seemed to be in a hurry. "Everybody seemed to be having a good time," said Dominique. They finished dinner at some point after 9 p.m. and got up to leave. As they approached the front door, Michelle disappeared for a few moments—Dominique and Heidi presumed she had gone to the restroom. She returned shortly thereafter.

Everybody had put on their coats and rushed to their cars to get out of the cold. Marty drove the four back to the psychology office and pulled the Explorer up next to Dominique's blue Trans Am.

The couples said their goodbyes. After Heidi and Dominique got out of the Explorer, the Theers drove away. Dominique started up his car, then stood outside with Heidi. They'd both smoked a quick cigarette—Marlboro Light—while the Trans Am got warm. They flicked their still-lighted butts onto the pavement, got into the car, and drove away, turning right on Raeford, heading south for home, at about 10:40 p.m.

Speaking with Heidi, Clinkscales asked whether she knew a friend of Michelle's named John. Heidi said she had in fact met a John about six months earlier when she and Michelle had gone to a Bennigan's restaurant after work. John and another man—Bill was his name, she thought—were there, too, and John spent some time talking to Michelle.

Heidi had known little more about John until recently. On the previous Tuesday—just five days before the murder—a man identifying himself as John had called the psychology office. Heidi'd answered the phone. John told her that he was worried about Michelle. John said Michelle had told him her husband abused her. John didn't say what this abuse was. But he wanted someone to call Michelle. Heidi says she passed the message on to her boss, Tom Harbin.

• • •

Michelle was still groggy, she would later claim, when Detective Clinkscales showed up at her home with Murphy at about 9:30 a.m. on Monday, December 18. She would claim that when she'd talked to them, it was against her wishes, that she was too sedated to properly answer their questions. Still, she said, they'd insisted on interviewing her again.

In his official report, Clinkscales made no mention that Michelle seemed sedated when he questioned her a second time after the murder. Instead, she again was calm and cooperative, and spoke openly about the Army sniper.

His full name, she said, was John Diamond. He was about 27 or 28 years old and both a soldier at Fort Bragg and a night student at Methodist College, near the base. He drove a 1995 or 1996 teal Pontiac Firebird. She acknowledged she had dated him over the summer while she and her husband were separated, but had broken off the relationship when she returned to her husband in the fall.

Michelle said that while she'd ended the romantic relationship with John Diamond, she did continue to speak with him—up until the day of the murder. She said she had spoken to him by phone on Sunday just hours before her husband was killed. She couldn't recall the exact time, but thought it was before 4 p.m. She said they'd spoken about her other car—a 1976 yellow Corvette—and what to do about a mechanical problem. She provided the detectives with John's cell phone number.

Before leaving to track down John Diamond, the detectives had one last line of questioning for Michelle. They asked about her husband's life insurance. She said that they had a renters insurance policy through USAA with premiums paid by direct deposit from their account at Bank of America.

The policy on Marty Theer was $500,000.

The sole beneficiary was Michelle Theer.

7

For two decades, a person who died violently in any of twenty counties in North Carolina stood a very good chance of ending up on the autopsy table of Dr. Robert L. Thompson, the veteran pathologist for the Office of the Chief Medical Examiner in Chapel Hill.

And so it was, at 1 p.m. on Monday, December 18, 2000, that in front of Thompson lay the naked body of what he would describe as a "well developed, well nourished white male." The body was delivered along with a paper bag of clothes: gray dress shirt, white T-shirt, black pants with belt, white Jockey type shorts, black socks with garters, brown shoes, a necktie and a pair of red sequined suspenders.

On the right wrist and left ankle of the body were military ID tags: CAPT. FRANK MARTIN THEER.

Marty had been in peak physical condition when he was killed. There was no heart disease or any other sickness in his body. His stomach contained 350 ccs of partially digested food, no doubt from the Christmas dinner at the Fox and Hound. He had no alcohol in his blood.

Thompson's cursory inspection of the outside of the body confirmed Detective Clinkscales' rubber-glove examination: that Marty had been shot five times. Four of the wounds were to Marty's chest, arms and legs, the shots the detective believed had hit Marty while he was at the top of the stairs. Marty also had two small scratches to the left forehead, three faint scratches to the upper back and small abrasions to the right knee and right ankle, from what the detective believed was Marty's tumble down the stairs.

The fifth and most serious shot was to the head, the one the detective suspected had been delivered as Marty was on the ground bleeding internally from the other wounds.

Looking inside the body, Thompson found that the bullet that hit Marty's right abdomen, leaving a corresponding hole in the shirt, had wreaked havoc inside the body. It had struck the liver, traveled up into the chest through the left lung, pierced the aorta, exited the chest wall and lodged itself in his left arm. The slug was recovered. No powder residue was found. The bullet—like the others in this series—had come from below Marty and hit him in the right side, going up into his body.

Another body shot had hit Marty in the left forearm, leaving a hole in the shirt, and traveled through the soft tissues of the arm, creating a second hole in the shirt, before re-entering the chest just below the left nipple, causing a third hole in the shirt and going slightly into the chest muscle.

The third body shot had struck Marty in the upper right thigh—a corresponding hole in the pants was found—and gone up into the muscle, moving through his pelvic bone and piercing his bladder before lodging in the abdominal wall, where the slug was retrieved. Again, this bullet had traveled upward, from Marty's right to left. He had essentially been shot in the butt from below with his back to the assailant, perhaps while turning away from the assault.

A fourth shot had hit Marty higher in the left leg—another hole was found in the pants—and rammed into the left thigh bone, cracking it, the bullet fragmenting on impact. This one had also been fired while Marty had his back to the shooter.

The worst wound was to the head. It had entered just below the left ear, traveled through the left side of the brain and exited out the right side of the top of his head. This was a "close-range gunshot wound," Thompson determined, based on the abrasions around the bullet hole caused by the burning and non-burning gunpowder shot out of the barrel along with the slug.

The coroner concluded:

> The autopsy reveals five gunshot wounds with the most serious of these being the wounds that involved the head and chest cavities. No natural disease is identified and the blood alcohol is negative. The cause of death in this case is due to multiple gunshot wounds.

8

At about the same time the coroner was completing his autopsy, Clinkscales and Murphy left Michelle's house and made the short fifteen-minute drive to Fort Bragg to find John Diamond. Inside the base, Clinkscales tracked down John's unit and spoke with John's commander Michael D. Trombley, the battalion command sergeant major for the 2/325.

From the brief description by Trombley, it was clear that Staff Sergeant John Diamond possessed the skills to have gunned down Marty Theer on a darkened stairwell with the deadly efficiency described in the coroner's report.

Trombley confirmed what Thomas Harbin had said: that John was an Army Ranger trained as a sharpshooter. The detectives told Trombley that they wanted to speak with John.

John was summoned to the sergeant major's office. He arrived shortly thereafter. When he walked in, it was clear he was a man a lonely military wife could easily fall for. He was 28 years old, tall—over six feet—with a lean and muscular build from his Ranger training, and a head of dark hair.

The detective told John that he was investigating the murder of Air Force Captain Marty Theer and that information had arisen that John knew Marty's wife, Michelle.

If John showed any reaction to this, Clinkscales never put it in his report, which doesn't mention so much as a flinch.

The detective asked John if he would come to the police station to talk. Trained to take orders, John not only agreed to go the police station for the interview, he said he preferred it. He didn't want anyone at his unit seeing him talking to police.

He arrived on time at 1 p.m. on Tuesday, December 19, two days after the murder, and sat before two police sergeants, Ralph Clinkscales and his boss William Mitrisin. Since John was not officially considered a suspect, the investigators didn't read him his rights. John had not brought a lawyer, neither private counsel, nor a military attorney, who would have been provided for free.

It was a golden opportunity for the investigators. They wanted to start questioning Diamond and see what happened. As with all the other interviews in the case, this one was not tape-recorded. Clinkscales and Mitrisin took notes and prepared reports.

The interview began with John being asked about his background. He told the investigators that he had been in the Army for ten years and was at that point in which he was considering leaving the military for civilian life.

From this interview and subsequent investigation, the detectives found that John had grown up a military brat; his father, George Diamond, served in Vietnam, an Army "tunnel rat" who probed the dangerous dark caves used by the Viet Cong.

After the war, his father was employed as a union ironworker, moving from job to job, state to state, finally setting in Killeen, Texas, another base town located adjacent to Fort

Hood. John joined the Army out of high school. He did his basic training at Fort Pope, Louisiana, and was stationed in Panama in 1998. He earned his sergeant stripes, got married to a local Panamanian woman named Lourdes and was transferred to Fort Bragg in 1999—the same year that Michelle's husband was transferred to Pope. Along the way he attended several schools: Ranger, surveillance, rappelling, air assault and sniper.

Like Michelle's experience, John's was typical. Career military, many stops between his home town and here, future uncertain.

John was next asked if he knew anything about the murder of Air Force Captain Frank Martin Theer. John said he had seen it in the news. The late Sunday killing had made the local television newscasts Monday evening and was carried in a story Tuesday morning in *The Fayetteville Observer* under the headline "Air Force Captain Slain." Written by Missy Stoddard, a staff reporter, the article gave only the basic details, saying police were investigating the "mysterious killing" of 31-year-old Air Force Captain Frank Martin Theer while his wife, Michelle, had been inside her psychology office picking up paperwork. The report identified the gun as a 9mm and quoted nearby business people as being shocked. Stoddard had called the Theer residence, but was told by "a woman who answered the phone" that Michelle "did not want to talk to the media." There was no mention of John Diamond.

With John saying he knew nothing about the murder other than what had been reported, the detectives shifted to the critical question. They asked him if he knew Marty Theer's wife, Michelle. Clinkscales' report doesn't provide any hints to John's physical reaction, but did note that he was forthcoming.

John readily acknowledged that he knew her—and on intimate terms.

They'd met, he said, after he answered her personal ad on the Internet that previous March, nine months earlier. Their first date was in Fayetteville at O'Charley's restaurant. Over drinks, they told each other that they were married but separated from their spouses. After that, they'd begun seeing each other regularly for sexual encounters in local hotels at least twice a month, taking turns paying for the rooms. Their time together was an open secret. Once, at It'z nightclub, Michelle had introduced John to her father, and mentioned to John that her parents were divorced.

The relationship, John insisted repeatedly, was purely sexual—the same thing that Michelle had told Clinkscales. "His attitude was as he was a ladies' man and Michelle was just one of the ladies that he was seeing," the detective later recalled. He said he had never met Marty Theer.

Where John differed from Michelle was on the duration of the relationship. Michelle had said she had ended the relationship in the fall when she got back together with her husband. But John told the investigators the relationship had continued to the present time. He said he'd had sex with Michelle as recently as the weekend before the murder, when they went to a nightclub called the Warehouse, then spent the night at the Holiday Inn in Raleigh on Saturday, December 9, 2000.

And he had last seen her, he said, as recently as the day before the murder, on Saturday, December 16, at a restaurant called Zorba's down the street from Michelle's office. Over a one-hour lunch, she'd told him she was planning to go to a dinner party that night with her boss, husband, and somebody from her office. This was also information that Michelle had left out. She had mentioned to Clinkscales that she'd called John the day of the murder to talk about maintenance on her Corvette; she'd said nothing of the Zorba's meeting or of the Holiday Inn encounter.

Another discrepancy concerned Michelle's Corvette. When asked about it, John said he knew that she drove a yellow Corvette and that she was very fond of it but he never had anything to do with the maintenance. If she ever asked him, he recommended that she take it to the shop. As far as he knew, the car was running fine.

Clinkscales made note of this and moved on. The detective wanted to know if John had access to any guns. John said that he didn't own any firearms and that the only guns he fired were for military training, with one exception. He said he did occasionally go to a firing range at Jim's Pawn Shop, where he would shoot rented handguns at silhouettes.

In fact, John said, he had gone to Jim's the day before—just hours after the murder. John said he had rented what he believed was a 9mm Beretta, the same caliber of gun that had killed Marty, and fired it in the range.

The detectives would later determine that John was telling the truth about going to Jim's. A receipt showed that from 10:17 a.m. to 10:45 a.m. he had been at Jim's Gun Jobbery and Indoor Range, facility with six rifle lanes and twelve pistol ranges. He had in fact rented a Beretta 92 FS, earmuffs and goggles. He was given one free target—a silhouette of a man—and bought two more. He brought his own 9mm ammunition for the gun, which is the civilian version of the military-issued M9 handgun.

Although there was the obvious significance of John handling a gun in the hours around the murder, his actions posed a problem for the detectives. They now couldn't swab John's hands for gunshot residue. His hands would be covered in it from the visit to the shooting range. Clinkscales didn't bother to take a sample.

The detectives wrapped up the interview by asking John the most important question of all: Where was he at the time of the murder?

John didn't flinch. He said that he was at home all Sunday night with his wife, Lourdes; their son and Lourdes' mother, Priscilla, who was in town visiting from Panama.

After putting the child to bed, John said, they'd watched a video of the Mel Gibson movie *The Patriot* and then he'd gone to sleep at around 10 p.m. He said he'd left the apartment the next morning.

He said that police were welcome to contact Lourdes to check this out.

The only requests he had were that he be allowed to call her first to alert her that police would be calling, and that the investigators didn't tell her about his relationship with Michelle Theer.

Clinkscales agreed to the terms. The detective was still trying to play good cop with John, not wanting to spook him. So far everybody was talking—and nobody was hiring a lawyer. With contradictions in the statements of Michelle and John, Clinkscales wanted to be able to question both of them again.

At about 2:30 p.m., John called Lourdes from the police station. The detectives couldn't hear what he was saying to her, but the call ended with John saying that Lourdes was ready to talk to the investigators.

After John left the police station, Clinkscales called Lourdes, reaching her at work at Hardy Hall Guest House at Fort Bragg, where she was a maid. The woman on the phone spoke in a strong Spanish accent, but seemed to understand Clinkscales clearly. He told her that they needed to ask her some questions. When Lourdes asked what this was all about, he simply told her that he wanted to ask her "some things," being deliberately vague. He didn't want to do this over the phone. Lourdes agreed to meet him later at her apartment.

At 4:35 p.m., Clinkscales and Mitrisin arrived at 974 Stewarts Creek Drive in Fayetteville. Lourdes' unit was No. 1, in the back. There the detectives were met by Lourdes, her mother, Priscilla Solis, and Lourdes' son Chance. The apartment was small, but not unlivable for three adults and a baby—two bedrooms, two bathrooms, kitchen and living room.

The interview began with Clinkscales telling the women the questioning concerned a "major investigation" into a "serious crime," but they didn't tell them that it related to the murder of Marty Theer, nor did they reveal John Diamond's link to Marty's wife. The detectives asked Lourdes about her relationship with John.

Lourdes seemed to have no problem understanding Clinkscales. She assured the detectives that although she was from Panama, she spoke and comprehended English. Her mother, on the other hand, needed Lourdes to translate for her.

Lourdes explained that although they were legally separated, John continued to spend the night in the apartment, sleeping in a different room. John didn't tell Lourdes what he did from day to day; all she knew was that he didn't tend to wear his uniform when he left the house, either to go to work on the base or to attend classes at Methodist College.

When asked about John's activities that previous Sunday night, Lourdes confirmed what John had said: that he had been with her. He had rented *The Patriot* that day and John, Lourdes and her mother started watching it around 7 p.m. until well after 9 p.m., when the adults went to bed. John had slept on the couch and Lourdes in the bedroom. She said she was a sound sleeper, so she couldn't say for sure whether John had gone out that night. The next morning, around 8 a.m., she found John asleep in their child's bedroom.

Clinkscales asked Lourdes to translate these questions for her mother, who confirmed everything Lourdes had said.

As the detectives left the apartment, they knew that John's alibi was good, but not ironclad. There was still room in Lourdes' account for him to have snuck out and done the murderous deed while his admittedly heavy-sleeper wife was in the other bedroom.

But so far this was only a theory. Beyond some vague idea that love or jealousy could have been at work, with the $500,000 life insurance payment serving as a financial motive, the detectives had no hard evidence that Michelle Theer or John Diamond had had anything to do with Marty's murder. Many marriages are fraught with troubles; often they involve one or both parties having affairs. And the $500,000 policy is not unusually high for a man of Marty Theer's rank and economic standing.

Neither the crime scene nor the autopsy had provided any evidence of who the shooter or shooters had been. There were no eyewitnesses. The neighbors had only heard the shots. The police dog's search had ended in a cul-de-sac.

The detectives needed more. Was there something that they didn't know?

9

They spoke for about an hour that evening in December 1999 in the coffee shop of the Barnes & Noble, conversation coming easily, the attraction mutual. Her real name, she said, was Michelle Theer. She explained that she used the Susan pseudonym because she was afraid that somebody she knew might have answered the "marriedbrunette" personal ad seeking the rendezvous man. She said that if that had happened, she would just pretend that she was in the coffee shop for other reasons.

The meeting came just three months after Michelle had arrived in Fayetteville from Florida. She had a new career and an empty house. Her master's and doctorate degrees in clinical psychology from the Florida Institute of Technology, along with a helpful referral, had gotten her the job she'd wanted, as a contract psychologist in Dr. Harbin's office, but the town, in her words, was a "shithole." Nothing like the Denver of her youth, or Melbourne, Florida, where she'd lived before coming to Fayetteville.

She had left behind warm weather and a pool, and brought with her a lousy marriage to a neat freak with symptoms of a premature midlife crisis. No sooner had they arrived in Fayetteville than Marty was on deployment—again—flying his C-130 and leaving her alone. That Marty wanted to bring children into her world of isolation galled her.

She wouldn't tell any of this to the man now sitting across from her, the former "Six8_01," Charles McLendon, from Sanford, North Carolina, separated but not divorced, looking for somebody interesting and hopefully local. Charles could have her name and perhaps her body, but not her secrets. They left the coffee shop separately, but kept in contact by phone and email.

They met again within days. Driving her yellow Corvette, Michelle arrived at Charles' house. On their second date, they had drinks, talked and had sex. Michelle didn't spend the night, returning the thirty-five miles to Fayetteville to the empty house on English Saddle Drive.

After that, they had regular sexual encounters about every other week, again at Charles' house. Usually, Michelle drove up in her Corvette. Sometimes, she arrived in a dark colored Ford Explorer. Once, when she drove home from his house, she got a speeding ticket. She returned to his house, upset, and showed it to him. That was the only time that Charles could remember Michelle spending the night.

Only once did they go to her house. It was in February 2000, and the rendezvous had involved planning. Charles drove to a predetermined location—a Hardee's restaurant off Interstate 87 near Fort Bragg—where he met Michelle, who was waiting in her Corvette. He wasn't familiar with the

Fayetteville area, so he followed her car to a business area parking lot, where he dropped off his car and got in the Corvette with Michelle. She then drove them to her house in a neat, quiet neighborhood.

They talked, then left for dinner and a movie. They returned to the house, talked a little longer, and "turned in for the evening," as Charles would later put it. It was the first and last time they would have sex in Michelle's home. When Charles asked about her marital situation, she explained that her husband was in the military and away for months, deployed in either Arizona or Alabama—he couldn't recall which—and she didn't want to talk about it anymore. He didn't press. The next morning, Charles went home.

Not long after that, Charles said, he "got the feeling that there was something strange going on about her," and he wanted to find out what it was. The key would be to crack into her electronic world.

Years later, he would give differing accounts of how he'd discovered Michelle's email password. At one point, he said he'd "stumbled" on it, at another that he'd simply guessed it.

Either way, he had it: "CHEATER."

He did it once, from his home computer, taking a peek at her inbox. He found names of several other men, no doubt contacts for sex, their screen names provocative. Throughout their three-month relationship, Michelle hadn't mentioned any other partners besides her husband, and Charles feared that Michelle had not only been screwing around, but had given him a sexually transmitted disease.

As he'd looked over her email page, he didn't have time to read the messages. Michelle had apparently logged on at the same time as he did, booting him off the server.

An hour later he called her. He asked if she was seeing other men. She responded by demanding to know how he'd found out about her private information.

He then asked her why she didn't just leave her husband.

She said she was planning on it, but didn't want to discuss it further.

The argument led to a break-up, in late February or early March 2000, and they never saw each other again. He would never know how hard she had taken the split.

But her computer records showed that she had lost none of her sexual drive; if anything, she experimented more aggressively after breaking up with Charles.

"Hello," wrote a man in a March 8, 2000, message, later retrieved from her computer. "I saw your ad posting . . . and was wondering if you are still looking for someone to play with."

She wrote back, describing herself as an "MFW alone in a life-style and just getting started. . . . Looking for partner and escort to CF functions"—personal ad speak for a married white woman looking for somebody to go with her to events sponsored by Carolina Friends, a swingers' organization that threw weekend-long parties in hotels in which the adventurous could meet new partners and swap old ones.

"Write back if you are still looking and might be interested in meeting," she replied, giving the name "Shelley."

Within hours, a man identifying himself as Nate wrote back to Michelle's marriedbrunette email address:

> Shelley, that sounds interesting. I'm 29. Also have brown hair, blue eyes and am in good shape. I enjoy good friends, conversation and have a lot of fun dancing at the functions as well as afterwards. . . . I'm at work now so I can't write for too long but would like to see a picture of you. I think you have one of me from my postings, but if you don't, I'll send you one.
>
> By the way, I love to give oral sex.
>
> Talk to you later,
>
> Nate.

Whether Michelle ever hooked up with Nate isn't known—the computer record isn't complete—but later emails clearly show that Michelle became immersed in the local swinger scene in the months after her time with Charles. No longer just hooking up with one guy, she apparently began going to swinger parties at hotels, having sex with multiple partners—both men and women, sometimes with more than one partner at a time.

The logistics for the liaisons were made on the Internet. So, too, were the post-coital post-mortems, as one graphic email exchange from March 16, 2000, showed. A couple giving their names as "Mark and Teri" wrote to Michelle about their apparent shared sex partners, including a woman named Dyell and a man named Chris, from a weekend escapade. From the wording of the couple's email, Michelle was still finding her comfort zone in the swinger world.

"When we kissed with Dyell in the car with us, I felt that you were a bit tentative," says the explicit email from one member of the couple—it doesn't say who.

> I was too, but at the time, she clearly seemed to enjoy it and when we talked later, she confirmed that. She said she really liked watching us and had wanted more. I know exactly how she felt. I was the same way watching the two of you together—though you would also like knowing that after we talked, Dy slid her clothes down, laid the seat back and had me play with her clit until she came. She was thinking all the while about being with you.

The email added that the couple also "took an immediate liking to Chris."

> You were totally right about that. Although we both want some time with just the three of us—and although

> Dy still isn't ready to play with another man—neither of us has any problems with Chris being a part of things when you want him to be.

The communication ends with the couple inviting Michelle and Chris on a "trip to Atlanta" and says it's "your choice" whether to bring Chris. "We'd both rather spend the weekend with you than go to Atlanta without you if you're unable or unready to go," the email says. "We're both totally agreed about wanting to give you the things you fantasize about, like MMF"—sex between two men and a woman—"and foursomes when you're ready for them. And don't worry, we don't do things out of obligation. It will all be fun. Last night was great. Talk to you soon."

Michelle responded under her marriedbrunette address.

> Hi, guys, Sorry it took me so long to answer your letter. A very good friend of mine came into town yesterday and I spent all day with him. Glad you made it home OK. We made excellent time and were in the sack long before you two. Of course, it sounds like you had an exciting drive back. Laugh. I'm glad you both liked Chris. He's up there near the top of my favorite people list. I did feel a little bad leaving him and going off with the two of you separately.

Michelle told them she still hadn't thought about the Atlanta trip, but would let them know soon. Either way, she wrote,

> That weekend is definitely a go—no matter if we got to Atlanta or not, though. If we go to Atlanta, I want to have Chris there, too. We really are partners in this

> new life-style and I wouldn't consider going without him. I'll try to catch you guys on line later. I'll be on line later tonight.
> Shelley.

Such emails were all over her computer in March and April—men of all shapes, sizes and sexual interests—with screen names like "Chopper Jack" and "Ohio Stallion" answering her personal ad. They ranged from "Tim," with the "athletic build" and "regressed sexual experiences to explore," to "David," who sent her pictures of himself shirtless, though he warned some of the pictures were old and he was "about five pounds heavier, no mustache right now, but I take requests." Michelle sent him pictures of herself. She checked out computer bulletin boards listing "gang bang parties," with "females especially wanted."

A month later, in early April 2000, Michelle wrote under her Shelley pseudonym to another couple—Jen and Dale—about hooking up with them and her partner, who isn't named.

> Hello, nice to hear from you. Write back if you're interested in meeting us sometime. We are looking forward to meeting you.
> Shelley.

They replied,

> Hi, Shelley, just a quick note to let you know that we got your photo. Here are a couple of others of Jen and I. I think that we are going to check out one of the Carolina Friends events over the next couple of months. We have a newborn and it isn't easy getting away.
> Dale.

And on it went, online trolling begetting real-world hotel encounters, never leading to serious relationships or even long-term friendships—until one message arrived that changed everything.

It was in April 2000, around the time that Michelle was talking dirty with Jen and Dale, and apparently during one of Marty's deployments, that she got a response to her ad from a man who matched Michelle's requirements perfectly. He was attractive, physically fit, fun-loving, Caucasian, 25 to 35 years old, drug and disease free, over six feet tall, with a full head of hair and a Fayetteville area address.

His name, his real name, was John.

10

Death brings a crowd. When the policewoman and the detectives finally left her in peace, Michelle spent much of the morning after the murder in seclusion in her bedroom. She was dressed in her pajamas and still groggy from the sleeping pills. But soon the quiet would be shattered.

First came her mother-in-law, Linda Gettler. Marty had adored his mother, calling her every week. A nurse, Linda had raised him on her own in Colorado. Marty had never known his father, a schizophrenic who'd divorced his mother and left him with only a last name and a jumble of feelings. For a father figure, Marty had turned to his loving grandfather, Al Dunbar, who'd taken him fishing and camping, helped him shoot Estes model rockets—Marty had dreamed of being an astronaut—brought him to Boy Scout meetings and fueled Marty's lifetime love of America. Marty had carried a photo of his grandfather and late grandmother in his wallet. Already in ill health, it would be a miracle if Al Dunbar survived the loss of his beloved grandson.

Michelle and her mother-in-law always got along well, and when Linda Gettler arrived at the Theer house just hours after her son had been gunned down, she gave Michelle a warm embrace and told her how proud Marty had been of her, the only girl he'd ever dated, the high-school sweetheart who became a psychologist. Michelle told Marty's mother that he'd been the best husband a wife could ever have.

Over the next few hours that Monday, additional relatives flew in—Michelle's mother, Ann Forcier, came from Colorado, her father, Thomas Forcier, from Louisiana. Also arriving were Marty's childhood friends Lonnie Carlson and his wife, Sherri.

Lonnie had been the best man at Marty and Michelle's wedding in June 1991, which took place just days after Marty'd graduated from the US Air Force Academy in Colorado Springs and while Michelle was serving in the Air Force reserves. Appropriate to their military status, the newly minted First Lieutenant Frank Martin Theer, then 21, wed Tech Sergeant Michelle Forcier, then 20, in the Academy's own chapel in a ceremony that Michelle's younger sister, Angela, remembered as "a fairy tale." Boyfriend and girlfriend since high school, neither had ever loved anybody else. "In Michelle, Marty had the perfect match—a true soul mate and life partner whom he dearly loved," one of Marty's Academy classmates would later write. "Watching the two of them together reminded us all of the goodness of life."

That life now over, Michelle reached out for support. As she called around the morning after the murder, she tried to find one of her best friends, Rafael Harris, who, unknown to her, police were interested in. Michelle had seen him as recently as a week before in Raleigh to celebrate his passing the

North Carolina licensing exam for psychologists. Michelle could only get his answering service. She dialed his employer, Appalachian State University, and left an urgent message with the security office, which finally reached him. In a phone call, Michelle told him that her husband had been killed, but didn't give details. As much as she wanted him there, she didn't ask him to be with her; it was too late for Rafael to change plans, so he continued on to Venezuela.

The days after Marty's murder were consumed with visits from friends and relatives and making funeral arrangements. The Air Force held a memorial for Marty on Thursday at the chapel at Pope Air Force Base. Michelle attended, as did her parents, Marty's mother and the Carlsons.

In between the flurry of activity, Michelle and the others close to her, particularly her father, had been contacting the Fayetteville Police Department seeking information about the crime. Little was being provided; the local paper was only reporting how senseless his murder seemed. "He didn't have an enemy in the world as far as we know," Marty's grandfather Al Dunbar told the *Observer*, which also reported that Marty had been murdered after returning from a Christmas party in Raleigh.

As Marty was being eulogized on base, nobody who had known him had any idea why he'd been killed, or by whom. The autopsy was complete and the body was released for burial—Marty was to be laid to rest that weekend at a plot near home, at the Air Force Academy—but the coroner had yet to provide a report of his findings.

With grief turning to frustration, Michelle and her family were clamoring for information. Finally, on Thursday—the same day as the memorial service—the police department invited Marty's friends and family, along with military representatives, to the station for a briefing by the lead investigator, Sergeant Ralph Clinkscales.

Michelle was pointedly not invited.

Hurt, angry and demanding answers, she insisted on attending, though she asked that police refrain from mentioning her affair with John Diamond. None of those mourning Marty knew about it. Police reluctantly agreed to allow Michelle to sit in on the briefing—and agreed to say nothing about the affair.

The session began at 1:40 at the police station on Hay Street. Seated in the major crimes conference room were Michelle, her parents, Marty's mother, the Carlsons and two military liaisons for families in crisis, Jenny Johnson and Scott Morris.

Using a chalkboard, Clinkscales and his boss, Sergeant William Mitrisin, gave a brief overview of their theory of the case, providing information that wasn't in the papers. They said they believed Marty had been shot by a handgun on the stairwell outside Michelle's office, stumbled down the steps, then been shot in the head. They explained the nature of Marty's injuries and said they believed that five shots had been fired. They said there was no physical evidence that they could discuss other than the brass 9mm casings picked up near Marty's body.

By all accounts, it was an uncomfortable meeting that left nobody satisfied. Word had gotten out that Michelle had not originally been invited. Also, the detectives were far from forthcoming. People asked a number of questions and got the same answer: "We can't tell you that as long as it is an ongoing investigation." The detectives still refused to provide copies of the autopsy or police reports, or a tape of Michelle's 911 call, all of which Michelle and her family had requested.

After giving the group an overview, Clinkscales spoke separately with the mothers, Ann Forcier and Linda Gettler. Michelle's father was also allowed a private briefing, but was so angry at what he saw as police stonewalling and the treatment of his daughter that he refused to talk to them. In the private sessions with the mothers, Clinkscales apologized for how the general meeting had gone and asked Ann and Linda if they had any information that would assist in the investigation. Neither woman did.

Most of the group then left for dinner at Huske Hardware House, a restaurant up the street from the police department.

Staying behind was military liaison Jenny Johnson, who not only was helping Michelle with the mountains of paperwork and procedures that follow the death of one of the Air Force's own, but had also become a friend. When the family members were safely away, Clinkscales called Jenny outside the meeting room and berated her for "not doing your job" by defying the police request to keep Michelle out of the meeting, Johnson would later recall. Clinkscales defined the job as to "represent Marty's best interests"—not Michelle's. Jenny returned to the conference room and started crying.

Michelle also stayed behind. She approached Clinkscales, asking to speak with him in private. They went into the witness room. Michelle said she had more information that she hadn't wanted to provide in front of the others. The detective said he still wasn't ready to speak with her again. But Michelle explained that she was about to leave for Colorado for Marty's burial and wanted to do this now.

Clinkscales agreed. He and Mitrisin interviewed Michelle for the third time, only now they had the benefit of the statements by John Diamond. As it turned out, this was one of the reasons Michelle was so eager to talk to the detectives in private. She had met with John the day before, and wanted to tell them what they she'd discussed with him.

She told the detectives she had called John and set up a meeting at the Village Coffee House on Boone Trail in Fayetteville. Michelle said she'd wanted to look John in the eyes to determine if he'd had anything to do with Marty's murder.

When they got together, she said, John expressed remorse

to Michelle and revealed that he had spoken to police about their relationship. She said that she'd then looked at him intently for any clues of what he was thinking—she was, after all, a clinical psychologist—but could find nothing.

She left believing in her heart that John Diamond had not killed her husband.

Her statements offered detectives an opening to ask her further about her relationships with John and Marty. She had come in without a lawyer and with no reluctance to talk; they wanted to take advantage of that. Asked again about her marriage, she said she and Marty had been wed for nearly ten years, and that it had only been rocky near the end.

From this interview and later investigation, Clinkscales and Mitrisin found that the Theers were very much like thousands of other military couples in Fayetteville—people who'd married young, struggled with the demands of a soldier's life, and finally didn't make it. Only this time, the marriage had ended in death, not divorce.

Michelle told the detectives that she and Marty had been high school sweethearts, growing up near each other in Denver in the '70s and '80s. They'd begun dating when Marty was 16 and Michelle was 15 and never considered being with anybody else up through their wedding five years later.

Born December 9, 1970, Michelle was the first of three children. Her mother was a homemaker and her father was in the Air Force, spending months away from the family when he was deployed. Her parents divorced in the mid-1980s, and a teen-age Michelle found adult responsibility when she was still in high school.

Mature beyond her years, Michelle helped raise her two younger siblings, Angela and Tom, when her mother went back to work. Michelle took her sister, who is ten years younger, to ballet lessons and watched her and Tom after school until their mother came home.

Academically mediocre in high school, Michelle never

had time for after-school activities except for volunteer work at the children's hospital, and had few friends, spending most of her free moments with her boyfriend, Marty. After their dates, she would bring him by the house, and he would play with her younger siblings.

At least twice, Michelle and Marty brought her brother and sister camping. Michelle also had a part-time job that helped pay for the repairs on the clunker car her father had given her.

Michelle finished her last year in high school while Marty—a year ahead of her—went to the US Air Force Academy in Colorado Springs seventy miles away. On weekends, she drove to the Academy to pick him up and bring him back to her house, returning him in time for classes Monday morning. Marty's classmates said he put in extra homework hours during the week so he could have his weekends free for Michelle.

When Michelle graduated from high school in 1988, she followed her father—and her grandfather before that—into the Air Force, joining the reserves. From summer boot camp, she went into college in the fall, at the University of Northern Colorado in Greeley. The GI Bill covered some of her costs; loans and her salary from the reserves covered the rest.

Two years into college, she volunteered for five months of service during Operation Desert Shield. Then her unit was activated for Operation Desert Storm, for which she served seven months, again in the United States. Her efforts in those operations earned her the Air Force Achievement Medal for Meritorious Service and she was promoted to tech sergeant and assistant noncommissioned officer in charge.

Shortly after their wedding in the Air Force Academy chapel, the newlyweds were uprooted. Marty abandoned his plans for becoming an astronaut when he saw the long waiting list, and opted instead for soaring closer to ground, as an airplane pilot. He was shipped off to Vance Air Force Base in Enid, Oklahoma, for flight school. Michelle followed.

Michelle brought her sister, Angela, out to stay with them over the summer, and Marty enjoyed showing the youngster his flight maps and telling her how pilots navigate. Michelle would tease Marty that he shouldn't make little Angela do his homework for him. Michelle's family—mother, brother and Angela—also visited them for Thanksgiving and Easter.

Michelle and Marty came out to Colorado for Christmas. The family would take turns opening presents. When Marty's time came, he would get out his pocketknife and very carefully cut the tape, then gently fold back the wrapping paper as people urged him to hurry up.

For her year in Oklahoma, Michelle was content as a military wife. She kept the house neat and orderly to Marty's exacting Air Force standards. When he was gone on a deployment, she had the company of their cockatiel Phoenix. She worked part-time in a day care center and spent about five days a month with her reserve unit at Tinker Air Force Base outside Oklahoma City.

In October 1992, the Air Force sent Marty back to Colorado for Flight Op School in Denver. With every milestone in his training came a certificate, each of which Michelle hung on the wall in an elaborate frame with silver wings. Their Christmas celebration at home included not only their immediate families, but Marty's classmates who were stranded in Denver for the short break. That same month, they had a family birthday party for Michelle, inviting her family and Marty's mother, Linda.

Michelle took interest in Marty's father. She helped track him down, and he and Marty reunited.

From Flight Op School, Marty was sent to Falcon Air Force Base near Colorado Springs, where he worked on his master's degree. Michelle followed him, finishing her college work—which had been interrupted by the Oklahoma and Denver moves—at the University of Colorado at Colorado Springs.

College awakened a mind dormant in high school. In 1994, she graduated magna cum laude with a BA in psychology and sociology, becoming the first person in her family to get a college degree. She also volunteered for Operation Provide Promise, the UN-led peacekeeping effort for what was then Yugoslavia, working for several months in Germany.

While in Colorado Springs, Michelle's bird Phoenix died and the couple acquired Topaz, a blue-and-gold baby macaw in sickly condition with no feathers. The bird became a part of the family; the Theers even sent out baby announcements. Michelle bottle-fed her to health, and Topaz would be her constant companion, through Michelle's most trying times, for years.

The couple kept in close contact with their families. Over Halloween, Marty and Michelle—by now in their 20s—dressed up in costumes and took Michelle's little brother and sister trick-or-treating.

When Marty graduated, the couple packed up Topaz and moved to Melbourne, Florida, where Marty was stationed at Patrick Air Force Base, flying C-130 transports. The couple bought a house with a pool and enjoyed all that Florida had to offer, going scuba diving, paragliding and, once, skydiving, which Michelle loved.

On holidays, Marty and Michelle would travel back to Colorado for paragliding in the mountains, and ski trips in Vail and Breckenridge, where they would be joined by her family, including her grandmother from Los Angeles. They also flew out for Angela's high school graduation and brother Tom's wedding, where Marty and Michelle danced to swing songs.

Over their first summer, Angela visited the Theers in Florida, and they took her to SeaWorld, Universal Studios and an alligator farm. Marty taught Angela to swim in the backyard pool.

Meanwhile, Michelle began graduate school, studying clinical psychology at the Florida Institute of Technology, with plans to become a therapist. From the very beginning, psychology fascinated her, even the darker aspects of human behavior. She volunteered at a rape crisis hotline and led therapy groups in prison.

The second summer in Florida proved much tougher than the first, the separations becoming more difficult on Michelle. Marty was stationed in Kuwait for several months. She tried to make the best of it. She sent him care packages of cookies and brownies she'd baked. She called her mom and urged her to do the same, telling her that, "He's stuck out in the desert." Marty sent back letters about dodging snakes and said he had drawn the envy of the other guys who didn't get so many good things in the mail.

But living in the house by herself weighed on Michelle. Angela came out for the summer again, and Michelle brought her to classes and to her volunteer activities.

In 1997, Michelle received a master's degree in clinical psychology. Her master's thesis reflected her military experience: "Women in Modern Warfare: Role of Personality Hardiness and Coping Skills." She paid to have her sister and mother come out for graduation. Marty was in town and his pride in Michelle's achievement showed. Usually calm and quiet, he couldn't stop talking about how excited he was, and he took Michelle out for a celebratory dinner. As a gift, he gave her skydiving classes to get her jumping certificate.

Two years later, Michelle received her doctorate in clinical psychology. Along with her academic work, she had built up extensive clinical experience, seeing patients individually or in groups at local Florida clinics. According to her résumé, she also counseled prisoners at the Brevard Correctional Institution in Sharpes, Florida.

She spoke at seminars or on radio programs on such subjects as date rape, substance abuse in college, gay and lesbian issues, eating disorders, communicating with your child and stress in the workplace. In 1998, she presented her master's paper at the annual convention for the Southeastern Psychological Association, tailoring her remarks about women serving in the Gulf War. She even spoke to Florida Institute of Technology's cross-country team on how to improve athletic performance.

Between Michelle's school work and Marty's flying, the couple spent increasingly more time apart—and eventually no time at all together. Talking to Detective Clinkscales, Michelle repeatedly complained of the pain and loneliness of the separations.

In 1999, Michelle had a long psychology internship in Alabama, and Marty was transferred to Moody Air Force Base in Valdosta, Georgia. They kept separate households and rarely saw each other. Michelle became more independent and for the first time began second-guessing why she had always worked so hard to keep the house clean and neat for Marty.

But their problems were deeper than the stresses of separation. Michelle told the detectives that while the couple was living in Florida she'd found something on his computer. It looked to her like evidence Marty was having an affair, perhaps with somebody he had met on the Internet. (It was a claim that would never be verified.) Still, the marriage continued—and so did the stresses.

With Michelle's completion of college and Marty's transfer in 1999, the couple was about to move again—to the sixth city in eight years. After completing five months at Moody, Marty headed to Pope Air Force Base. This forced Michelle to find a job in or around Fayetteville, a city she had never heard of before.

As it turned out, the search was not as difficult as it could have been. A university connection helped get her a meeting with Dr. Thomas Harbin, who had an office in Fayetteville.

Impressed with Michelle, Harbin signed her on as a contract psychologist, working out of his two-story office on Raeford Road.

She got a provisional license in North Carolina, which would be upgraded to full license in a year. It meant that she couldn't bill many major insurance carriers yet, but she would be able to build a caseload. She found additional work as an adjunct faculty member at the Webster University Graduate School at Pope and at Campbell University at Fort Bragg.

Though she was now, at age 29, finally beginning her professional career, she never warmed to Fayetteville. She made some friends within the military community, becoming close to Michelle Montgomery, the wife of Marty's commander, Paul Montgomery. She also kept up her friendship with FIT classmate Rafael Harris, who would find a counseling job at Appalachian State University.

But her family—to whom Michelle was closest—still remained two thousand miles away in Colorado, unable to give her support just as she was entering the most uncertain chapter of her life. The move to Fayetteville had jolted her out of the protected and structured world of education into the vast unknown of the work world. She was approaching her 30th birthday and Marty was making noises about having children, something she wasn't ready to do without being closer to family to provide help.

By the spring of 2000, Michelle told detectives Clinkscales and Mitrisin, her marriage was more strained than ever. Michelle ticked off the many things that Marty did that irritated her, including "his exceptional tidiness," and the ongoing debate about children.

It was around this time, she told the detectives, that she'd met John Diamond over the Internet and begun a sexual relationship with him. At the same time, she insisted, she was still trying to work out her problems with Marty, but her husband was always the stumbling block. Michelle told Clinkscales and Mitrisin that over the summer before the murder she had given Marty an ultimatum: attend couples counseling or the marriage was over. When he refused, she said, she walked out.

She rented a furnished unit in the Applewood Village Apartments from July through September in what she called a "temporary therapeutic separation." When asked by Clinkscales about her love life, she said the only affair she had had while living in North Carolina was with John. Pressed on whether she'd had affairs while living other places, she refused to answer. But she insisted to Clinkscales that Rafael Harris was a platonic friend.

She acknowledged that she'd continued to see John Diamond longer than she had initially said to Clinkscales. And this time Michelle confirmed what John had said: that they'd had sex as recently as the weekend before the murder, on December 9 at the Holiday Inn in Raleigh after going to a club called the Warehouse to celebrate her 30th birthday. She had slipped away from home by herself by telling Marty that she was visiting Rafael; Marty knew him and felt comfortable with her being with him.

Asked how deeply she felt about John Diamond, Michelle said she didn't love him, though John had at times said he loved her. Overall, John treated her well, she said, though he had twice used profanity to her, calling her a bitch when she didn't return his calls promptly.

Clinkscales and Mitrisin then asked Michelle about the day of the murder. Michelle again said that she had called John before 4 p.m. to ask him questions about repairs on her Corvette. She said nothing about seeing him on Saturday, the day before the murder. Clinkscales pressed her on whether that Sunday phone call was the only time she'd had any contact with John that day. She insisted that it was.

Then Mitrisin threw Michelle a curve. He told her that as

the investigation progressed, police might have to check her phone records to see if she were telling the truth.

"Well," she told the detective, "I just remembered I did call John Diamond while I was at the Fox and Hound restaurant. I don't have the exact time, but I went to the ladies' room and used my cell phone, but got no answer."

Her admission that she had tried to contact John about an hour before the murder would change the course of the investigation.

That phone call from the ladies' room could have been Michelle's way to summon John to the murder scene. Even if he hadn't answered, it could still have been a signal to murder: Her number could have popped up on John's caller ID.

That Michelle admitted to this was doubly fortunate for police. If the call had not been answered, as she said, it would never show up on phone records. Mitrisin's threat to check the records meant nothing, since unanswered phone calls aren't recorded.

The interview concluded with the detectives asking Michelle for two things. They wanted her to take a lie detector test. And they wanted her to wear an electronic listening device—a wire—the next time she met with John Diamond.

Michelle said she would consider both.

11

The letter was found on his grave by Marty's mother.

Marty Theer was laid to rest three days after Christmas, December 28, 2000, at the US Air Force Academy in Colorado Springs. The service was conducted with military honors.

Five pages long and typed, the letter was addressed to "My Dearest Marty."

> I know you can hear my heart screaming out in pain, reaching out for your soul in my dreams, waiting for you to walk in the door and tell me the whole thing was a mistake. If you came home today, I would never be angry for anything. I would kiss you all over and hold you until my arms collapsed in exhaustion.

Skeptics would question whether Michelle Theer had meant the letter as a private message to her murdered husband, or as a really self-serving missive to the police detectives who she felt were closing in on her. It was written not long after her meeting with Clinkscales and Mitrisin, at a time when Michelle's father was urging her to hire a lawyer because it was becoming increasingly clear that she might be a suspect in Marty's death.

Either way, the letter marked Michelle's most detailed account of her feelings.

"I wish I could say that I wanted to be at your gravesite today, but it's not true," she wrote, saying that she would have preferred to have had him cremated and his ashes spread. "But my daddy told me that I had to give you back to your mom now, so I chose the Academy because it seemed so important to her and your grandparents."

As for herself, "I feel empty and alone," she wrote, "helpless and hopeless. Many times I have contemplated swallowing a bottle of pills and seeing if I can join you in whatever afterlife there may be, if there even is one." With all of her "hopes, dreams, plans, and adventures" having centered around Marty, she said she now felt "like a shell with no direction. Even worse, a scared shell that is consumed and filled with fear. . . . I feel buried under a mountain of despair."

A mountain, she wrote, caused in no small part by the Fayetteville Police Department. "They have handled the investigation with glaring incompetence," she wrote, "I am sorry I did not do a better job making sure the perpetrator was caught and brought to justice." She wondered if she could have chased "the shadow I saw in the corner of my eye and gotten a glimpse of a license plate, a description, something."

But love kept her with Marty. "I did not want to leave you," she wrote. "You were breathing and I don't know if you could hear me or not, but I wanted you to hear me telling you how much I loved you and convince you that everything would be OK once the ambulance got there. I'm sorry I did not get them there soon enough."

She was sorry, she said, for a lot of things: that her work was so important they'd had to return to get her book, that she hadn't insisted on him coming inside with her, that they hadn't gone in through the better-lighted front door. She thought of the children they might have had. "I feel guilty now that I kept delaying having a baby," she wrote, but added, "At the same time, I wonder how I could function now with an infant, or if I were pregnant."

Marty's death, she said, had even been hard on the pets—Topaz the bird and Kramer, their sheep dog. Topaz had been prone to screaming fits and Kramer had lost the taste for bones. "You see, we all miss you. We need you. Why did you have to leave???" she wrote. "I wonder what the next years will be like, and cannot envision anything. Please come to me in my dreams. I need your comfort." She signed it, "All my Love and Forever yours, Michelle."

12

As much as Michelle disliked the city of Fayetteville, she hated the local paper even more. Since her husband's murder, Michelle Theer had been contacted repeatedly by reporters from *The Fayetteville Observer*. Each time she refused to comment.

At the same time, however, she was trying to get the paper to run what she considered a proper obituary for Marty, something longer than a paid notice that had run on January 5 and one that didn't have the taint of the murder investigation.

The paper considered her request, and in early January the managing editor, Michael Arnholt, wrote her back:

> Dear Mrs. Theer,
>
> I am writing regarding a clarification of the obituary information you provided about your husband, Marty Theer. Below is a copy of the obituary that we intend to publish free of charge on our obituary page. It includes the information that we typically include in news obituaries—or obits. Though we cannot include additional information, I would like for you to verify that what we are publishing is correct.
>
> I assume, for example, that you go by Michelle Theer rather than Michelle Forcier and that you are living in Fayetteville. We will publish it immediately when I hear back.
>
> Sincerely,
>
> Mike Arnholt, managing editor.

He then attached a draft of the obituary:

> *Marty Theer, 31, of Denver, died December 17th. Capt. Theer was a C-130 pilot stationed at Pope Air Force Base. A graveside internment service with full military honors was held December 28th at the United States Air Force Academy cemetery in Colorado Springs, Colorado. Capt. Theer is survived by his wife, Michelle Theer of Fayetteville, his mother Linda Dunbar Gettler of Denver and his father Frank Martin Theer of Denver. Memorials may be made to the Capt. Marty Theer Memorial Fund at First Citizens Bank for a charity to be chosen.*

This was not what she had been looking for. Michelle fired back a letter taking issue with the text—she said Marty had had military honors, not full military honors, and "if you want to be accurate, correct that." Also, there was a word missing in the last sentence; it should have read "memorial *contributions* may be made" to the fund.

"Ninety-eight words is a piece of shit obituary," Michelle wrote to Arnholt.

> I would also like a refund for that pitiful paid advertisement you squashed in the corner of the page on January 5th. In addition, you can inform your reporters to stop calling me any time in the future. I will never have any comment or interviews for your rag. I think you are a piece of shit newspaper and I intend to spread the news.
>
> Please let me know what date the obituary will be published in the obituary section so I can purchase my last ever copy of your rag.
>
> Michelle Theer.

As frustrated with the newspaper as Michelle was, it was still her primary source of information about the investigation into her own husband's death. After the briefing for her family, detectives cut off all communication with her. She and her father called the police department for updates and copies of reports and the 911 tape, only to be told, "No comment," or given the run-around.

She could find no more answers from the local paper she so despised. On December 30, two days after Marty's funeral in Colorado, the *Observer* reported that "police say they still do not have a suspect or a motive" in Marty's murder. The paper didn't even report the results of the autopsy conducted nearly two weeks earlier, noting that the pathologist, Dr. Thompson, was out of the office.

Instead, the paper printed the concerns of people who lived and worked around Michelle's office. "Ever since the murder happened, I don't feel like coming to the office late," Jake Lee, a web page designer who worked in a building on Raeford Road, told the paper. A couple named Lee and Adam Walker were quoted as saying that they now thought twice about bringing their 2-year-old son to work. "You just don't know," he said.

With the silence from police becoming unnerving, Michelle in the first week of January hired two criminal defense lawyers, H. Gerald Beaver and Haral E. Carlin, to try to get more out of the police than she could. She also needed their advice about the last things Clinkscales had requested: that she wear a wire when she talked to John Diamond and that she take a polygraph test.

Her attorneys repeatedly contacted the police department, but they couldn't get any information either.

Michelle had good reason to be concerned. Behind the scenes, the investigation was building momentum.

Unknown to Michelle, very early on, police were searching the darkest parts of Michelle and Marty's lives. On December 29, Clinkscales interviewed Marty's former commander at Patrick Air Force Base, Lieutenant Colonel Michael Sweeney. He told Clinkscales that in January 1997, nearly four years before the murder, while Marty and Michelle were still living in Florida, Marty's work performance had begun to suffer. He did so poorly on one flight evaluation that the base nearly grounded him. Marty finally confessed to his boss what the problem was. "His wife had found out about the Internet communications and became very angry," Clinkscales wrote in his report about his interview with Sweeney.

According to the commander, it was porn, not an affair as Michelle had suspected, but either way it was trouble. Marty stopped viewing online porn for a time, but returned to it in 1999, "causing turmoil in their marriage," according to Clinkscales' report. The commander had recommended marriage counseling, but before he could find out if Marty had followed through, Marty's squad was transferred to Moody AFB and he was out of Sweeney's jurisdiction.

The next part of the investigation focused on Michelle. Acting on an anonymous phoned-in tip, Clinkscales got a lead on a man said to have critical information about Michelle's personal life. Charles McLendon got a call in early January asking him to come to the Fayetteville police station for an interview. Late the morning of January 5—the same day *The Fayetteville Observer* ran that little obituary on Marty that would draw Michelle's ire—McLendon sat before Clinkscales spelling out in detail his experiences with Michelle.

After recounting how he'd responded to her personal ad and met her in the Barnes & Noble coffee shop, McLendon told the detective about keeping in contact with Michelle for about a week before having sex with her at his house, the first of a half-dozen liaisons. McLendon also spoke of how

Michelle hadn't wanted to talk about her husband except to say he was gone for months at a time on deployment for the Air Force. And he told Clinkscales about how he'd cracked into Michelle's email account and found evidence that she was hooking up with other sex partners.

Clinkscales asked McLendon if he remembered Michelle's password, and that's when he told him it was "CHEATER."

The interview not only exposed Michelle's hidden sex life, it caught her in a lie. She had told police that John was the only man with whom she'd had an affair. Now there was Charles McLendon, and quite possibly others.

To find out more about the relationship between John and Michelle, Detective Clinkscales interviewed John's Army buddies. They said they had seen John with Michelle and recounted that John referred to her as his girlfriend. But they knew nothing about John ever being angry at—or jealous of—Michelle's husband. And Marty's murder hardly seemed to concern him. According to Clinkscales' report of the interviews, John and his friends "laughed and made jokes about the situation because they were sure that Diamond did not kill Michelle's husband."

Clinkscales, however, was less certain. From the start, the detective had been skeptical of the alibi provided by Lourdes, John's estranged wife with whom he still watched movies, ate dinner and overnighted. It wasn't just the gap in time that concerned the detective—with Lourdes unable to account for John's whereabouts all night—but the nature of their relationship. If they were separated, why had John been there?

Police checked court records after the murder and found that on Monday, December 18, 2000—the day after Marty was killed—John had filed for divorce from Lourdes. She was served with the papers the following day—the same day that Lourdes was interviewed by Detectives Clinkscales and Mitrisin, yet she never mentioned any of this.

Clinkscales decided to interview Lourdes again—this time without letting John Diamond alert her first.

At 3 p.m., the detective showed up at the Hardy Hall Guest House while she was working. He asked her the same questions about the night of the murder, and got the same response: John had been with her and her mother and the baby, watching the video of *The Patriot* until 9:30 or 10 p.m., then they'd gone to sleep in separate rooms, with Lourdes finding him on the sofa in the morning. She reiterated that she was a sound sleeper, so really couldn't say if he'd ever left the apartment late that night.

Clinkscales asked more about her marriage to John, and she acknowledged that she knew he had seen other women in the past. But she insisted that John could not have been involved in a murder.

Then Clinkscales turned up the pressure. He told Lourdes that John had admitted to being involved with a woman named Michelle Theer. He said that John and Michelle had met in hotels the previous summer, and that as far as John was concerned, the relationship was still ongoing. He told her that John may have been planning to run off with Michelle, perhaps to Florida.

Expressing his deepest sympathies, Clinkscales said it saddened him to see how John was treating Lourdes, that she didn't deserve it.

Lourdes burst into tears.

It didn't take long for John to find out what Clinkscales had done. On January 18, shortly before John met with Michelle, Clinkscales called asking if he would take a polygraph. John refused and lashed out at the detective. According to Clinkscales' report, "Diamond said that thanks to me, his wife knows about his situation. He said that I had betrayed and him and because of this he would not take a polygraph."

That same day, Clinkscales called Michelle, asking her again if she would submit to a lie detector test. Michelle said she would have to consult with her newly hired attorneys. After talking to the detective, Michelle called around to friends to see if they knew anything about the police investigation. The news wasn't good. The investigation had expanded from the Fayetteville Police Department to the military police. She got word that agents from the Air Force's Office of Special Investigations were interviewing Marty's crewmates from the 2nd Airlift Squadron at Pope.

The next day, January 19, her friend Jenny Johnson—the base liaison who had been berated by Clinkscales at the police station briefing with Marty and Michelle's family—called Michelle to say that she had just been interviewed by OSI agents, who made it clear that investigators saw Michelle as refusing to cooperate. According to Jenny, they accused Michelle of refusing to turn over documents and balking at taking a polygraph. Michelle said the first part was untrue and the second part was premature: she still hadn't even spoken with her attorney about the polygraph. To Michelle it appeared that police, failing to find any real evidence, had launched a campaign to pit people against her and John. She was determined to not let them succeed.

Just days later, on January 23, 2001, Clinkscales turned up unannounced at Michelle's office with another investigator, to discuss the polygraph. Michelle replied that she might be willing to take a polygraph as long as it was not administered by the Fayetteville Police Department. To ease her concerns, the detectives explained that the test would be given by a top-notch—and impartial—examiner from the State Bureau of Investigation. "However, this information was not convincing enough for Theer," Clinkscales wrote in his report.

According to the detective's report, Michelle had rattled off a number of reservations. "Theer said that she was naturally an anxious person," wrote Clinkscales. "She knew that the polygraph measures levels of anxiety. This might cause her to fail the test while giving truthful answers." She also cited statistics on the low reliability of the test, and questioned the qualifications of the examiner, including his background, education and field experience.

"Theer said that she has lost faith in the FPD and that we had spread unfounded rumors about her having several sexual extramarital affairs," wrote Clinkscales. "She said that everything that she told us was the truth, but we were not sharing everything in reference to the investigation with her." For instance, Michelle sought—but couldn't get—information about John Diamond, including whether police had conducted a gunshot residue test on him and whether he'd had an alibi for the night of the murder.

Michelle later said she'd refused to take the polygraph both on the advice of her attorney and for technical reasons. "As a scientist, I had evaluated the research on the validity and reliability of polygraph results and found the procedure to have an extremely high error rate," she would later write. "That from a purely scientific perspective, it was not possible for the machine to distinguish truth from untruth." Two days later, Detective McLamb called her, asking again if she would take the polygraph. Once more, she refused.

Michelle next clashed with military police. She phoned Pope Air Force Base to obtain Marty's death certificate and autopsy report—both of which she was unable to get from the civilian police. When a woman she identified as Master Sergeant Lisa Urenda told Michelle that they couldn't provide those documents, she grew angry and decided to pay a personal visit.

On January 26, Michelle went to Fort Bragg to speak with agents from the OSI. Accompanied by Marty's commanding officer, Paul Montgomery, Michelle was brought to an interrogation room at 11 a.m. She later complained that they'd made them wait thirty minutes before an investigator named Agent Vince Bustillo and a woman Michelle described only as "a scraggly haired female" came in. Michelle says she asked them several questions—what the OSI's investigation was about, what their role in the Fayetteville police investigation was, and whether they were communicating or cooperating with the Fayetteville police—and she kept getting the same response: "We are not answering your questions."

The female particularly seemed to grate on Michelle, who quoted her as saying, "We know what you are doing."

It ended, according to Michelle, with Bustillo asking Michelle if she had any statement to make.

"If you have no questions for me and you won't answer any of my questions," Michelle snapped back, "then I guess there is nothing else to say."

Everybody, it seemed, was against her. Even those supposedly trying to help seemed to have an agenda. One weekend morning, Michelle's clock radio went off to a local Crime Stoppers program report seeking the public's assistance in solving Marty Theer's murder. The report used language that Michelle found overly blunt and disrespectful. The only example she could recall was the broadcaster saying that Captain Theer had been "shot in the head," but whatever was aired left a mark on her.

"I was traumatized," she later wrote. "I was incoherent, called my father crying, shocked at the vicious wording of the report." She suspected the police had put the Crime Stoppers people up to it "to harass and hurt me."

She called the Crime Stoppers hotline to complain, but it was a weekend and nobody was there, so she left a message. The following Monday, somebody called Michelle back. She demanded to speak with a detective. She was told he was out sick and that he would have to call her back. Michelle said he never did.

That same day, Michelle went to work and, at about lunchtime, looked out her window to see three OSI agents walking around in the grass. Office manager Heidi Mougey also saw them and called the office to report some "goons" nosing around, according to Michelle. Tom Harbin went downstairs and saw agents with metal detectors looking around the grass and pavement. Agent Bustillo flashed a badge and Harbin went back to his office.

That night, Michelle called her attorney—"fed up," she would later say. A couple of days later, this letter arrived at the police chief's office:

> On January 3, 2001, Ms. Michelle Theer, the wife of the deceased, retained the services of our law firm to assist her in her dealing with the Fayetteville Police Department. She had been requested by Detective Clinkscales of your department to assist the Fayetteville Police Department by wearing a wire and engaging in conversation with suspect John Diamond. At that time, she was willing to assist your department in any manner that she could to uncover evidence that may lead to the arrest of the person responsible for her husband's death. After a long string of unpleasant encounters with the detective involved with this investigation, which I will not detail at this time, she has lost trust in your department and therefore, desires no further contact by your officers.
>
> Therefore, I request you inform your detectives assigned to this investigation to have no further contact with Michelle Theer during the course of their investigation. Should the need arise for contact to be made with Ms. Theer, please contact either H. Gerald Beaver or myself and we will assist you in setting up a meeting. However, one of us will be in attendance at

> all times during the meeting. I truly regret that it has come to this and would be more than happy to discuss this matter in more detail if you desire.
>
> Signed,
>
> Haral E. Carlin.

Michelle would never speak to a law enforcement person again. But her quest for details about the police investigation didn't end. In her anger and frustration, she did something her lawyers specifically told her not to do.

She met with John Diamond.

13

On January 17, Michelle and John went to The Spy Shoppe, a Fayetteville store that sold such amateur sleuthing devices as little cameras and secret recording equipment. According to store employee Wanda Stolarski, the pair asked about purchasing a device or service that could search for electronic bugs in Michelle's house. The Spy Shoppe had just such a service—an employee could go to the house and look for eavesdropping devices. Michelle and John booked an appointment, leaving Michelle's home phone number as a contact.

But Michelle apparently had second thoughts. Several days later, the appointment was canceled. Then, Michelle changed her mind again, came back into the store and re-ordered the bug sweep. An employee went to her house with an electronic detector searching everywhere, including the phones, for hidden bugs. Nothing was ever found.

Around this same time, Michelle's neighbors saw suspicious activity in their Hunter's Crossing subdivision. On January 21, Felicia Montgomery, who lived close to Michelle in a cul-de-sac, asked her son to let the dog out. He came back in to tell her that a teal two-door sports car was parked in front of their house.

She called 911.

"By us living in that dead-end area we were kind of curious that maybe somebody was in the woods," recalled Montgomery, who is not related to Marty's commander. "So I called the sheriff, because my kids and I are by ourselves most of the time."

A deputy responded and tried to reassure her, saying that nine times out of ten a suspicious parked car is evidence that somebody is having an affair. The deputy asked if she wanted the car towed; Montgomery said no.

The next morning, at 5:45 a.m., the car was gone. But it returned the next night, and almost every other night through the end of January and into February, usually arriving in the evening and often being left there all night.

Finally, one night, Montgomery saw the driver. After getting out of the car, he was walking across a yard toward Michelle's house. Montgomery shouted out to him to move the car, but he didn't stop walking.

After several attempts to get his attention, she finally yelled out that her husband parked his truck where the sports car was and "he might just back over it."

The man turned around and moved his car across the street, then again walked toward Michelle's house. From then on, he parked it there or on another street.

Montgomery kept a close eye on it, not just because she was worried about robbers in the neighborhood, but also because she had read in the paper about the murder of the husband of the woman who lived in the house, now being visited by the man in the sports car.

For a time, the man had been parking his car in between

Michelle's house and her next-door neighbor, Norman Zaldivar. "We've been having some break-ins and talking to the law-enforcement agencies," recalled Zaldivar. "They were telling us to report any suspicious activity, because there was a trail that goes into two other subdivisions from the back."

Zaldivar called a couple of friends—officers for the Cumberland County Sheriff's Department—and gave them the make and model of the car to see if it was stolen or involved any crimes. It wasn't.

But soon, as the man had been seen walking across Zaldivar's lawn, people were looking at Zaldivar in a funny way. "It was just annoying to me," he said. "The neighbors were coming to me and saying, Who is the guy walking in front of my yard?, thinking my wife was having an affair."

Finally, he went next door and confronted Michelle. He had been on good terms with her; shortly after the murder, he'd helped her set up an alarm system. This time he told her he didn't appreciate having this guy park in front of his house, and all the whispers that came with it. The car was gone the next day.

The man in the sports car, police would later determine, was John Diamond.

On January 27, Michelle and John met for dinner at a local restaurant. They discussed everything that had happened in the last six weeks. Michelle took detailed notes and later wrote a summary.

In it, she made it clear John was her best source not only of information but of emotional support. John was the key. Although their meeting—if revealed—would only heighten suspicion, having John beside her provided the best chance of fending off the police and the press.

John Diamond could now be much more than a lover.

He could be her salvation.

14

In terms of rank and education, the man now sitting in front of Michelle Theer in the Fayetteville restaurant was a step down from her husband. John Diamond was a staff sergeant to Marty's captain—an enlisted man to Marty's officer—with only a high school education to Marty's master's degree.

And that's what made him special. John was everything Marty was not: spontaneous, action-oriented, self-assured to the point of cockiness, and primal.

In January 2001, John was an infantryman assigned to the Headquarters and the Headquarters Company, 2nd Battalion, 325th Airborne Infantry Regiment at Fort Bragg. He was nearing what he hoped would be the end of his career in the military, the only job he'd ever had. Preparing for the transition to civilian life, John attended night classes at Methodist College, close to the base, doing well enough to make the dean's list.

John and Michelle had met, as they both told police, on the Internet in the spring of 2000 when he responded to her personal ad seeking a "rendezvous man." At the time, Marty was on deployment; John was technically married, but separated, in a way, from Lourdes.

The relationship was electric. For somebody who fashioned himself as a ladies' man, John Diamond had finally found his match in Michelle. He became infatuated with this woman who was an intelligent, accomplished professional by day and a dynamo in the bedroom at night. Sexually, she knew no bounds, introducing John to a world he could only have dreamed about.

John showered Michelle with fawning emails, with many of the subject lines saying, "I love you," "Good morning, baby," "Sexy," "Words can't describe," "I miss you," "Incredible weekend," "Wonderful night," "Soul mate," "Eternal" and "Forever love."

With Marty on deployment, Michelle and John did little to keep their relationship a secret. Jim Marshall, a friend of Marty's who lived in the same cul-de-sac as the Theers, was mowing his lawn one day when he saw John and Michelle pull out of her driveway in her yellow Corvette. Michelle smiled and waved at him.

Other times, Michelle could be prickly. Neighbor Timothy Greenhaw said John came by more than twenty times. Once, Greenhaw asked Michelle as she was getting her mail, "Are you and Marty getting a divorce?"

Michelle asked him what would make him think something like that. Greenhaw answered that Marty seemed to be gone a lot and another man was coming by the house.

"No, no, that's just a family friend," she said defensively, and then walked back into her house. That was the last she ever spoke to Greenhaw.

With his Army buddies, John was completely open about Michelle, even boastful. One night, John came by the barracks dressed up. "I asked him where he was going. He told me he and Michelle were going swinging," his Army buddy Rickie Bizon recalled. "I asked him what swinging was, and he explained to me that he and Michelle would go to a swing club and meet other couples and swapped partners. He told me they went 'swinging' a lot."

Army Sergeant Mark Dash, a fellow squad leader with John in the same company, saw them at a local nightclub called It'z. And Sergeant John Pickett once saw Michelle driving her yellow Corvette onto the post to pick up John. Another time, John brought Michelle to the barracks, according to Rickie Bizon. The pair watched the movie *Vampires* and ate chicken.

"I believe Michelle and Sergeant Diamond were exclusive, because he never talked about any other females," said Pickett. "Sergeant Diamond once told me that he and Michelle went away for the weekend a couple of times and also went to clubs."

Bizon said, "John Diamond told me he met a psychiatrist and that she was pretty wealthy. [He] said that she makes quite a bit of money. He told me she made about $4,500 a month." At the time, John was making about half that as an Army sergeant, listing on a college aid application a 1999 adjusted gross income of $22,958.

The only ones who didn't seem to know about the relationship were Lourdes and Marty.

Even when Marty returned home from his deployment in April 1999, not long after Michelle had started the affair, he still appeared unaware. His presence—often sporadic due to shorter term deployments—posed only a minor inconvenience. Instead of going to Michelle's house, John and Michelle snuck away to motels in Fayetteville, Raleigh, Charlotte and Wilmington, taking turns paying for the rooms. And when Marty was out of town, John would return to the Theer house, again doing little to avoid the neighbors' eyes.

Lourdes, too, was clueless, though John having an affair wouldn't have surprised her.

A native of Panama, Lourdes met John when he was stationed there in 1995. At the time, he was 22 years old and she was 29. She thought he was the most handsome man she had ever met—a thought that occurred to more than a few women. John's family said that he always attracted women. "When he was younger, he never ever had to look for women, they always came to him," his mother, Kris Diamond, said. "He loved women. He never got serious about anybody, though." His sister, Deborah Dvorak, recalled in a television news interview, "He took two girls to the senior prom. He's never been in love with just one woman. He was always one woman after another."

When John met Lourdes, he fell hard. He told her almost immediately that he wanted to get married.

But the relationship had problems from the start. Lourdes later told *The Fayetteville Observer* that John wouldn't let her visit him in the barracks. When she called him at work in the afternoon, she would be told in Spanish that he had "gone home," a phrase that in Panama meant he had a family.

Then, one night at dinner in a restaurant, a woman came up to them and asked John how his baby was. When Lourdes demanded an explanation, he said that until recently he had been married and that he had a daughter whom he never saw back in the United States. He had never told Lourdes.

In fact, John had gotten married shortly after joining the military, but was divorced when he left for Panama.

This left Lourdes shocked and angry. But in what would become a pattern, she forgave him, and the relationship continued, better than before. On October 23, 1996, they got married. Two years later, Lourdes gave birth to a son.

But a second shot at marriage and fatherhood did nothing to stop John's wandering eye. One day, the phone rang at their home in Panama and Lourdes answered. The caller was a woman asking what time John would be picking her up to go to the beach. Another time, after he had been out late frequently, John told Lourdes that he was participating in night exercises; it turned out he was, but they were not of the military variety. Lourdes found love letters in John's pockets from a Panamanian woman.

Every time Lourdes confronted John, he'd tell her, "You're crazy." And every time, Lourdes forgave him.

"I always had hope in my heart, because I loved him, and I had hope that when we moved to the U.S. we start a new life," she told the *Observer*.

That happened in early 1999 when John was transferred to Fort Bragg in North Carolina. Lourdes moved first to John's parents' house in Killeen, Texas, while he got settled in North Carolina. In the fall of 1999, Lourdes and their year-old son moved into the two-bedroom apartment with John not far from the base.

At first, life in America was as good as Lourdes had dreamed. And the fact that she spoke almost no English proved only a minor problem. She got a job as a housekeeper on base, and could speak Spanish with the other Latina workers as she slowly learned English. There were Spanish language programs on television. And John was fluent in Spanish. John kept regular hours, returning each night for dinner, and she believed that he had left his womanizing in Panama.

But within months, the old signs returned. John would stay out all night, offering lame excuses. Once, a woman called their apartment for him.

When Lourdes confronted John, he would become angry. "He treated me real bad," Lourdes recalled. "One night, when we started to discuss our problems, he tried to grab me and he told me he was going to kill me so bad that my son would see the blood. He was verbally abusive by always saying things to me that offended me. I remember one time that he told me that he got tired of old pussy. He always got mad I couldn't leave with anybody, because he was always watching my time. He would get very mad if I wasn't on time."

In November 1999, they got a legal separation, and John found himself spending many nights on Army buddy Rickie Bizon's sofa in the barracks. But the Diamonds never split for long. John would return to the apartment and spend the night with Lourdes, who clung to the hope that they could reconcile and live happily ever after.

John frequently told her that despite everything, he loved her. And just as frequently, he disappointed her.

In the spring of 2000, John underwent surgery on his knee to repair an injury. Lourdes decided that she would surprise him by visiting him in the hospital. She went into his room, sat down and told him, "I came to see how you are."

"No," he said, agitated, "you have to go."

Lourdes wasn't willing to leave.

"No," she told him, "I want to stay here because I want to see what happened with the operation, how you are."

Angry, John summoned a nurse to say that Lourdes was bothering him. He told the nurse that she was an ex-wife and wouldn't leave.

"I'm not your ex-wife," Lourdes snapped back. "I'm your wife. But I'm going to leave because I don't want problems."

As she left, Lourdes saw a brunette woman go into John's room. At the time, Lourdes didn't know what Michelle Theer looked like.

Lourdes wouldn't know about Michelle until Clinkscales told her.

Now, in late January 2001, the woman whom Lourdes had first seen in the hospital was meeting John for dinner to compare notes. Each had been interviewed by police; each had disclosed the affair, though gave differing versions of its duration and intensity, with Michelle suggesting it was over and John saying it was still ongoing. Michelle had revealed to police that she'd called John from the Raleigh restaurant just hours before the murder. And police had made it clear to Michelle that they not only felt John was a suspect, but that she was under scrutiny, as well.

That's why Michelle's lawyers had advised her to stay

away from John Diamond. But at this point, Michelle felt she had nothing to lose. She needed to know everything she could about the investigation.

Later, Michelle said she'd taken detailed notes on what John had said, then gone home and typed up a question-and-answer memo for her attorneys. The Q&A, which police would later find on her computer, reflected what Michelle claimed were John's recollections and feelings as police were bearing down on him.

It portrayed John as confident, defiant, and as angry with police—in all, very much on the same wavelength Michelle. In fact, it would never be known for certain how much of the remarks were her words or John's. Still, the Q&A memo would be the only record of what John and Michelle had discussed that night in January.

It began with John being asked about the early days after Marty's murder on Sunday, December 17, with John telling her that Clinkscales—Michelle spelled his name "Kinkscales"—and a second detective described as "some little gray-haired white guy with a moustache and glasses" showing up at the barracks.

"Did you know why they were there?" Michelle asked.

"No," John said, according to the notes. "They asked if I knew Frank Theer. It didn't ring a bell right away and I said no. They asked if I know Michelle Theer. I said yes and they told me he is her husband. They asked if I've been reading the paper or looking at the news, and I said I only watch CNN. I asked what was going on and what was this all about. They told me he had been shot and killed Sunday night. They wanted me to go downtown and ask some questions about our relationship."

John told Michelle that he went to the station where he spoke to police, who didn't read him his rights or record the interview. The investigators, he said, honed in on his relationship with Michelle.

"They asked how we met, how we knew each other, if we talked about our spouses with one another," John said. "Then they asked where I was Sunday night. I told them I was with my wife and her mother visiting my son. I spent the night there that night."

John recounted how police asked him if he had owned a gun—he told them no—and inquired about his military training.

"They keyed in on sniper school and all my Ranger training and started alluding to the fact that I had all the training and I was a good enough shot that I could have done this," he said.

"What did you say to them about that?" Michelle asked.

"I told them there are thousands of other guys on post who have done all the same things and it doesn't mean that any of us had done it," John said. "Then they asked if you ever had fights with your husband, and if you could have done it, or if you could have hired someone to do it."

"What did you tell them?"

"I said no. She is not the kind of person who could have done it or hired anyone to do it."

John said he told police that he and Michelle met on the Internet, and "that is when they told me you do this a lot. I asked what they meant 'does that a lot'? They said you go on the Internet, pick up guys, go and have sex with them, stuff like that. Then they asked if it made me mad to hear that you did that."

"What did you say?"

"No, that I didn't believe that and even if you did, we are just friends," said John. "Whatever you do in your private life is your business. We're just friends.

Michelle then asked: "Did they ask you to let them swab your hands for gunpowder residue?

"No," John said.

Up to this point, the Q&A corresponded roughly to what

Clinkscales and Sergeant Mitirisn—the "little gray-haired white guy"—recorded in their reports, though some of the timing was off. When police interviewed John on the Tuesday after the murder, they still did not know about Michelle's Internet activities—that information came later.

In the Q&A, Michelle showed how eager she was to find out how much police knew and suspected about her—and what John was saying. She asked him if police revealed anything else "about me or our relationship that would make you think they were labeling us as suspects."

"They said that there was a large life insurance policy and it would be real convenient for something to happen to him because you would get all the money," said John, according to Michelle's notes. "They also pointed out that we were having an inappropriate relationship. They mentioned you were having marriage problems and asked if I knew about it. I told them, no—no more than anyone else and that we didn't talk about things like that."

"Were they harassing you, trying to push any buttons?"

"They were trying to get me riled up and saying that you were just using me and a lot of other guys, and that I shouldn't try to protect you," said John. "They were really trying to get me to point the finger at someone."

Michelle then asked John about the follow-up interview with his wife, Lourdes.

"This is when they told her they had to tell her some information," said John. "That is when they told her about us and our relationship. They told her that we were suspects in your husband's death. Then they told her that she shouldn't protect me because we were planning on moving and I had no intentions of seeing her or my son again, that I was not going to pay child support and would leave her high and dry.

"How was she reacting to this?" asked Michelle.

"Crying, upset. They asked her the same questions over

and over again, telling her not to protect me, that they would ruin my son's life."

"She stuck to her story, though?"

"Yes, even though she was upset. She told them she was not trying to protect me and that she was telling the whole truth."

The Q&A went on to say that police also interviewed Lourdes' mother, his friends in the barracks, his sergeant major and his first sergeant and his mother. All were asked if John owned a gun and if he had ever talked about killing anybody. All said no to both questions. To his superiors, police asked what kind of soldier John was, if they knew about his extramarital affairs—an important question because adultery is a crime in the military—and whether they though he was capable of murder.

Each said he was a model soldier. Police even interviewed John's mother, Kristine Diamond, in Texas.

"They asked if she thought that I had done it, asked what she knew about our relationship, and that if she was hiding something she shouldn't try to protect me," John said. "They told her they would ruin my life until I confessed."

"What did she say about their questions?" Michelle asked.

"She told them I would never do anything like that, and that she doesn't know anything about my private life. As far as she knows, I am just a playboy. Then they told her again that if I didn't cooperate with what they wanted, they would make my life miserable."

With everyone backing John, the harassment was stepped up. Another detective called John's cell phone and asked John to take a polygraph. John told him that he had to talk to his lawyer first.

"I did tell him at that time I felt unsure about taking it through their agency because they were lying to me, lying to my wife, lying to my friends and I felt like they were trying to coerce false information," said John.

"Tell me more about what lies they told your friends and family?" asked Michelle.

"That I was a raging jealous person that couldn't stand that you were married, that we were going to run off together, and I was going to abandon all my responsibilities, that you were hopping from bed to bed and I was being manipulated by you."

According to the Q&A, John went back to his lawyers to ask them what to do about the polygraph. The lawyers told him that a lie-detector test was a lose-lose for John, and that police were fishing; if they had any good evidence, they would have already arrested him. He was advised to pass on the polygraph."

Police told John they would continue to pressure him, that they would make his life difficult until they ruled him out as a suspect.

"They also told me that if I didn't cooperate they were going to prevent me from getting out of the service," John said.

Along with the Q&A with John, Michelle prepared a detailed timeline of her interactions with police and others since her husband's murder. Again, she insisted that this document was intended for her attorneys, though authorities would challenge that, calling it instead a private diary.

In either case, starting around the time that she met with John at dinner and going through February 15, Michelle meticulously recorded her versions of events and conversations, offering not only factual details, but a window into her mindset in the weeks following her husband's murder.

What she didn't know at the time was these documents—the Q&A with John and her timeline—would be retrieved from her computer.

She also didn't know that she would soon be under surveillance.

15

It was an anonymous call that tipped her off to police. "A neighbor of the Theers on English Saddle Drive called with suspicious activity at Theer's house," according to the report of the call, which came in at 8:30 a.m. on February 1, 2001. "A man comes to side of house and parks. Has done this three days. The caller's son saw the man enter thru the garage and into the house two times. The son saw this at 2:30 pm."

The car was described as a Pontiac Formula, late 1990s, painted teal, with the North Carolina license plate NPA-9417. A vehicle registration check found that the car belonged to John Diamond.

The report was forwarded to Detective Ralph Clinkscales, who called OSI Agent Vince Bustillo asking for surveillance on the house and daily updates. Soon, six Air Force vehicles, including rented civilian cars and a pickup, were following Michelle and keeping watch on her house.

On a rainy Thursday, February 8, Michelle left her house. It became evident that this would be for something longer than a grocery run. Police didn't know it at the time, but she was headed for Florida.

The exact destination was Melbourne, her former home. She planned to meet a former college psychology professor for three days of intensive trauma therapy to cope with her husband's death and the stress from the police investigation. For a companion on the trip, she'd initially called Rafael Harris. Michelle later said that he'd first agreed, but then backed out because he was on call that weekend at the psychology clinic. Another friend who had previously said she would love to go to Florida with Michelle any time declined.

"I was very distressed," Michelle wrote in her timeline memo. "I was afraid to drive myself. I am afraid to go out alone at night. I mentioned my dilemma to JD"—John Diamond—"and he offered to drive down with me."

John's sister, Deborah Dvorak, lived about an hour from Melbourne. John agreed to have Michelle drop him off there for a visit while Michelle went on to the home of her friend Donna Miller-Brown, another classmate from the Florida Institute of Technology. After Michelle finished her therapy, she would return to Deborah's house on Monday to pick up John for the 70-mile, 9-hour drive back to Fayetteville.

"It was not a romantic weekend getaway, as I am sure the police department would believe or tell others," Michelle wrote in her timeline. "Still, I did realize before leaving Fayetteville that going out of town with JD would not look good, but had no reason to believe anyone would ever know."

They left as planned on Thursday for John's sister's house in Citra, arriving late at night or early Friday morning. John did much of the driving while Michelle slept. When they arrived at his sister's house, Michelle went inside briefly to use the restroom, then returned to the car. As scheduled, John stayed behind and Michelle drove by herself to her friend's house in Merritt Island, near Melbourne.

That weekend, Donna took Michelle to one of the professors for the therapy. As they traveled, Donna realized that she hadn't seen Michelle recently and "I was really shocked to see that the roots of her hair were turning white," recalled Donna. "To me, that was a sign of stress."

On Sunday morning, February 11, Michelle left Donna's house for a gas station in Ormond Beach, where she waited for John to arrive. His brother-in-law, Victor Dvorak, dropped John off in the parking lot without speaking to Michelle. All he remembered was that she was driving a newer model Trans Am–type car, possibly blue, matching the description of John's car. John and Michelle drove back to Donna's house to spend the night.

Donna recalled that they didn't act like a couple, and slept in separate rooms. The next day, they drove back to North Carolina.

Michelle later wrote in her timeline memo that when they'd arrived in Fayetteville, she stopped at her house to unload her luggage, then took John to his car, which was parked at Fort Bragg in a lot across the street from the barracks.

"At his car, John realized immediately that his car had been broken in," Michelle wrote, a victim of what she called "an extremely rampant problem on Bragg." She wrote that the passenger-side window was shattered and the car was soaked inside from the heavy rains over the weekend. When John looked inside, he found "several items" had been stolen from the back seat, Michelle wrote, and that the center console was emptied.

When he reached under the seat, he started cursing.

"I know the cops did this," he said, according to Michelle.

John told her, she wrote, that he had borrowed a handgun from a friend the week before.

According to Michelle's account, John said that he had planned to shoot the 9mm pistol at the range over the weekend, but stored it under the seat when he'd decided instead to take the trip to Florida.

"He had left the weapon in the car because he could not bring it in to the barracks, could not leave it with his ex-wife because she is not speaking to him due to the lies and the harassment by the police," Michelle wrote in her timeline, "and he did not want to even have a weapon in my presence or leave it at my house because he knows how easily certain things make me break down."

Unknown to Michelle at the time, police were amassing

evidence undercutting key parts of her story. While John and Michelle were on the road on their way to Florida, Fayetteville police had tracked down one of the most important witnesses of the case.

16

They found him from calls logged on John's cell phone. Obtaining the phone records by subpoena, police pored over the calls recorded in the days surrounding Marty's murder. One number was dialed on John's cell phone at 10:43 a.m. on Monday, December 18, 2000—the day after the homicide. From their investigation, detectives knew that this was at almost the exact time that John had finished firing his rental 9mm at Jim's Pawn Shop.

The number was traced to a man named Peyton Ross Donald, an Army sergeant at Fort Bragg.

On Monday, February 12—the same day that Michelle and John were returning to Fayetteville from the weekend in Florida—agents from the Army's Criminal Investigation Division found Peyton on the post and told him Fayetteville police wanted to talk to him.

At 3:15 p.m. the sergeant reported to the Fayetteville police station for an interview with Detective Clinkscales and OSI Agent Bustillo. Peyton explained that he and John had met in Panama in the mid-1990s when John was his squad leader. They'd renewed their acquaintance when both found themselves stationed at Fort Bragg in 1999. John attended college classes down the street from Peyton's house and would stop by occasionally.

Peyton knew little about John's personal life, though he

did know about Michelle. He said he'd met her once "as far as I remember" at a dinner with his wife and with Michelle and John at Tony Roma's barbecue restaurant. John had told Peyton that Michelle was married to an Air Force officer.

A couple of days later, Peyton saw Michelle again, only this time with a different man. Peyton later described him to John, who said it was probably her husband, Captain Marty Theer.

Bringing the interview closer to the case at hand, Detective Clinkscales asked if Peyton owned or had access to a firearm.

He said he did, a Smith & Wesson 9mm pistol that he had purchased in Panama. The detectives asked Peyton if the gun had ever left his custody or if it could have recently been used in a crime. Peyton initially said no. He had always had it and was happy to go home and bring in the gun for police to see.

There was something in the way that he answered that left Clinkscales and Bustillo concerned, for they then asked him if they could follow him home while he got the gun.

Peyton changed his answer. He said he had in fact let the gun out of his possession, but it had gone to a trusted friend.

John Diamond.

Clinkscales asked if John had had the gun in his possession on December 17, 2000, the day that Marty Theer was fatally shot.

Peyton said that he had.

The sergeant said that John hadn't kept it, however. He'd returned the gun to Peyton a few days later, only to borrow it again. The last time John had taken the gun was just two weeks ago. He'd never said why he wanted it again.

Even as he spoke to police, and the implications of what he was saying were becoming evident, Peyton insisted he wasn't worried about the gun, because he trusted John.

Clinkscales asked Peyton to call John to see if he still had the gun. The detective asked to record the conversation, which made Peyton uneasy. Peyton said that if John had nothing to hide, then everything would be OK, and recording was unnecessary.

Clinkscales continued to press, asking if he could at least listen in on another extension. Again, Peyton refused. He was certain that John still had the gun and would be happy to show it to police to test.

The investigators agreed to the terms. But because they still wanted to see the gun registration paperwork, they asked if Peyton could call John from home. They followed him to his house on Tartan Court in Fayetteville. He first showed the detectives a US Forces Panama Weapon Registration Card, identifying the gun to be a Smith & Wesson model 5906 with a four-inch barrel—overall length of 6 inches—with serial number TDE1713.

It was a 9mm—the same caliber of gun that had killed Marty Theer.

At 4:36 p.m., Peyton called John's cell phone. It wasn't known where John was, but this was around the time that Michelle would claim that John was with her, coming back from their trip to Florida.

"Hey, man, do you have that handgun?" Peyton asked, as the detectives listened to only his end of the conversation. "Do you have the pistol? Fayetteville PD wants it."

When John asked Peyton why they wanted the gun, Peyton said, "They want to shoot some rounds through it."

The detectives couldn't hear John's reply. But from Peyton's reaction, they knew it wasn't good. His face fell. He appeared confused.

"OK, well I will talk to them," he told John. "I will tell them that you don't have it."

He hung up the phone and leaned back in his chair, not saying anything for a moment. He then told the investigators he couldn't believe what John had said. He was stunned.

They asked him to call John back. Peyton was reluctant,

but Clinkscales pressed hard. He told Peyton that this was serious business, that this gun—his gun—may well have been involved in a homicide. And now it was missing.

"Just give me a minute," Peyton said.

Peyton composed himself and called John back at 4:37 p.m.

"Where is it?" Peyton asked. "Do you know when you can get it? So what am I supposed to do? You don't have it?"

Over and over, John told him he didn't have the gun anymore.

"They want it now," Peyton said. "I want it now."

Peyton hung up again and told the investigators that John insisted he didn't have the gun anymore, and that if the police had any more questions, they should talk to John directly.

The detectives asked Peyton to try to talk to John himself one more time. Ten minutes later, Peyton called John. This time, John said he wanted to talk to Peyton later that night.

"OK," said Peyton, now spent. "I don't like being involved in anything like this, and I don't like them questioning me. Come clean."

After he hung up, the investigators decided to leave. Three phone calls to John and it was obvious he wasn't going to reveal anything to Peyton Donald.

At the investigators' request, Peyton gave them ten rounds of 9mm Luger ammunition that he used in the pistol, and they started to walk out of his house. Just as they got to the door, Peyton's cell phone rang. He spoke to the caller and then motioned for the investigators to stop.

It was John. He said he had the gun after all. It was in his car, and he would bring it to Peyton later that night.

An hour after that phone conversation, the Military Police at Fort Bragg got a call regarding a car break-in in the parking lot near Gavin Hall. An MP, Private First Class John Mc-

Cann, responded at 6:14 p.m. There he found Staff Sergeant John Diamond standing next to a teal Pontiac Firebird with a busted passenger-side window.

Asked what had happened, John told the MP that the car had been parked there for four days, since Thursday, February 8, and that when he returned, he'd found the window broken and several items stolen, including a number of compact discs and a handgun.

McCann had handled smash-and-grab cases on the base before and was familiar with the way a car looks after a break-in. This one didn't fit the pattern. He found broken glass on the passenger seat and floor, but none on the driver's side. Typically, a smash-and-grab leaves a mess, with glass strewn about the interior. If anything, this one looked like the passenger door had been open when the window was broken, evidence that this was a fake break-in.

That would be a topic for later exploration. Right now, whether this was a real or staged break-in, John Diamond was in a lot of trouble. In telling McCann that a handgun had been stolen, Diamond was admitting to an offense under Article 92 of the Military Code of Ethics failure to obey an order by possessing a privately owned gun on base.

McCann frisked and handcuffed John. Just then, a woman drove up in a four-door Honda sedan. She was in tears. McCann assumed that this was John's wife.

At the time, the MP knew nothing about the murder investigation into John Diamond and didn't recognize Michelle Theer driving a borrowed Honda. McCann also was unaware that agents from the Criminal Investigation Division had been tipped off to John's reported break-in and had quietly arrived outside Gavin Hall about the same time as McCann, secretly watching as the MP arrested John.

Michelle drove away and John was transported to the MP station. At 6:50 p.m., he was taken to a holding room and questioned further by McCann. But within minutes, the MP received an order to stop the interview. The case was being handed to investigators from CID. One of its agents would conduct the rest of the interview. McCann stopped his work, and for the next several hours, John remained at the MP headquarters, waiting.

It was CID Special Agent Patrick J. Conner who had phoned ahead asking the MPs to halt the interview. Conner was one of the military investigators assigned to the probe into Captain Marty Theer's murder. On his way to the MP headquarters to speak with John, Conner stopped to look at John's car. Like McCann, Conner thought the break-in was suspicious. In addition to the lack of shattered glass on the interior, the car stereo hadn't been damaged and nothing had been taken from the glove compartment. The car was wet inside, but not as wet as Conner thought it should have been from the heavy rain. The floorboards and cloth seats were damp, but there was no pooled water.

After looking at the car, Conner went to the MP headquarters, where he was joined by two other investigators: another CID Agent, David A. Rudd, and Fayetteville police Detective Ralph Clinkscales, who had been summoned to the base after John had reported the break-in and was arrested.

By now it was past 10 p.m. on day that had started early for John, nearly 500 miles away in a different state. John was read his constitutional rights to have an attorney and to remain silent—he waived those rights—and settled in for what would be a two-hour interview by Conner and Rudd, stretching into the early morning hours of the next day.

Clinkscales secretly observed the interview from behind a one-way glass.

No transcript of the interview exists, but according to reports later filed, the agents began by asking about the break-in. John told them the same thing he'd told the MP: that he'd returned to his car that evening after being away for a few days, only to find the window broken and $30 in cash, a collection of CDs and an unloaded Smith & Wesson all missing. The gun, he said, had been stashed under the seat.

The agents asked him where he had gotten the weapon. John said he had borrowed it from his friend Peyton Donald, because he was thinking of buying it. He said this wasn't the first time he had borrowed it; he had used it before in January to shoot at a range in Hope Mills, North Carolina. He couldn't recall the name of the range or the exact location of it, because he had never been there before and had simply followed directions from a friend in his unit. He said he'd only fired the gun that one time.

Asked why the gun had been left in his car, John explained that he hadn't given the gun back right away because he'd planned on shooting it again. He acknowledged speaking with Peyton Donald earlier that day, but claimed Peyton had never asked for the gun back to give to the Fayetteville Police Department.

As for his whereabouts over the weekend, John said that on February 8, he had left for Florida with Michelle Theer in her black four-door sedan. He'd visited his sister and looked in the area for a college to attend, as he planned to "ETS"—exit the service—the next month, March. John told the investigators he was planning on going to a civilian school, either the University of Florida or the University of South Florida.

Michelle, he said, was visiting a former professor to treat her for post-traumatic stress. During the trip, John said, Michelle had slept most of the way because of medications.

Asked about their relationship, John—unaware that Clinkscales was watching him—gave a different account from the one with Fayetteville police, describing his relationship with Michelle as platonic. (Adultery is a crime in the military.) John said they'd met at a Barnes & Noble bookstore—he said nothing of answering a personal ad on the Internet—and gone out for the first time to O'Charley's restaurant. They would occasionally go to clubs, but just as friends, and they corresponded on line once or twice a week using Yahoo with the log-on losdiamantes. Michelle's log-on was drmichelle, but he didn't know what server she used.

John said he had spoken to Michelle about her husband's murder. She told him that on the night he was killed she and Marty had come back from dinner with her and gone to her office to get a book she'd needed for class. While in the office, she told him, she'd heard something outside, and went out to find her husband.

John said that at the time of the murder he was with his wife, son and mother-in-law. Despite the alibi, John complained, police treated him like a criminal. As Clinkscales secretly watched, John accused the detective of harassing John's wife Lourdes and threatening to put her in jail. The police investigators, John said, had told him that Michelle whores around quite a bit.

"[He said] if the police had something on him, then they would have arrested him by now," Clinkscales wrote in a report on the interview. "He would not put himself in a situation like this, being the boyfriend kill the husband and have the police target him for the homicide. He mentioned that if your spouse cheats on you, then you must not be doing what you are supposed to be doing in the first place."

The interview ended around midnight, and John was released for the night. He was driven back to the barracks, where Michelle picked him up. He had been ordered to be at the CID office at 1 p.m. the next day, Tuesday, February 13.

After John left, the investigators on both sides of the one-way glass compared notes. John's account of the break-in was untrue. They had more than Peyton Donald's statements. They also had videotape.

17

Again, it was a neighbor who turned on Michelle.

He was a former Army soldier named Shannon Wayne Mack. Several days earlier, Shannon had called Air Force OSI agents to report that a man was paying nearly daily visits to the widow of slain Air Force Captain Marty Theer. Shannon was transferred to Agent Vince Bustillo, who convinced Shannon to cooperate with the investigation.

After conferring with Fayetteville police, Bustillo arranged to have surveillance technicians install two military intelligence–grade Sony video cameras at Mack's home behind a vent in a storage space above the garage, with the lenses aimed at Michelle's house and the street in front.

One camera had a Fuji 140mm lens with a doubler, the other had a 300mm lens with night vision capability. A pair of recorders were placed on a garage shelf and loaded with videotapes that could handle up to twenty-four hours on one tape. An internal battery kept the cameras running and the time and date stamps current in the event of a power outage.

Installation began Saturday, February 10 while Michelle was in Florida with John, and the equipment was up and running at 6:42 p.m. the next evening. In exchange for $150 and a 12-pack of beer, Mack agreed to change the tapes each night at 9 p.m. For the first day, there was nothing to shoot. John never arrived at Michelle's house and Michelle was nowhere to be found. The cameras quietly photographed an empty house.

But the next day, Monday, there was activity. According

to the time log on the video, at 4:28 p.m., a black Honda driven by Michelle pulled up in front of her house. Police later learned that Michelle had borrowed the Honda from a woman who worked as a casualty affairs officer at Fort Bragg, helping spouses after a loved one is killed or dies. The woman had lent her the car because Michelle told her she was too upset to drive the Explorer.

Just after Michelle arrived, the video showed John's teal Pontiac Firebird pulling into the driveway. This was the same car that John would later claim had been parked all weekend at the base and which he'd found burglarized in the parking lot.

The video showed Michelle getting out of the Honda and checking her mailbox. She returned to the Honda, unlocked the door and turned the light out on her car, then walked up to her house. About a half-hour later, the videotape showed, Michelle walked out of her house to the Honda carrying a bag in one hand and two bags over her shoulder. She put something in the trunk, then opened the driver's-side door and put two of the bags in the back seat.

She got into the car and drove away from the house, while behind her, John pulled out of the driveway in his Firebird. Michelle made a U-turn somewhere out of the camera frame and drove up in front of her house, where she idled the Honda next to John's Pontiac. They could be seen speaking briefly. The Pontiac did not have a broken window; the reflection from the glass was visible on the video.

Both cars were seen on the video driving side-by-side on English Saddle Drive, leaving the Hunter's Crossing neighborhood at about 5:10 p.m.

It was during the time between Michelle's arrival home and the pair's conversation from their cars that John had spoken to Peyton Donald about the borrowed handgun.

And less than an hour after the cars were taped leaving Michelle's neighborhood, John had called the MPs to report that the same Pontiac Firebird had been broken into and Peyton's gun stolen.

Between the videotape and Peyton Donald's statement, investigators knew they could arrest John Diamond for charges much more serious than weapons possession and adultery.

John apparently knew it, too. When his company assembled in PT formation at Fort Bragg on the morning of February 13, John was missing. He had been ordered to return at 6:30 a.m., and no one knew where he was. His commander put out the word to look for him.

Eventually, at 1 p.m., John showed up, explaining that he had been talking to CID officers. But CID said he hadn't been with them. For those seven hours, John was considered AWOL. Now seen as a flight risk, he was ordered to remain on the post under close supervision.

But he disappeared again. Members of his unit fanned out and found him 100 yards away in the North Carolina woods. He was hauled back and placed on barracks restriction indefinitely.

That meant he wasn't allowed to go to Methodist College classes at night. Worse, he was forbidden from communicating with Michelle—not by telephone, email, letters or in person.

The separation proved excruciating for both of them.

18

"I have no idea when he will contact me again."

Sitting at her computer, making another entry into her timeline, Michelle's anger swelled. It was the police, she was convinced—Clinkscales and the others—who were destroying her life.

"I believe it is their intention to keep us from communicating so they can manipulate either of us in any way they please and prevent communication," she wrote after she found out about John's arrest, "that the more we talk to each other, the more their incompetence is revealed."

For comfort, she turned to where she always had: the Internet.

On February 13, the day John went AWOL, she found an email from her friend Michelle Montgomery. The Montgomerys had stood by Michelle from the beginning. It had been the Montgomerys who'd arrived at the murder scene to see Michelle.

> Dear Michelle,
>
> I can only imagine how hard Valentine's Day is for you. I hope your memories of love carry you through the day.
>
> Michelle Montgomery.

Michelle Theer wrote her back.

> Dear Michelle,
>
> Thank you so much for all your support and help

> in this ordeal. I don't think I ever got the chance to tell you, but I have always thought you were the best commander's wife I have ever encountered, and I am third generation Air Force. I do have a favor to ask of you and your husband. My attorney is asking me to gather statements from anyone who had direct interaction with the police and any knowledge of the interactions between myself and the police. I would like both you and Paul to write a statement if you are comfortable doing so.
>
> The statements should be "as you remember it and in as much detail as possible," What we would like you to include is everything you remember about that night, then notification, your arrival at the scene, what you were told, the message you were given that I was not interested in your help.
>
> Only write what you remember to the best of your ability, but please include everything you felt was improper or harmful.

She also asked that Paul include in his statement his observations of how agents from the OSI had treated her when she'd tried to get information from them about the murder investigation.

> This case is very likely to go unsolved, and I would have trouble five years down the road when no one will remember anything. Please have the statements notarized, if that is possible.
>
> I'd love to get together with you soon. What do you say we go get a manicure and pedicure and a start to the year of Michelle. I'm free all day Friday and next Monday.
>
> Warmest regards.
>
> Michelle.

◆ ◆ ◆

The next day, Valentine's Day, came and went, with Michelle, who once had so many romantic partners, now faced with no one to be with but her platonic friend Rafael Harris. He had returned from his trip to Venezuela and was spending a couple of days at Michelle's house. It was the first time he had seen her since the weekend before the murder, when Michelle had arranged to meet him in Raleigh to celebrate his passage of the state's licensing exam for psychologists. But Rafael was surprised when Michelle showed up with John Diamond. All night, at the restaurant and later at a club, Rafael felt like a "third wheel," and that evening, Michelle and John retired to the same hotel room at the Holiday Inn.

Now, after so much had happened, Rafael asked her about the man she had been with during that weekend in Raleigh. Michelle said that John was being confined to the post because investigators thought he might have been involved in the murder of Marty.

That was all she said, and Rafael didn't press. He thought that if she wanted to say more, she'd tell him. But then, sharing her feelings about John had been virtually impossible for Michelle.

Being away from him, as she was now, seemed unbearable. Friends like Michelle Montgomery and Rafael Harris weren't the same.

In the summer of 2000, Michelle had been free to see John as much as she wanted. She'd moved out of the house and into a furnished unit at the Applewood Village apartment complex. She had a three-month lease. John regularly came by and made himself at home, so much so that when one of John's Army friends visited, he remarked that the two looked like a couple.

After the separation, Marty had finally agreed to see a marriage counselor, creating a situation in which Michelle was still secretly seeing John, while also making an effort to save her marriage. She was living, as she had been since going on the Internet, a double life.

On June 27, 2000, Michelle and Marty attended their first session with Kenneth Kastleman. Although in the same profession as Michelle, his academic credentials were stronger. A Harvard undergraduate, Kastleman received his clinical psychology degree from the University of North Carolina, and was licensed by the state as a marital and family therapist and as a psychologist. He had nearly twenty years more experience as a therapist.

When the couple came into his office at 3 p.m., all Kastleman knew were Michelle's name—he had been told only that her husband would be attending—and that they had been referred by Dr. Tom Harbin for marital counseling.

Addressing complicated marital problems takes time, and the session for the Theers, as for other couples, began slowly, with Kastleman making an initial evaluation, dissecting and analyzing the relationship. As such, he would want to try to determine the nature of the relationship, the couple's conflicts and connections, and the level of motivation that existed by one or both to undergo therapy, to make things better. This evaluation could take more than one session, and might involve speaking separately with each member of the couple.

Kastleman wanted to find out early on whether there was any drug or alcohol abuse, physical violence or neglect involved in the relationship. Such a finding could send the process outside his office into a hospital or a jail cell.

According to his notes of that first session, substance abuse and domestic violence didn't exist. That left finding out what other problems plagued the Theers and beginning to chart a course for action.

As Kastleman spoke with the Theers, he jotted down his impressions and selected direct quotations from the couple that he felt reflected certain issues that may have to be dealt with later.

"I've changed and I think Marty needs to recognize that," Michelle said.

Marty, in turn, said, "I don't understand why Michelle isn't able to work this out with me."

From the first, Kastleman realized the couple existed in "an atmosphere of significant disagreement" and that much of this disagreement stemmed from "long-standing conflicts." Among the most critical conflicts, he found, was the issue of autonomy: Michelle wanted more freedom, and Marty was struggling to understand and deal with that.

"She has grown distant from Marty over the past several years of their marriage," Kastleman recalled, based on his notes. "Marty reports that he doesn't see why Michelle is so upset about things and thinks they can reconcile their differences."

Marty said the couple had just returned from a trip together—Kastleman's notes don't say where—that was intended to help them work out their problems and get along better. At the time, Kastleman was not told that the couple lived separately, Marty in the house, Michelle in the apartments. And Michelle would never tell him about her affair with John Diamond or her experiences in the swinger world.

The session ended with the couple agreeing that they needed to continue seeing Dr. Kastleman, and a follow-up was scheduled for the next week, on July 6, 2000. Kastleman put in his notes that he hoped to gather more information about the couple's ability to tolerate differences, resolve conflicts and see each other's viewpoints.

"These two individuals, in my impression during that session, were locked in a pretty significant disagreement," recalled Kastleman. "They were both articulate and they weren't giving very much. And so I wanted to know a little bit more about Marty and Michelle and how they were able to be flexible in building bridges between them."

In his appointment book, he initially wrote down that both Marty and Michelle would be returning. He later scratched out Michelle's name, and on July 6 only Marty Theer showed up at noon. Kastleman's notes don't say why Michelle didn't attend, and years later, when asked about it, he couldn't remember if an explanation was given. Either way, the session went on without her, with Marty still befuddled about his problems with Michelle.

"I don't understand why she doesn't want to be together," Marty said. "I guess she just doesn't love me anymore."

Marty said that over the years, he had been generally pleased with the marriage and that the problems had begun only recently. He felt like he was the only one putting any energy into saving the marriage. Michelle was the one pulling away, he said.

In trying to see Michelle's side of things, Marty acknowledged that some of his expectations—among them that she keep the house neat and clean—probably bothered her, but not enough for her to want to leave him. He also spoke of debating whether to re-enlist in the Air Force, and said that his decision would be influenced by whether he and Michelle stayed married.

Kastleman made a note that Marty had "developed a style of being quite persistent and insistent," though he was not overly aggressive or threatening. "He simply had a strong opinion and is forceful about it," Kastleman recalled.

He noted that he may have to discuss with Marty how to become better at listening to Michelle and discussing her feelings. Still, Marty seemed willing to do what he had to do to make the marriage work, and a third session was scheduled for a week later, on July 11 at noon.

But the day before the session, Michelle called to cancel.

Kastleman's notes don't give a reason, but the session was reset for July 27 at 6 p.m., and this time, Michelle attended with Marty. This session focused on the issue of boundaries.

"He needs to respect my privacy," Michelle said.

Again, Marty was perplexed, telling the therapist, "I don't see why she has to live in a separate place."

This was the first time Kastleman realized that the two weren't living under the same roof. When he asked about their separation, Michelle explained that she was living in her own apartment and, according to the session notes, "She wants Marty to respect the boundaries she has established."

Among her main concerns was that she wanted Marty to call first before coming to her apartment. Michelle never mentioned anything about John Diamond, whom she was continuing to see while living in the apartment. Rather, the session continued with the clueless Marty questioning why Michelle wanted to live apart, even though he said he was trying to be more understanding.

As he had in the last session with Marty, Kastleman asked Michelle about the history of the marriage. She said that in the beginning she was satisfied to be a homemaker and to accept Marty's needs for a tidy house. But during graduate school and after they'd moved to Fayetteville, she said, she'd become less tolerant of what she saw as his excessive need for order.

Marty responded that he had loosened up recently and couldn't see why Michelle was still upset.

The session ended with Kastleman putting in his notes that it appeared Michelle was in fact the one who was "establishing some distance" with her requests for privacy and complaints about Marty.

Continuing with the evaluation phase, Kastleman wanted to further explore Michelle's issues with boundaries, perhaps in an individual session at some point, to determine whether she was motivated enough to take the next step—therapy—to find ways to make the marriage work.

The Theers left his office agreeing to return, together, a week later, on August 1, at 6 p.m. Prior to the next session, Kastleman got his answer about Michelle's motivation.

She left a message on his answering machine. He called her back. His notes don't reflect exactly what Michelle had said, but her intent was clear: "She terminated the marital evaluation."

Kastleman would never see the couple again. On August 10, he closed the books on Marty and Michelle Theer, summing up what he had gleaned from two sessions with the couple and one with just the husband: "The couple seemed to be stuck in a conflict that was currently unresolved. It would appear that the wife is attempting to distance herself from her husband. The husband is frustrated by the fact that there has been a distance established by his wife over issues he feels could be reconciled."

Later, Michelle expressed dissatisfaction with Dr. Kastleman. "I got us in to see a psychologist who had difficulty working with our schedule and did not seem to be able to help us negotiate the main issues," she wrote. After he told her that he was going on vacation for a month—a scheduling issue not reflected in his notes—she dumped him. "We were frustrated and I finally agreed to see the chaplain with Marty."

Twice in late August 2000, they visited the chaplain at Pope Air Force Base, Michelle said. "The first session we discussed our difficulties and gave the chaplain a chance to hear my side of the story," she later wrote. "In the second session I confronted Marty with the affair"—the affair that Michelle believed Marty was having, based on what she said was the Internet personal ad she'd discovered in Florida. "He admitted it," Michelle wrote. She said that Marty admitted to "looking" for a woman, but never actually having sex with one. "[He] tried to justify it as loneliness and boredom and claimed it was not significant," she wrote.

The chaplain had heard enough, Michelle wrote. Professing to be ill-equipped to continue with these kinds of issues involved, particularly for two agnostics like the Theers, the chaplain said he could no longer counsel them, according to Michelle. "He noted that I was clearly suffering from depression," Michelle wrote, "and that Marty needed to validate my feelings of abandonment."

Michelle said that after the failed efforts with Kastleman and the chaplain, she'd turned to a psychiatrist, who prescribed medication, but it "helped little." Michelle was diagnosed with depression and, over the next four months, prescribed various combinations of the antidepressants Celexa and Paxil, the anti-anxiety medications Xanax and Klonopin and the sleeping pills Ambien and Sonata.

In late September 2000, Michelle's apartment lease was up and so was the separation. She moved back in with Marty, despite the failure of therapy to solve their problems. "I felt that extending what was intended as a therapeutic separation would not be helpful. Marty of course wanted nothing more than for me to come back," Michelle later wrote. "As I feared, once I was back in the house, Marty was happy with the status quo."

But not Michelle. Being back with Marty meant less time with John. Around the same time she returned to live with Marty, Michelle made plans for a second separation—this one permanent.

The island of Saba is a five-square-mile dot in the Caribbean off the coast of Florida, with 1,200 local residents living in a resort-based economy. For visitors, the island offers, in the words of the Saba Tourist Bureau's website, "a secluded haven" with "peaceful and friendly surroundings" and plenty to do or not do, from scuba diving to nature hiking to lying in a hammock. The four small villages on this little Dutch island are "as quaint and charming as the gentle, friendly manner of the Saban people, descended from hardy 17th Century pioneers."

The island is also home to the Saba University School of Medicine, where fifty new students a year are admitted to receive what the school calls "a comprehensive basic and clinical medicine education program that produces physicians who are proficient to meet health care needs in the Netherlands–Antilles and other countries."

In June 2000, around the time that Michelle moved into the apartments, she applied for a job as an instructor at Saba University. How she found out about the school isn't known; however, the university was advertising for a psychology instructor in the sorts of journals that Michelle would have read: *Academic Physician* and *The Chronicle of Higher Education*, and those of the American Psychological Association.

She received an employment application in mid-September, around the time she moved back in with Marty, and sent it back on September 26. It landed on the desk of University President David Fredrick. He was impressed.

He found that Michelle not only possessed the right balance of clinical and teaching experience for a psychology instructor, but her station in life suggested she was more suited to moving to an isolated island. On her application she wrote she had no dependants. Under "Name of spouse," she drew a line.

"I thought, well that actually is a very good possibility for us because single people have less difficulty making a transition," Fredrick recalled.

He affixed a sticky note to her application noting she was 29 years old, single, no children and a strong candidate. Then he called her. Michelle confirmed her academic and employment background and her single status. She told Fredrick she was interested in the position and available to start after the first of the year, but wanted to see the island.

The university has a policy against paying for every promising candidate to come in for an interview. "Otherwise, we'd be flooded with people who want to go to the Caribbean for a visit," Fredrick said. But he was so impressed with Michelle that a compromise was struck. Michelle would pay the airfare and the university would provide lodging and meals.

Michelle had only one other matter to discuss. She said that although she was unmarried, she did have a fiancé who would like to go with her to visit Saba.

"She was interested in the position," recalled Fredrick, "but it would be very helpful if the fiancé also had some activity that he could be involved in while she was there."

Michelle thought perhaps her fiancé could complete his bachelor's degree there at the university. She prepared a letter for Fredrick asking him to review the Methodist College coursework of John Diamond.

By fall of 2000, both were openly referring to each other as their fiancé or spouse. On an application seeking federal financial aid to attend Methodist College, John listed two references, his father, George Diamond, and Michelle Theer, whom he called his "fiancée." And in his psychology class there, John was so good at answering questions that one of the students asked him how he knew so much about the subject. "My fiancée is a psychologist," he said.

A day or two after Michelle spoke to the president of the Saba University School of Medicine, John used her email account to send a message to the Saba Deep dive shop. "Hello, my name is John M. Diamond," began the message, sent September 28, 2000. "Myself and my wife are relocating to San Saba on March 1, '01."

John explained that he was a Special Operations soldier

finishing his Army tour after ten years and that he had many skills. He said he was certified as an advanced diver and in dive rescue and would soon be certified as a dive master. He had a security clearance, spoke fluent Spanish and instructed Brazilian jujitsu and aikido.

"My wife will be teaching at the medical school, and we will be in San Saba for the next three years. So I will have great longevity for work," he wrote. "If you have a position available, I would be very interested in hearing about it. Looking forward to living and working in San Saba. Hope to hear from you soon."

He signed the message, "Sincerely, John Diamond, Staff Sergeant, U.S.A."

John received a quick reply from Donna Cain-Lockhart at the dive shop:

> Hi, John, right now we are at full staff, but by all means keep in touch. Typically, we hire instructors only, so if you would like to take that course up there or possibly here on the island, it would be a benefit to you. In the Caribbean you never know when an opening will come up. If you have any questions about Saba, we would be happy to answer them. It is quite a piece of paradise. Congratulations to your wife.
>
> On a personal note, would you be interested in teaching jujitsu or aikido to children and adults on the island? We had a Tae Kwon Do instructor here that left the island over a year ago and left a void in activities for the youth to be involved in. Let me know your thoughts on this. I am on the board that coordinates the adult education program. I hope to hear from you soon.

The next day, John responded by thanking Donna for her time and saying that he did plan to take the instructor course.

"I would be interested in teaching kids," he said. "Up to now, I've only taught military special operations soldiers, but the transition would be fairly easy. So if you could provide me with the information on that, it would be great."

Donna's reply gave him the lowdown on working on the island. Even if John got a job as a scuba instructor, he could expect to make only $5 an hour. She said he could charge what he wanted for the martial arts classes, with a quarter of the money going to the adult education program for use of the facility.

> You will have to get permission from Immigration/Government to work here, takes sometime, but as long as you are not taking a job away from a local, they will usually grant you permission. We have virtually no unemployment here. You will need a police record, passport, etc. Probably much of that you already need to establish residence, along with a letter requesting permission and what the classes would entail.

On October 5, John sent his last email to the scuba shop, confirming that he would be arriving on the island on the 18th. Donna replied the next day that she might not be there—she had a possible overnight off the island—but "the guys" would be. "Just ask for Mike," she said. "They are both named that so we can't go wrong."

She told him that the Saba Deep dive shop's office was on the windward side in the same building as The Swinging Doors, the island's Western saloon, in the center of the village. The staging area for dives was in Fort Bay, downstairs from the bay's only restaurant, called In Two Deep. "So you can't miss either location," she said. "I have told both Mikes about you, so they will be looking out for your visit."

At the university, meanwhile, administrator William Cornell was given the word that a prospective instructor was on her way to the island. He was asked to set up a dinner with the dean, the dean's wife, the associate dean and the associate dean's wife and himself. "Just a feel-good dinner," recalled Cornell. "It's also kind of an interview process, and they wanted some feedback from me on whether or not she would be a good candidate for the position."

John and Michelle arrived as scheduled at Saba on October 18. They were greeted warmly, with the university treating them to dinner at a restaurant called Bean's Garden. Michelle introduced John to the deans and their wives as her fiancé.

While dining on a 273-dollar meal of soup, garlic bread, grouper and duck, the conversation inevitably turned to island vs. mainland life. The dinner party's host, Administrator Cornell, asked John how he expected to stay busy on an island as small as Saba while Michelle worked at the university. John said he didn't expect to have a problem. He said he was athletic and would enjoy runs around the island. He said he was a certified dive master and would like to do some dive work.

They discussed whether there might be demand for a karate school for kids or adults. Cornell noted that there was a university student about to graduate who had a black belt and taught martial arts. There was some talk of John replacing him. John noted that nearby St. Martin had a sky-diving club, which piqued Cornell's interest, since he had done "a little jumping" in his college years. John seemed interested, in fact "very much so," recalled Cornell. "More so than her." In fact, in Cornell's eyes, they were a mismatched couple. John was tall and handsome, "the life of the party" and "the charmer," while Michelle was "a little dumpy." Still, they looked in love. "Very bubbly," he said of them, particularly John.

The dinner seemed to be going well until Cornell started talking about his own background. Before becoming a university administrator, he'd worked for fourteen years as a prosecutor in California.

"Mr. Diamond's conversation noticeably dropped off," he said. "At that point in time, neither Mrs. Theer nor Mr. Diamond partook in much of a conversation. There was still conversation, but it was noticeably less."

After the tour of Saba and the university, John and Michelle didn't go directly back to Fayetteville. Computer records showed that she booked a room for three days and two nights, October 20–23, at Club Orient, a clothing-optional resort on St. Martin.

The reservation was held under the names "Mr. and Mrs. Theer."

19

On the same day that Michelle was emailing her friend Michelle Montgomery for help and talking to her other friend Rafael Harris, investigators were conducting a follow-up interview with Sergeant Peyton Donald. In the session at Fort Bragg on February 13, 2001, Peyton provided more details about the gun he had loaned to John.

The first time John had borrowed the gun was in early December 2000, when he called to ask if he could use the 9mm to shoot at a range. He picked it up at Peyton's house, kept it for three or four days and returned it.

John then borrowed it again around December 14—three days before Marty's murder—according to Peyton.

The next time Peyton heard from him was on Monday, December 18, the day after the murder, when John called him at home asking if he had read the morning newspaper.

"No," Peyton replied, "but I am online and can look it up."

"Look in there under 'Theer,' " John said.

Peyton did a search and found the story of the murder of the Air Force captain late at night.

"That was Michelle's husband," John said.

"No shit," said Peyton. "That's pretty messed up."

"Yeah, I know," John said.

One or two days later, John returned the handgun. Peyton couldn't remember if John had said anything about it. Peyton recalled telling John to place it on the stairs and he'd put it away later. The gun was in the same condition as when John had picked it up, smelling of cleaning fluid.

The gun remained in Peyton's house for the next six weeks. Then, in late January or early February, John borrowed it a third time, asking Peyton if he was interested in selling it. He said he was because he never used it. That was the last time Peyton saw the gun or spoke to John about it—until the day before, when police had Peyton call John.

About two weeks after the follow-up interview, on a Sunday in late February, Peyton Donald found a message on his answering machine. It was Michelle Theer telling him that she had something to give him. Up until now, Michelle had no idea that Peyton had spoken to the police in detail about loaning John the gun before the murder.

Before he had a chance to call her back, Michelle called a second time, late at night. She wanted to meet with him immediately. He said he was getting ready to go to bed and asked if they could meet the next day, Monday. She said yes.

They agreed to meet at a Chili's restaurant near the mall in Fayetteville. After Peyton hung up, he called Detective Clinkscales, who told him to go ahead with the meeting.

The next day, police fitted Peyton with a wire to record the conversation, and he headed for Chili's.

When he got there, he didn't see Michelle. He called her

from his cell phone. She asked him if he knew what was going on with John and the murder case—and whether John had confided anything to him. Peyton said he didn't know anything about any of that.

He asked her about their meeting. She told him she'd decided against it after all. It didn't feel right to her. She feared he might be wearing a wire.

Although the meeting never happened, the fact that Michelle had tried to contact Peyton, combined with Peyton's statements about loaning John the gun and John's lying about the break-in were the final pieces of evidence investigators needed to make a case against John Diamond.

Quietly and without any publicity, he was transferred from the barracks to the brig at Camp Lejeune, North Carolina.

20

The military is a strictly hierarchical system, with a sacred adherence to chain of command, and a proud tradition of formality and order.

And so, from the moment Staff Sergeant John Diamond was hauled into an interview room after reporting the car break-in, this enlisted man who'd spent his entire adult life in the armed services knew that his fate—as a soldier and an American—would be decided by those he called "sir."

John's journey through the military justice system, then, began in the office of a superior, a captain, Magistrate Heather J. Fagan. It was her task to make a cursory review of the case against John and decide whether he should remain locked up at Camp Lejeune while he awaited a so-called Article 32 hearing, the military equivalent of a preliminary hearing, in which a judge determines whether the accused should stand trial in a military court-martial.

In a report drafted on February 20, eight days after John's initial arrest on post, Fagan said she had read statements presented by both John's military accusers and his appointed defense attorney, the military version of a public defender. She also heard testimony from investigators and one of John's Army buddies. The legal standard to keep him locked up was not an onerous one. Fagan had only to find that it was "more likely than not" that John was guilty of certain crimes and was a threat to flee if let out of jail.

The first alleged offense that Fagan considered was the easiest to decide. She found it clearly more likely than not that John had committed adultery. He was, by his own admission to civilian police detectives, a married man having an affair with a married woman, and in the United States Army, that is a crime. In John's case, the relationship with Michelle Theer appeared to have continued after the murder, based on his many visits to her house.

Fagan also found it clearly more likely than not that John had committed a second offense, violating lawful order by having that pistol stashed under his car seat. Although a military post is obviously awash with weapons of all sorts, it is a crime to violate the order against possessing a private gun on post.

As for the more serious potential charge of murder, Fagan noted that John had borrowed the same model of 9mm pistol used to kill Marty, only to have it disappear from his car under questionable circumstances. "It is unlikely it was a break-in," said Fagan, citing how clean the car was, the lack of glass, and Rudd's theory that the passenger-side door was actually open when the window was broken. Later, John's mistress Michelle had suspiciously called the man from whom John borrowed the gun, saying that she had something for him, Fagan noted. Lourdes' alibi for John on the night of the murder was only slightly more believable than the break-in report. "Mrs. Diamond could not verify that her husband was at home at the time of the murder because they sleep in separate bedrooms and do not keep tabs on one another," wrote Fagan.

In considering flight risk, Fagan said, "Sgt. Diamond's behavior has grown more erratic." She noted his disappearance when his unit searched for him and found him 100 to 150 yards away in the woods, a place that Major Donovan characterized as "where someone would go if he wanted to hide."

This proved to Fagan that less-restrictive forms of restraint, such as putting John on post restriction or assigning him an escort, "have been tried and are inadequate," and that his night school enrollment and having a child prove insufficient motivation to remain put, the magistrate wrote. If John were sprung from jail, she said, "It is also more likely than not that Sgt. Diamond may also engage in serious criminal misconduct."

"Confinement is necessary because Sgt. Diamond is a flight risk," she wrote. "His repeated absences combined with the seriousness of the charges and the maximum penalty of life in prison demonstrate that he will likely not appear at future proceedings. His conduct has shown that he will likely depart the area and not return on his own accord."

At 5:20 p.m. on February 20, John was notified of the decision. Under military law, he could remain in jail for 120 days without official filing of charges. If those charges were filed, he could stay in jail another twenty-one days before his Article 32 hearing. Once that ended, the matter would go up the chain of command, with John's brig commander submitting summarized findings to the division commander to decide whether John should face a court-martial. If that happened, an arraignment would be held within five days.

In all, John was looking at spending the next five months, minimum, in jail before a trial, longer if his attorneys sought delays.

There was also the chance that he would be transferred to a civilian jail, if jurisdiction in the case shifted from the military to the state of North Carolina. Investigators and prosecutors from both Cumberland County and the military had yet to make a decision on who would prosecute John, though the military had the inside track because he was a soldier facing charges of murdering another soldier. Also it was commonly believed to be easier to win a conviction in a court-martial, particularly if it was an enlisted man accused of killing an officer, than in a civilian court.

As he sat in jail, John had only sporadic updates of the investigation and case against him. His lawyers told him what they knew, but police and military investigators continued to keep information under wraps. He still wasn't allowed to have any contact with Michelle.

Michelle was particularly worried; she didn't know if she would be the next to be arrested. In trying to re-establish communication, they found a go-between in somebody on John's approved visitor list, his sister, Deborah Dvorak. After John was arrested, Michelle called Deborah, whom she had met only a couple of times. Deborah appreciated Michelle's help and concern and was comforted by her calm in the face of the crisis.

John's arrest had predictably stunned his family, who had never known him to get into any trouble, much less something like this. His father, George Diamond, started shelling out tens of thousands of dollars on legal assistance, hiring a private attorney, Coy Brewer, a former judge in private practice in Fayetteville, to go with the appointed military counsel.

When Deborah poured out her fears, Michelle, the trained

psychologist, offered a sympathetic ear and encouragement, telling Deborah, "He didn't do anything, so don't worry about it."

Michelle and Deborah spoke increasingly often after John's arrest, with Michelle asking Deborah to reveal what little she knew about John's case. And when Deborah drove up to North Carolina from Florida to visit John at Camp Lejeune, Michelle would give her messages to relay to John.

Michelle told Deborah to keep these communications secret, for the protection of Deborah and her brother. Michelle often asked Deborah on the work being done by John's military counsel, Captain Martin. Deborah's reports didn't impress her. Michelle referred to Martin as a bitch and part of a military conspiracy against John.

From his jail cell, John tried to find creative ways to get Michelle past the Camp Lejeune guards. On his request sheet applying for visitors, John listed two people: Deborah Dvorak, sister, and a Dr. Theer, whom he identified as his "family shrink" and "family psychologist." She was not approved as a visitor.

John's arrest and the looming uncertainty over her own fate weighed on Michelle. She tried to take her mind off things, visiting her father and grandmother in New Orleans over Mardi Gras in late February. Her sister Angela flew in from Colorado for what grew into a major family gathering, with about 100 aunts, uncles, cousins and friends squeezed into her grandmother's little house. It was around the time of Marty's birthday, and Michelle kept talking about how much she missed him and how wonderful he had been. Angela went with Michelle to parades, but the weekend did little to lift Michelle's spirits. The whole time, Angela said, Michelle was "sad and drawn."

Michelle's return to Fayetteville was traumatic, as the whispers about her grew louder. While making a phone call to a claims examiner for the Zurich life insurance company, which had still not paid out Marty's half-million-dollar policy, Michelle's cell phone rang. The examiner could overhear her telling the caller with exasperation, "No, sir, I did not kill my husband. Those are just nasty rumors." She told the caller, whoever he was, that he could come to her office if he wanted to discuss it further.

Despite the mounting problems, Michelle tried to continue working as a psychologist in Tom Harbin's office. As she had during her marital woes, she expressed her frustrations to her boss, whom she felt she could trust. "Her attitude was that investigators were incompetent, that they were spending too much time investigating her and not getting on with the proper investigation of whomever else the guilty party might be," recalled Harbin. "It was also her opinion that they were spending too much time investigating Sergeant Diamond."

Harbin urged Michelle to be "less antagonistic and more cooperative" with police, telling her that she was only making herself look worse. "She would insist that there was nothing that made her look bad," Harbin said, "and I would counter there were some things that didn't look good."

Calling John from the restaurant after Christmas dinner shortly before Marty's murder was among those things, Harbin told her. But Michelle insisted that there was nothing sinister about the call—her car was being worked on and she had been trying to arrange for a ride the next day.

Michelle continued to hurt herself. In early March, she logged on to eBay and changed the personal information on her account, now calling herself Michelle Forcier of New Orleans. She then auctioned off her murdered husband's possessions, including his flight suits, uniforms, computer games, even memorabilia from his beloved Denver Broncos. Michelle's detractors found it galling that she would be liquidating his belongings so quickly after his murder. Her sister would later come to Michelle's defense, saying that her family had been encouraging Michelle to start selling Marty's things; Michelle had to go through eBay because her name and address had been widely reported in the local media and it would have been worse to have a garage sale.

All the while, Michelle hungered for information about the police investigation—and began to wonder if there were details out there that police were ignoring. Or details they shouldn't know. On the same day she put Marty's items up for eBay auction, Michelle called her former marriage counselor, Dr. Kenneth Kastleman, requesting records of their sessions. Marty had been to counseling without her. She needed to know what he had said in private.

At the time of Michelle's call, Kastleman was swamped with work and somehow had managed to miss all the publicity about the Theer case. He only spent two days a week in Fayetteville and seldom read the local paper.

He hadn't even known that Marty Theer was dead. Following procedure, Kastleman prepared a standard release form for Michelle to sign to get records of the sessions she'd attended. For Marty's solo session, in which he'd bemoaned that Michelle no longer seemed to love him, a separate consent form would be needed with Marty's signature. He sent Michelle the consent form and waited, thinking little of it.

Not long after that, on March 19, 2001, Michelle returned the release form to Kastleman. It included only Michelle's name; she had handwritten Marty's name and then wrote, "Deceased."

Kastleman was surprised by Michelle's request. As a licensed psychologist like himself, Michelle had to have known that she had to provide documentation proving she had the legal authority to view Marty's private records. Even a spouse involved in couples therapy has no right to see records from an individual session in the state of North Carolina.

"In an effort to expedite the process of getting information to you," Kastleman said in a letter to Michelle, "I am writing to you to explain several issues so that I can get your response. Firstly, I want to say that I was shocked and saddened to hear of Marty's death. My heartfelt condolences go out to you and to those others who grieve with you."

He went on to say that "as you know from your work as a psychologist," complex rules govern information disclosure and that if she represented Marty's legal interests, she would have to provide documentation for his files.

"But if, for example, other persons now legally represent Marty's interests, my disclosing information about him could in their view represent a violation of his rights," he wrote, requesting some "further explanation" of the "forensic matter" at issue so he'd know what to do.

"Let me assure you," he concluded, "that I am attending to this matter with the utmost consideration for your interests and needs."

When Michelle received the letter, she called Kastleman, saying she didn't understand why he wouldn't release the notes from Marty's session. He spelled it out for her again, this time in a letter sent certified mail. "I must have a release from the person or persons who are legally authorized to request the information on Marty's behalf," he wrote. "If that is you, then I would need to have that information on file before releasing the information."

Far from understanding, an angry Michelle called Kastleman a second time, reacting the same way with him as she had with the newspaper editor who wouldn't run the obituary the way she wanted. The psychologist now found himself locked in an "atmosphere of disagreement" similar to the one that he'd identified in the Theers' marriage.

Michelle told him on April 2, 2001, that he was frustrating her efforts, and believing the newspaper stories about her. "That was the first thing that alerted me that there was something in the papers, because I hadn't been reading the papers," Kastleman said later. "I really didn't know."

Finally relenting, Michelle asked him exactly what kind of documentation she needed to provide, and he reiterated that she needed written proof that she was legally authorized to request records on Marty's behalf. He suggested that an attorney could help her do this. Michelle countered that an attorney was going to cost money. Kastleman apologized, but maintained that legal assistance would probably speed the process along.

Michelle said her attorney would draft a letter that day. Kastleman repeated that he was sorry she was in this predicament, and hoped that whatever the lawyer came up with would resolve the issue quickly.

He never got a letter from an attorney. It was the last time he spoke to Michelle.

That Kastleman refused to release the documents was understandable. That he had missed the media attention was odd, as the investigation into Marty Theer's murder intensified and was on the brink of becoming front-page news.

Police had returned to the Fort Bragg barracks where John Diamond, when he was on the outs with Lourdes, spent the night in the room of Army friends Rickie Bizon and John Pickett. The pair gave written statements to investigators on March 2, providing more damaging evidence against John. Bizon said that "some time" between December 16 and the night of the murder, John had been attempting to call Michelle from Bizon's barracks room. "But she was avoiding him," said Bizon. "He finally made contact with her while he was in my room to find out why she had been avoiding him." Bizon had left the room while John was talking to her.

Bizon and Pickett had returned to Bizon's room, and John

was off the phone and sitting on the couch. "Usually, when he finishes using my phone, he'll get up and leave, but this time he was just sitting there," said Bizon.

Bizon asked what was up. "He told me to close my door," recalled Bizon. "He told us Michelle was raped by her husband and that she was thinking about hiring someone to kill her husband. He told her that it was not a good idea."

Pickett and Bizon told John that if it were their girlfriend, they'd beat up the husband. John said he had in fact offered to do that very thing. "But Michelle told him to leave him alone," said Bizon. "I didn't know what to think of the conversation and did not take it seriously."

Bizon eventually left the room.

After giving their statements, the pair allowed investigators to cart off the WebTV computer that John had used to send emails to Michelle.

The case against John was now complete. One week after the interviews with Pickett and Bizon, the public information office of the U.S. Army's 82nd Airborne Division at Fort Bragg announced that one of its own, Sergeant John Diamond, was being held in a military jail in the investigation in the December 17, 2000, murder of Captain Frank Martin Theer.

This marked the first official word that John was a suspect, but few details were provided except that police expected to meet with the district attorney to discuss the case. *The Fayetteville Observer* reported that John's father had arrived in town that week in support of John, his ex-wife, Lourdes, and their 2-year-old son.

"I'm going to see him tomorrow," George Diamond told the paper in a story published March 10. "He has never been in trouble with the law. He has been a good soldier." Marty's mother, Linda Gettler, was quoted as saying, "I'll be glad when we know the whole story and that Marty has justice."

The paper also carried a comment from Michelle Theer, who up until now had shunned the *Observer*. "There have been a lot of lies and a lot of misinformation going around," she said. "I prefer to keep my private life private right now." As for her relationship with Diamond, she called it a "friendship," but wouldn't say how they knew each other. She did say that her husband's death "has turned my life upside down."

All of this publicity had escaped Dr. Kastleman's attention. Not so that of the man who had referred the Theers to him. Michelle's boss and confidant, Tom Harbin, who had been interviewed the morning after the murder, spoke on March 13 with Detective Ralph Clinkscales, the first in a string of increasingly revelatory—and damaging—interviews.

Harbin reiterated his statements from the night of the murder, telling Clinkscales that the Theers' marriage was troubled. He added some details, now recounting how Michelle had told him about her suspicions that Marty was looking for a woman on the Internet and how Michelle blamed this as one of the reasons for her separation that previous summer.

Asked about his own relationship with Michelle, Harbin said it was business and non-sexual—Clinkscales wrote "plutonic friendship" in his report. Harbin said he had taken Michelle out for dinner and drinks about two weeks after the murder, picking her up at 6:30 p.m. and returning her at 8:30 p.m. He couldn't remember where they'd gone, but offered police his credit card information to check. Harbin left the police station.

That same day, a meeting was called in the office of Cumberland County District Attorney Ed Grannis to discuss jurisdiction in the John Diamond case. Attending were Clinkscales, his boss Sergeant Mitrisin, military prosecutor Major Randy Bagwell and other civilian and military brass. The group decided that John would be prosecuted by the military.

The announcement came the next day. According to the Army statement issued March 14, as a result of a joint investigation by the Fayetteville Police Department, the Criminal Investigation Command at Fort Bragg and the Office of Special Investigations at Pope Air Force Base, Staff Sergeant John Diamond was being charged with five criminal counts: Adultery; wrongfully transporting and storing a privately owned weapon in a privately owned car on post; impeding an investigation by wrongfully disposing of a Smith & Wesson 9mm pistol; conspiring with a woman to commit murder; and murdering Air Force Captain Frank Martin Theer.

John's civilian attorney, Coy Brewer, told the media that his client "unequivocably denies his guilt of the offenses charges." John was a strong man and was "confident that this matter will be resolved in his favor," Brewer said. It was noted in media accounts that John's ex-wife could provide an alibi in court.

All Brewer would say about John's relationship to the murder victim's wife—and uncharged co-conspirator—Michelle Theer was that the Army investigation had found that they had met at a local bookstore several months before the shooting.

Michelle was again unavailable for comment. But John's sister, Deborah, would later tell a local television station that when Michelle found out she was named as a co-conspirator, she was livid.

"How could they do that? If they knock on my door, I'd kill myself or run away," Michelle said, according to Deborah.

Michelle told Deborah she might go to Louisiana, because it was closer to Mexico.

The day after the charges were announced, Tom Harbin was again talking to Detective Clinkscales. Harbin said he had more information about Michelle's past. He said that in the spring before the murder, Michelle had confided that she'd become pregnant with Marty's child, but gotten an abortion from a doctor friend in Charlotte. (No independent evidence of her claim would ever emerge.)

Then, in June or July 2000, when the Theers were separated, Michelle had told Harbin that she was waiting for Marty to get his re-enlistment bonus—from $60,000 to $200,000—so she could get her share. Around this same time, she confided that she'd applied for a job as a psychologist somewhere in the Caribbean, though he didn't know what had come of that.

The media attention angered and depressed Michelle. She tried to give herself a break by flying out to Colorado to visit her family. Her sister Angela gave Michelle and their mother a tour of the campus of the University of Colorado in Boulder, where she was a student, and then the women hit the mall. But the stress showed. Michelle had lost weight since Angela saw her last over Mardi Gras. She was by turns quiet and manic, saying little and spending a lot. Michelle shelled out more than her sister knew she had, buying jewelry for herself and necklaces for her mother and sister.

When Michelle returned home, she found out about Tom Harbin's increasing cooperation with the police. She was so angry that she quit the practice and stormed out of the office, though not without a parting remark. As Michelle walked away for the last time, she warned him that if things went badly for her, "It would, "according to Harbin," be on my head."

Then Michelle endured the worst publicity of the case: many of her secrets were coming to light. In an affidavit filed by Detective Clinkscales to search Michelle's house, he stated that Michelle and John had admitted to police they'd had an affair, meeting in various motels, using cash and credit cards. Their last liaison before the murder had been the previous weekend in Raleigh, the affidavit revealed.

Clinkscales also wrote about John borrowing the gun before the murder, John and Michelle's February trip to Florida together and the suspected fake break-in on post. Finally, it suggested a motive, noting that Michelle had been the sole beneficiary of her husband's estate, life insurance policy and military benefits.

The affidavit convinced a judge to let police search Michelle's home on English Saddle Drive in March, seizing a laptop and desk computer software, three floppy discs, numerous letters and notes, a will and photographs.

And it branded Michelle Theer as a slut and perhaps a murderess. Friends and in-laws were deserting her. Michelle's relationship with Marty's mother, Linda Gettler, crumbled. Once supportive of Michelle, embracing her the day after the murder and again at the funeral, sharing tears and memories of Marty, Linda made no secret that she felt Michelle might have been involved in Marty's murder, and stopped talking to her former daughter-in-law.

To try to regain Linda's trust, Michelle, sent her a twenty-four-page, handwritten letter intended to set the record straight.

> Dear Linda,
>
> These last few months have been so difficult—not only because of the loss of Marty, but the way this investigation has been conducted. I know it is difficult for you to read the papers and that is why I am writing. It is true that I can "explain" away many of the things written in the paper, but that you feel uncomfortable talking to me about them. The paper and the detectives paint me as an evil, cold-hearted woman who held no love for her husband and had him killed for money.

Asking Marty's mother to "step back and look at this situation objectively," Michelle conceded that "I am not perfect" and that "at times I did things to hurt Marty."

But, she said, "Marty was not perfect either."

Michelle told Marty's mother that her son may have had an affair with a woman he met on the Internet. This made Michelle curious about cyber dating, she told Marty's mother, and prompted her to go online herself.

> I never had any intention of starting a relationship—sexual or otherwise—but was just looking to see how people interacted in order to understand for my own personal reasons (my husband's affairs) and because this issue has come up numerous times in my professional practice. These are not excuses for cheating on my husband, but an explanation of how things happened. Despite what the police tell everyone, I am not a whore, slut, dressed-up piece of trash, predator, user, manipulator.

Michelle asked Marty's mother to "pull away from the hearsay, conjecture, and theories presented by the police" and ask herself if Michelle was truly capable of murdering Marty. When analyzed objectively, Michelle said, there was no evidence—no weapon, no shell casings, no DNA, no cell phone records, no witnesses and no confessions.

> Ask yourself if you think this is how our fairytale love life, high school sweethearts could come to an end. I loved Marty with all my heart and I always will. Never, ever in the worst of times did I consider (emotionally) tearing out half of my heart and ending my life.

Michelle wrote, "I love you. You gave me the greatest gift I'll ever have. I wish I had something to give back to you—and I don't want it to be a legacy of hate and conspiracy.

Please talk to me and ask me questions. I won't try to hide anything to protect you anymore."

> Please call so we can put all this to rest.
> I love you,
> Michelle.

Linda Gettler did call, and it was a disaster. Michelle now was no longer seeking to explain anything to anybody. She was angry at the world. She said her lawyer was mad at her and threatening to quit. Then she turned her ire on Marty's mother, yelling at her and saying she "wrecked everything."

When Linda refused to return Michelle's later calls, Michelle left her a recorded message saying Linda was so passive-aggressive she couldn't answer Michelle's call and that it was no wonder Marty was unable to have a relationship because he was just like his mother.

At Camp Lejeune, John had his own problems. His life on the outside was destroyed. Once a good student with dreams of attending a university after leaving the Army, John received a letter at the end of February from Robert C. Perkins, Ph.D., associate dean for academic affairs at Methodist College. Perkins was informing the onetime dean's list student about his absenteeism, having taken eight of his eleven allowed absences.

The North Carolina State Bureau of Investigation completed its forensic analysis of the bullets found in Marty's body and the casings recovered from the crime scene. The report confirmed that the jackets and bullets had come from the same gun—a Smith & Wesson Model 639 or 5906. John had borrowed a Model 5906 from Peyton Donald.

A second forensics report, this one looking for the presence of gunshot residue on Michelle's hands, was only partly helpful. From the samples taken by crime-scene analyst Carrie Sonnen, the bureau did find residue on both of her hands, but that could be easily explained: It could have come from cradling John's wounded head.

The best friend John had in the world was his father. While Michelle refused to talk to the press and continued to say and do things that only made her look worse, George Diamond was an outspoken advocate for his son. In an interview with *The Fayetteville Observer*, he blamed John's plight on his rank.

"He's an E-6 and they're trying to stick it to an enlisted man," he said in a story published April 19. "All because he happened to know the wrong person at the wrong time."

The charges, George Diamond said, had been filed to pressure John to turn on Michelle. "Since they didn't have any evidence, the best chance they had was to break him down," he said. "I'm a Vietnam vet, and the best way to break a person down is mentally. And since they have no case, he's being told his family deserted him and the woman has turned on him, trying to get him to confess. You ain't gonna confess to something you haven't done."

Even as the working class family's legal costs were already $30,000 and rising, George refused to abandon his son.

Which was a good thing, because within days John would suffer a crippling blow.

21

From the first time John Diamond had spoken to police, he knew that his liberty hinged on the determination of a woman he'd cheated on repeatedly and whom he had filed divorce papers against.

He worried about Lourdes' resolve even more after he was arrested. On his second day in jail, he found out that Lourdes had spoken with his lawyer. John placed a collect call to her asking her what she had said.

"The truth," she said.

Even over the phone, Lourdes could sense the anger welling up in him.

"The truth?" he snapped.

"Yes," Lourdes said, "that we had watched movies that night."

John calmed down.

Despite everything, Lourdes still loved John. She sent him cards in jail and believed him when he said he loved her and that when it was all over, they would make a new life together, maybe in Texas where his parents lived. She defended him even as police continued to hound her.

When Clinkscales showed up at her apartment one afternoon in February, claiming to have a tip that Lourdes had indicated to John's family that she might recant her alibi statement, she said that was all wrong. She said she'd merely spoken to John's parents when they'd called to check on her welfare. She insisted, again, that John was with her the night of the murder, watching *The Patriot*, then going to bed.

Still, even behind bars, John could rankle Lourdes. He wrote a letter saying that Michelle Theer was trying to help him and now wanted to meet Lourdes so they could put their differences aside and become friends. Lourdes tore up the letter.

But the more she thought about her relationship with John Diamond in the spring of 2001, the more she began to wonder. When he would pledge his love for Lourdes and their son, Chance, he seemed so believable. Then later, Lourdes would ask herself if John really cared at all about them, and whether he just said those things to take save himself.

In April 2001, Lourdes began to consider what really

was in the best interest of herself and Chance. The stakes were getting higher. As John's Article 32 hearing and, possibly, court-martial neared, Lourdes was going to have to do something that until now she hadn't had to do: testify under oath.

She didn't know much about American laws, so she called a friend in Pennsylvania to ask what was going to happen in court. The friend said that Lourdes would have to swear before God to tell the whole truth. Being caught in a lie could ruin her life. It could mean a jail term, deportation, even loss of her son, Lourdes was told.

Lourdes loved Chance deeply. The thought that the government could take him away from her sent her into tears.

And then she realized. She not only loved her son, she loved him more than she loved John Diamond.

In late April, Lourdes made another round of calls. She spoke to John's defense attorney, Captain Katy Martin, and asked what would be expected of her in court. Martin said that Lourdes would have to tell the truth. She spoke to John's father, who was staying outside their apartment in his camper. George Diamond always treated her with respect and kindness. He told her to listen to her heart, but reminded her that she had repeatedly said that John had been with her the night of the murder.

After a long and difficult night, Lourdes went to the MP office at Fort Bragg on Sunday, April 22, two days before John's Article 32 hearing. She asked for directions to the Criminal Investigation Division headquarters.

She said she had something important to say.

22

John Diamond was all Army Ranger, calm, composed, exuding the confidence of a highly trained soldier prepared for what he knew would only be the first battle of a long campaign. Observers at the first day of his Article 32 hearing on Tuesday, April 24, were struck by his Hollywood looks, tall, lean, muscular, with a handsome face and curly brown hair.

He took his seat at the counsel table at the 82nd Airborne Division Trial Defense Field Office, a staff sergeant surrounded by majors and captains. Serving as the judge in this proceeding—he is called the investigating officer—was Major Michael A. Oacobucci, who was empowered to hear the evidence and draft a recommendation on whether John should be court-martialed.

Beside John was his military lawyer, Captain Katy Martin, and facing off against him were the two Army prosecutors, Major Randall Bagwell and Captain Sean E. Summers, from Fort Bragg's Office of the Staff Judge Advocate General known to TV viewers as JAG.

Two men in business suits stood out in this sea of military dress: John's civilian attorneys, Coy E. Brewer and Ronnie M. Mitchell, who would share defense chores with Martin.

Noticeably absent was John's uncharged alleged partner in love and crime, Michelle Theer, who refused to testify on the grounds that her statements could incriminate herself.

As the prosecution called its first witnesses, John's side knew the proceedings were stacked against him. An Article 32, like a civilian preliminary hearing or grand jury session, is a speed bump on the road to trial. The best John could hope for over the next three days was to get a good enough look at the prosecution's case to help him better prepare for the court-martial.

The most important witness of the first day was the lead police detective in the murder investigation, Ralph Clinkscales, who took the oath and began describing his work, which had begun late the night of December 17, 2000: finding the body, inspecting the crime scene and interviewing Michelle Theer.

"Mrs. Theer couldn't think of anyone who might be an enemy of her husband or anyone who might have done this," Clinkscales testified. It wasn't until his second interview with Michelle, after her boss had revealed her relationship with an Army sniper named John, that Michelle admitted she'd had an affair with the accused, Staff Sergeant John Diamond, but claimed that it was over.

Clinkscales recounted how he'd tracked down Diamond, who'd also admitted to being involved in an affair with Michelle, with their last sexual encounter just the weekend before at a Raleigh Holiday Inn, "At which time a light bulb went off in my head, because Michelle said she had terminated the relationship and he seemed to think it was still ongoing."

John said he had an alibi—he was at home watching *The Patriot* with his wife—and Lourdes Diamond had confirmed that he was there, retiring to the other room to sleep when the movie ended, and being there the next morning when she woke up.

Clinkscales also revealed the big breaks in the case, when Michelle had admitted to calling John from the Fox and Hound restaurant the night of the murder, and when Sergeant Peyton Donald had spoken of loaning John a 9mm pistol.

On cross-examination, Clinkscales said that police never found any record of a phone call from Michelle to John from the Fox and Hound, and that the only evidence of such a call was Michelle's statement. "Her phone company said if there was no answer, then the call would not show up on the phone records," said the detective.

As for Michelle's possible role in the murder, Clinkscales said, "We have not made a determination that probable cause existed with respect to Michelle Theer at this point." He added, "We have not found any evidence in regard to an agreement to do an unlawful act between Michelle Theer and any other person."

The case against her, he said, remained under investigation.

After more testimony from other officers and the evidence technician at the crime scene, the first day of the hearing ended. The stage was set for the most important witness of the hearing.

Lourdes Diamond.

23

On Wednesday, April 25, Lourdes Diamond took the oath that had so concerned her, and settled in for questioning. She spoke in Spanish, her testimony translated by an Army interpreter. Her voice wavered, but her words rocked the courtroom.

"I did not tell the police the truth," she said. "I lied because he told me to do it."

With that, Lourdes laid out what she said had really happened in her apartment the night of December 17, 2000—the account that she had told the Army prosecutor the day before the hearing.

The night began as she had always claimed, with John coming over with *The Patriot*. The two of them and her mother had settled in at 8 p.m. after putting son Chance to bed.

John never made it to the final credits.

"After we put the movie on, I remember he got a call on his cell phone because I heard his phone ring," Lourdes testified. "He grabbed his phone and went into his son's room."

Lourdes didn't know what he'd said, or whether he'd even answered the call. But the timing matched: right when Michelle Theer said she had dialed John on her cell phone from the Fox and Hound.

"After the call he got dressed real quick and he left," she said. "He said he wasn't going to watch the movie, that he had already seen it, and he left. I didn't see him again until the next morning."

After John walked out of the apartment, Lourdes and her mother had finished watching the movie without him, then gone to bed. Lourdes didn't see him again until the next morning when he was on the sofa. She was a sound sleeper and hadn't heard him come home.

But her mother had. "She knows that it was late, because she had been sleeping for a while," said Lourdes. "She heard the house door that night when he came in, and she heard that he was using the clothes washer, and that that was weird because who would wash clothes at that time of night?"

As she spoke, John shook his head and grimaced. There was nothing else to do.

The morning after the murder, Lourdes said, John told her that he had gone to the barracks. When police called her on December 18 to set up an interview, John had already told her what to say. "He told me to remember that we were watching movies that night," she said. "I told him that it wasn't true, because he wasn't in the house that night. He then told me again to remember that we were watching movies that night."

In explaining why she'd lied about the alibi, Lourdes placed her marriage with John in context, telling how they'd met in Panama, how she lived in the United States on a visa, how she'd always loved John despite his infidelities—always forgiving him, always hoping that the latest transgression would be the last and they could live happily ever after in this new country of opportunity.

"Every time he called me from the jail, he said, 'Remember, we are going to be together, because I love my son a lot and I love you a lot and you are the only one I have ever loved,'" she said. "I changed my statement because I realized that he never loved his son, nor did he ever love me. I love my son more than I love him."

Cross-examination was futile. Just days before, John's own lawyer had counseled Lourdes to tell the truth. Lourdes said she couldn't pinpoint the exact time of that the phone call, but could come close: She and her mother had finished watching a Spanish-language TV show at 8 p.m., it had taken about twenty minutes to put her son to bed, and then the movie had started. Everyone in the courtroom knew that was close enough.

Lourdes wrapped up her testimony by saying she had a newfound confidence. She said that she still lived with her mother and son and had no boyfriend. "I have male and female friends now," she said. "I have a lot of friends and I believe that I am a single divorced woman and I have the right to have all the friends I want to have.

"No one has offered me anything or promised me anything to change my statement. It's just me and my conscience, because I am scared more of the laws of men than the laws of God."

The rest of days 2 and 3 of the hearing were anticlimactic. Even Peyton Donald's appearance, as important as it was, because it put a gun in John's hands, couldn't measure up.

It was just one numbing blow after another for John, ending with the playing of the surveillance video of the outside of Michelle's house, which laid to waste his break-in story. OSI Agent Vince Bustillo then summarized the interview with John's barracks friend Rickie Bizon, who'd spoken of John's phone call with Michelle shortly before the murder: She'd said Marty had raped her; she was thinking about hiring a killer.

Then Bizon himself testified, saying that when Marty actually had wound up dead, "We would always rag on [John] that he was going to get busted."

The prosecution ended its presentation on Thursday, April 26, and the defense didn't put on a case. In closing remarks, prosecutor Major Randy Bagwell called the case an emotionally driven conspiracy. "Soldiers kill out of necessity, but he was killing out of passion," he said. The key evidence, he said, was Lourdes' testimony. "He thought he had a rock-solid alibi, but it crumbled at the last minute."

Defense attorney Coy Brewer argued that the case lacked the critical elements of an eyewitness, physical evidence, a co-conspirator's testimony and a confession. He noted that Michelle had still not been charged and that her emotions at the murder scene were real. "Unless she is an actress of Academy Award–winning quality," Brewer said, "her reaction was genuine shock and surprise."

Over the next two weeks, the Army brass looked at the evidence and prepared a recommendation for Major General John R. Vines, who could order a court-martial, reduce the charges or dismiss the case. John and his family tried to remain optimistic—and realistic. His father was resigned to a court-martial.

"I wouldn't be the least bit surprised, with the way they have treated him so far," said George Diamond, claiming the accusations were trumped up because John was an enlisted man accused of killing an officer. The truth, George told the local paper, would come out in trial, and his lawyers "guaranteed him" an acquittal.

"His mental thinking has a changed a lot," George said. "He's feeling confident. After hearing their evidence, he was grinning. He's upbeat. He's looking forward to his day in court."

Michelle had a considerably darker outlook. In May, she left for Vero Beach, Florida. A former professor had recently built a house and invited her to stay in the old home until it was sold. Michelle also spent a week in Los Angeles visiting her grandmother. Her sister and mother also were there. Michelle continued to lose weight, and her compulsive shopping worried her family. Although she had no job and no insurance money coming in, she bought artwork, a floor lamp and costume jewelry for herself, and a table fountain for her mother.

Her spending habits were escalating along with her paranoia.

On May 9, she received an email from an old male friend named Shawn.

> Michelle,
>
> I recently heard that you are going on in your life. I am sorry for your loss. Are you doing OK? Please let me know how you are doing. Just worried about you.
>
> Shawn O.

When once such an email would have provided a secret thrill, now it only depressed her. She fired back a reply late at night questioning Shawn's motives for contacting her.

> Sorry if this sounds skeptical, but I don't have people jumping out of the woodwork offering me help

> right now. They seem to fear being tainted by the black cloud hanging over my head. Did OSI interview you or ask you to contact me? Complete honesty is appreciated.
>
> I don't have the energy for any more games, and trust me, you don't want to be connected to me in any way if they are interviewing you. Just don't believe anything they say. They are liars, users and backstabbers.
>
> Michelle.

Two days later, on Thursday, May 10, a recommendation on court-martial was drafted. A memo prepared by Colonel Curtis M. Scaparrotti reviewed a history of the John Diamond case and noted the relatively low legal threshold to bind him over to court-martial, the "reasonable grounds" burden, or "more likely than not."

In the stilted language of military law, the memo recommended these charges with these specifics:

> CHARGE I: Violation of Article 92
> SPECIFICATION: In that Staff Sergeant John M. Diamond, U.S. Army, did, at or near Fort Bragg, North Carolina, on or about 12 February 2001, violate a lawful general regulation, to wit: Chapters 4 and 5(a), XVIII Airborne Corps and Fort Bragg Regulation 190-12, dated 3 January 2001, by wrongfully transporting and storing a privately owned weapon in his privately owned vehicle.
>
> CHARGE II: Violation of Article 134
> SPECIFICATION 1: In that Staff Sergeant John M. Diamond, U.S. Army, a married man, did, at or near

Fayetteville, North Carolina, on diverse occasions between February 2000 and February 2001, wrongfully have sexual intercourse with Michelle Theer, a married woman not his wife.
SPECIFICATION 2: In that Staff Sergeant John M. Diamond, U.S. Army, did, at or near Fort Bragg, North Carolina, on or about 12 February 2001, wrongfully endeavor to impede an investigation in the case of the murder allegations against himself, knowing or having reason to believe there would be criminal proceedings pending, with the intent to impede the due administration of justice, by wrongfully disposing of a Smith & Wesson 9mm pistol.

CHARGE III: Violation of Article 81
SPECIFICATION: In that Staff Sergeant John M. Diamond, U.S. Army, did, at or near Fayetteville, North Carolina, on or about 17 December 2000, conspire with Michelle Theer to commit an offense under the Uniform Code of Military Justice, to wit: murder Captain Frank M. Theer, and in order to effect the object of the conspiracy the said Staff Sergeant John M. Diamond did with premeditation murder Captain Frank M. Theer by means of shooting him with a handgun.

CHARGE IV: Violation of Article 118
SPECIFICATION: In that Staff Sergeant John M. Diamond, U.S. Army, did, at or near Fayetteville, North Carolina, on or about 17 December 2000, with premeditation, murder Captain Frank M. Theer by means of shooting him with a handgun.

It was, as expected, a prosecution slam-dunk. Major General Vines reviewed the memo and on May 26 ordered

John to face a court-martial on all the recommended charges.

An across-the-board conviction would send John to prison for life without the possibility of parole. John's attorney, Coy Brewer, expressed no surprise. "We believe the Army would want to resolve this issue with a jury trial," he told *The Fayetteville Observer*. "John's frame of mind is as it has been throughout this period. He is very strong and emotionally and psychologically he is prepared to confront the hardships he must [face] to get through this tough time."

John's father, a free talker since coming out to North Carolina, now issued a carefully worded statement. "While we know this trial will be an ordeal, and appreciate the uncertainty of any criminal trial," he said, "we are confident that justice will prevail."

John would have little time to wait before confronting those hardships about which his lawyer spoke. His court-martial would begin just three months after General Vines' decision, during which time John and his lawyers had their own difficult decisions to make. Although there was plenty of evidence to bind John over to trial, there was reason for guarded optimism. Prosecutors only had strong evidence against John on two of the lesser charges. John's admissions and voluminous witness testimony sunk him on the adultery count, and the surveillance tape showing the car break-in to be a lie nailed him on the gun possession charge.

But as Brewer had pointed out in his Article 32 summation, the case against John on murder and murder conspiracy was much weaker. Lourdes' new testimony gave credibility to the belief that John had had the opportunity to kill Marty Theer, but there were still no eyewitnesses or physical evidence to prove that he really did. John didn't admit to anything, and the prosecution could produce nobody who said he did. And if the defense could show that

John hadn't been involved in the murder, then the conspiracy rap evaporated.

Now that Lourdes had shown what she was going to do under oath, there was only one wild card left for John.

Michelle Theer.

24

It was the first time that Michelle had seen John since he was arrested. She had not attended his Article 32 hearing. She and John had only communicated through his sister, Deborah.

As Michelle walked through the courtroom at Fort Bragg at about 1 p.m. on July 30, she passed John. They exchanged smiles, but said nothing.

Michelle was in court for a pre-trial hearing of great importance to both sides in the case: the admissibility of a memo called "Documentation of My Interactions with Law Enforcement."

This was the timeline that Michelle had prepared, her ongoing diary of the events—and her feelings—from the day of Marty's murder through February 15, three days after John's arrest.

A sobering reality of the personal computer age is that nothing ever really vanishes. It may come as a shock to anybody who has ever faced the agony and frustration of losing an important file or accidentally deleting a critical email that this information is actually still there. It's just hiding.

In reality, virtually everything ever written on a computer—every Word document and spread sheet created; every email sent, received or placed in the trash, every photo downloaded and every webpage visited—may well be forever preserved, somewhere, somehow, in some of the strangest places.

It takes a skilled computer sleuth with the most advanced software to find the information. But it can be found.

Michelle Theer found this out the hard way.

In March 2000, two of her computers—a laptop she shuttled to and from work and a desktop she kept at home—were seized by search warrant and shipped to military computer experts for an electronic autopsy. The dissection by these and other technicians would take years to complete, and much data would still elude them, but from the tens of thousands of pages of letters, emails, websites and downloads would emerge an intimate picture of Michelle—and damning evidence for John Diamond.

When extracted from the computer by technicians using a special investigative software called EnCase, the timeline document took the form of a 10-page, single-spaced memo with no paragraph breaks.

In it Michelle included damaging statements about John and information contradicting what the two of them had told investigators. Since Michelle was unlikely to testify in the court-martial—she would in all likelihood take the Fifth—the introduction of this document could, in a manner in speaking, get Michelle's testimony before the jury anyway.

Michelle's attorney, Gerald Beaver, objected to allowing the document to be introduced at trial, claiming it was written for him at his request, making it privileged and protected attorney–client communication. Army prosecutors countered that nowhere on the document did it say anything about it being written for her lawyer. They said that Michelle, as a licensed psychologist knowledgeable about confidentiality issues, would have clearly stated on the document that this was private communication with her lawyer to avoid this very problem.

The judge assigned to preside over John's court-martial, Colonel Patrick Parrish, considered these arguments at a hearing, and deferred a ruling. He wanted to hear first from the document's author.

Michelle's first appearance in court would not be a pleasant one. From the very beginning, the judge had little patience with her. After taking the oath and stating her name—Michelle Catherine Theer—Captain Sean Summers, an Army prosecutor assisting Major Bagwell, asked Michelle for the city and state in which she resided.

Michelle started to say, "My permanent address is PO Box 540043 . . ." when Colonel Parrish snapped, "Ma'am, I really don't want your box, just a city and state, because there's no need for everybody in the world to know your post office box."

"All right," Michelle said, "I don't have a current address at this time."

"OK," the judge said, "go ahead then."

At the time, Michelle was still house-sitting in Vero Beach for her former professor, trying to start a new life in Florida. Having disposed of Marty's possessions on eBay, she now dumped his name. She was no longer Michelle Catherine Theer as she'd claimed in court. At her request, the Social Security Administration had changed her last name to Forcier. She'd also contacted the Colorado Department of Motor Vehicles to say that she was widowed and had taken back her maiden name. She'd changed her name on her bank accounts, and asked Sprint to start sending her cell phone bills to an address in Florida.

According to authorities, she'd also restarted her love life, after meeting a man in a Florida bar and spending three days with him in his mother's home.

She'd had less success in getting her career back on track. She wrote to the Florida Department of Health to apply for a psychology license. After the board informed her that her application had been received and that a date was set for her to take the laws and rules exam, the licensing process hit a snag.

Fayetteville police Detective Ralph Clinkscales had sent a memo to the psychology board saying that Michelle Theer had not been cleared of criminal wrongdoing and was still under investigation. Florida health rules forbid issuing psychology licenses to criminal suspects. The Florida Department of Health's Medical Quality Assurance Board of Psychology tabled her license request until September so it could consider additional information about the criminal case.

On the witness stand, Michelle explained that she had written the timeline document on her laptop at both her home and office at the request of her attorneys after one of their first meetings in January 2001. The purpose, she said, was "to document the facts surrounding the ongoing investigation around my husband's death." The document found on her computer was only a draft, and not the final memo sent to her lawyers, and she had deleted it, she said.

Summers led Michelle through the document, seeking to show that by its own contents it wasn't meant for her lawyers, including the reference to contacting the Beaver Holt law firm.

"What I'm confused about is, you're writing a letter to your attorney telling them you're contacting your attorney?" asked Summers.

"I did that for my own purposes and my attorneys' purposes because I was working with two different attorneys and I wanted a record of the date that I initially contacted them," she said.

At other points, Summers asked, if she was writing to her lawyers, why did she refer to them in the third person as "my attorney" instead of just "you"?

Peeved, Michelle answered, "I don't know. I guess I'm not perfect."

Summers then turned to the attachment, the question-and-answer section that summarized Michelle's dinner meeting with John Diamond. Michelle said that she'd typed that up after talking to John, based on handwritten notes. She'd never shown the Q&A or the timeline to John, she said.

Michelle's frustration appeared to grow as Summers revealed that authorities had not only read this material, but documents about Michelle's patients, including psychological evaluations. Summers brought it up to show that the patient documents were clearly marked "confidential" while the timeline and Q&A were not.

The tension mounted when Summers read a sentence from the timeline section on the trip that John and Michelle took to Florida just before John's arrest: "We did not take his car because of the fear that he is being followed or his car was bugged."

"That's not true, is it?" asked Summers.

The defense called for an objection, and the judge sustained it.

Summers argued that the question was permissible. He said the fact that Michelle had lied to her attorneys—when she knew that because of privilege she could tell them the full truth, even confess to murder, and nobody would know—only proved that the timeline was not written for the lawyers.

"When she puts these lies in here, essentially it's lies to tell the police, to keep her lies straight, in her diary, in her mind," said Summers.

As he spoke, Michelle shook her head and rolled her eyes.

"Mrs. Theer," the judge snapped, "I'll warn you once, neither witnesses nor spectators may make comments, gestures, or any facial reaction to the testimony. If you do not agree with the question, you don't sit there and shake your head.

That's the way it's conducted in every courtroom in this country and it will be conducted in this courtroom as well."

"Yes, sir," she said.

The judge reiterated that the objection was sustained—no questions about lies—and Summers moved on, asking Michelle about her relationship with John Diamond. At the advice of her lawyers, Michelle then refused to testify, taking the Fifth Amendment. The only testimony about the relationship was when she denied that John had looked over her shoulder while she was typing the timeline and Q&A she'd made about him on January 27.

"Was Sergeant Diamond living with you on January 27?" asked Summers.

"Sergeant Diamond never lived with me," Michelle said.

"Was Sergeant Diamond staying over at your house?"

"Occasionally," she said. "Many other people also did."

The hearing ended after lengthy arguments by both sides and the judge delaying a ruling.

Michelle left Fayetteville for the comfort of home, flying to Colorado to be with her mother and sister.

While she was away, the pre-trial wrangling continued, this time with a reluctant Deborah Dvorak being brought into Fort Bragg for a deposition by the Army prosecutors. It was a combative Deborah squaring off on July 31 against Captain Summers and Major Bagwell as they attempted to elicit details of conversations between her and her brother and Michelle.

The prosecutors were trying to build the case that the communication—and thus the murder conspiracy—between John and Michelle had continued even after his arrest and incarceration, with Deborah Dvorak serving as the intermediary.

But Deborah proved that they would have to build it without her. She repeatedly claimed a faulty memory, until an exasperated Summers snapped, "Do you understand the difference between not wanting to answer the question and not remembering?"

The question, clearly improper, got the inevitable objection from her civilian lawyer, Ronnie M. Mitchell.

Bagwell, however, made clear that the prosecutors thought Deborah was lying.

"I think at this point what we have is a hostile witness," he said. "The government has noticed a pattern with this witness that she has a pretty good memory about a lot of events, and then you get to certain events, she doesn't remember certain things, even though they may have happened last week."

He then turned to Deborah and said, "I understand you're in a terrible position, but you are under oath and we do expect you to answer truthfully."

"And I'm trying," she replied. "I'm trying very hard to answer."

Indeed, the pressure was intense. On top of working long hours as a nurse and raising a 3 1/2-year-old child, Deborah was enduring both the emotional toll of seeing her brother being accused of murder and the very real cost and time of driving 500 miles to Fayetteville to visit him.

At the time, she was still fond of Michelle, seeing her as one of the few people helping John and showing any understanding of Deborah's plight. She had spoken to Michelle so many times on the phone from work that her bosses admonished her to stop taking personal calls. Deborah's husband, Victor, who had never liked Michelle, became so fed up with the frequent phone calls, the travel to North Carolina and the expense that he threatened to leave Deborah if she kept in touch with Michelle.

Desperate to help her brother, Deborah maintained the contact with Michelle in the face of this adversity. Michelle tried to ease the stress by giving Deborah a prepaid phone card. When Michelle visited Deborah's house in Florida, she made sure to do it when Victor was away. The women planned that if he ever came home unexpectedly, Michelle would hide.

Deborah relied so much on Michelle that she entertained Michelle's most outrageous ideas. At one point, Michelle hired a psychic who conjured up an image of the killer as a woman with brown hair. Though a brunette herself, Michelle interpreted this to be a description of a woman with whom Marty was having an affair. At another time, Michelle said that her grandmother was a witch who could put an evil spell on prosecutors during John's court-martial.

When asked at her deposition about her relationship with Michelle, Deborah downplayed all this, saying only that they were friends who spoke once a week. And when asked about her brother's relationship with Michelle, she said, "All I can remember is him saying that they were just friends, and I think I do remember him mentioning they had, you know, been together. But I don't know because he's with a lot of women, I don't know who."

What she did know was that she talked to John every day and that he was distressed by the charges. She summed up her family's feelings: "He's confused, too, just because he's friends with somebody, he says, or just because he was friends with somebody that was married to this person, he's a scapegoat."

A scapegoat about to go on trial.

Michelle Theer, arriving at Fort Bragg through a throng of reporters in July 2001, told a military judge that her detailed time line of events and emotions was intended only for her attorneys' eyes. The judge disagreed and allowed it into evidence.
The Fayetteville Observer

Captain Marty Theer, who piloted transport planes out of Pope Air Force base, was often away from home on deployments. His lonely wife, Michelle, turned to the Internet for companionship. *David Britt Johnson*

Looking toward a life after the military, John Diamond took night classes at Methodist College near Fort Bragg. He told classmates that his "fiancée" was a psychologist, a reference to Michelle Theer. *David Britt Johnson*

The 160,000-acre military base where John Diamond served as a staff sergeant in the Army. Every facet of military life influences, for better or for worse, neighboring Fayetteville. *David Britt Johnson*

After meeting on the Internet, Michelle Theer and John Diamond had their first date at O'Charley's Restaurant in Fayetteville. Later, John had considered proposing to her there but changed his mind. *David Britt Johnson*

Michelle Theer began her professional career as a psychologist in this Fayetteville office on Raeford Drive. It was a bitterly cold night in December 2000 when Michelle and her husband, Marty, returned to the office after a Christmas dinner. It was Marty's last night alive. *David Britt Johnson*

The stairwell where Marty Theer was gunned down. Michelle said that she had gone into her office to pick up books when she heard the gunfire outside.
David Britt Johnson

Michelle Theer ran to this video rental store down the street from her office to call 911 after her husband was shot. She claims that she locked herself out of her building and didn't have a cell phone with her. *David Britt Johnson*

John Diamond's wife, Lourdes, steadfastly stood beside him in the face of mounting pressures from police—until she began to doubt John's love. *The Fayetteville Observer*

After the murder of Marty Theer, John Diamond fired a rented gun at this pawn shop shooting range, providing a plausible explanation for the gunshot residue on his hand. *David Britt Johnson*

The tall and handsome John Diamond, whose tumultuous affair with Michelle Theer served as the backdrop to murder, is led away from court after being found guilty in 2001. *The Fayetteville Observer*

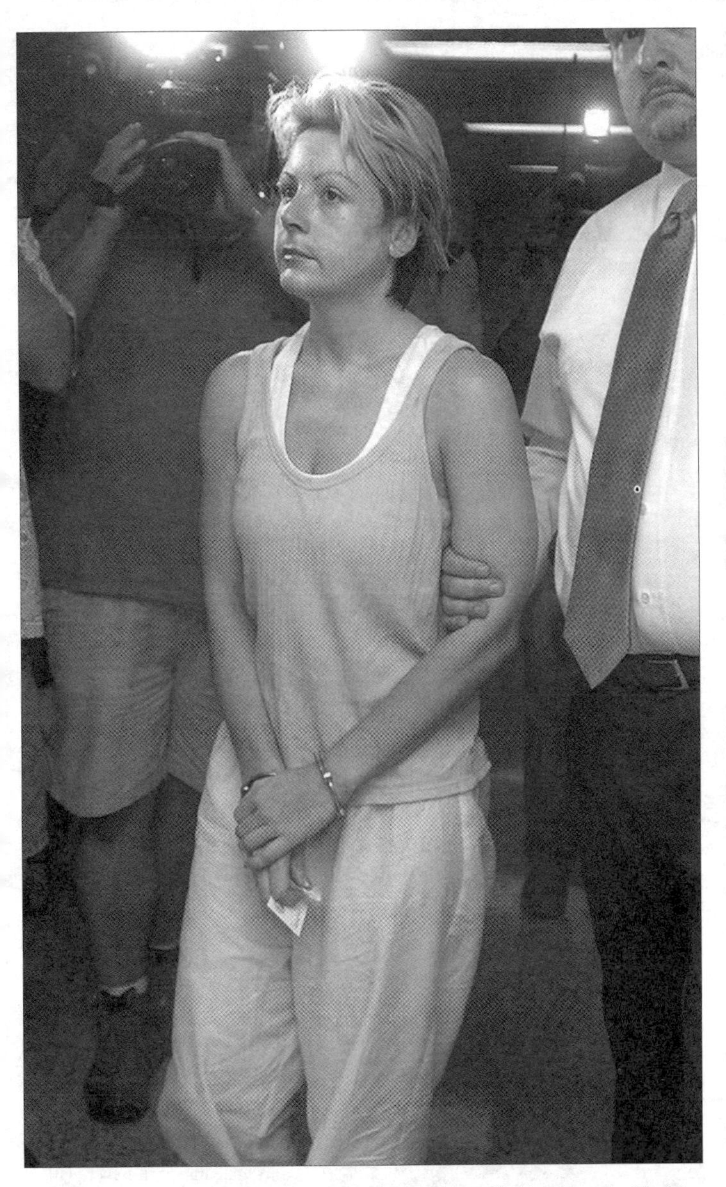

Michelle Theer, as she looked to federal agents who tracked her down in Florida. She was driven up to North Carolina after her arrest. *The Fayetteville Observer*

Neighbors say they often saw Michelle Theer bring John Diamond to her Fayetteville home while husband, Marty Theer, was away on deployment.
David Britt Johnson

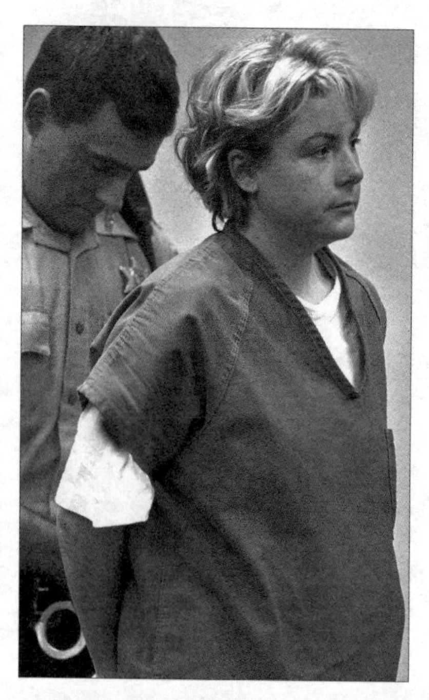

Michelle Theer, with a new hairstyle and a face altered by plastic surgery during her time on the run, is handcuffed by a sheriff's deputy after her first court appearance in Fayetteville in September 2002.
The Fayetteville Observer

25

Military trials work very much like their civilian counterparts. The defense sits at one side of the room, the prosecution at the other, the judge rules on matters of law and the jury considers the facts and decides guilt or innocence.

The prosecution carries the burden of proving that the defendant is guilty beyond a reasonable doubt, a standard no higher or lower than in municipal, state and federal courts across the United States.

Procedurally, the rules of evidence are basically the same—military hearsay is just like civilian hearsay, and the basis for an objection is the same in a court-martial as in a civilian trial. Military lawyers must still establish the proper foundation to introduce evidence. And witnesses must still tell the truth.

But one look at the courtroom at Fort Bragg on the first day of John Diamond's trial, made it glaringly obvious that this was not the county courthouse.

The color palette was not business suit gray and dark blue, but military green and khaki. Nearly everybody wore a uniform and carried a rank, from the judge who was also a colonel to the prosecutor who was also a major. Military lawyers address the judge as "sir," not "Your Honor". And it was not unusual for a soldier witness to answer, "Roger, sir," rather than yes.

By outward appearances, John Diamond fit in. He was dressed in his best Army uniform, the ornamentation from a career that had taken him from Texas to Panama to North

Carolina decorating his broad chest. But as his trial unfolded, John would always be reminded of the limitations of those sergeant's stripes.

Under military law, he had a choice of who would stand in judgment of him: the judge colonel could hear the case himself, or John could have a jury comprised of either six officers, or four officers and two enlisted personnel like himself. John predictably picked the jury with enlisted men. But the numbers were still stacked against him. Unlike the unanimous verdict required for conviction in civilian court, a military trial requires a two-thirds vote for conviction—the same as the percentage of superior officers on the jury.

John began his trial with other strikes against him. The judge earlier ruled against key defense pre-trial motions, including a change-of-venue request. The defense had argued that the jury pool would be tainted by the intense local publicity and that mere instructions from the judge to set that publicity aside wouldn't be enough of a remedy. The judge snorted back, "Do you think members of the military tend to disregard instructions?" and later ruled against the motion.

At 8:11 a.m., the judge took the bench and said, "Accused and counsel, please stand."

This was the moment that John would play his first defense card, a risky gambit acted out in front of his friends and family and those of the man he was accused of killing.

The courtroom was too small to accommodate everybody who wanted to be there. Watching the proceedings via closed-circuit TV in another room upstairs were John's parents, George and Kris Diamond, and his sister, Deborah Dvorak. In the same room were Marty's mother Linda Gettler, along with his lifelong friend—the best man at his wedding—Lonnie Carlson and his wife, Sherri, and Marty's cousin Richard Theer.

The judge said, "Staff Sergeant John M. Diamond, how do you plead?"

John's defense team had reviewed the evidence and decided there was no hope for him on the lesser counts. John decided to plead guilty to wrongfully transporting and storing a privately owned weapon in a privately owned vehicle on January 3 and to committing adultery with Michelle.

The hope was that when the jury heard about this, it would bolster John's credibility: that he wasn't wasting their time fighting charges he knew were true. Then, when he went on trial for the more serious charges of murder, conspiracy and obstruction of justice, he would get a fair hearing. At least that was the hope.

As John stood, the judge explained that a guilty plea "is equivalent to a conviction and is the strongest form of proof known to the law." But that the plea would not be accepted until the judge was convinced that John fully understood the ramifications of his actions. The judge explained in detail the elements of the charges to which John had just pleaded guilty.

"Any questions about those elements and their definitions?"

"No, sir," said John.

"And you understand that your plea of guilty admits that those elements and definitions, taken together, correctly describe what you did?"

"Yes, sir, they do."

In civilian court, the judge would have asked a couple more questions about the defendant's comprehension of the plea and its implications, then issued a sentence. But military court draws out the ordeal.

For John, this meant answering questions, starting with the circumstances of the weapons offense.

"Sir," John said, "on the week of February twelfth, I borrowed a gun from a friend of mine and stored the gun in my car under my passenger seat, unloaded," said John. "During that time, I went to and from my residence and work, sir."

"Were you taking it to any location authorized by your unit commander?" asked the judge.

"No, sir, I was not."

"In fact, did anyone even know you had the weapon? Your unit commander did not?"

"No, sir, he did not."

The judge asked, "Are you willing to admit," that the gun regulation "is, in fact, a lawful regulation?"

"Yes, sir, I am."

"And are you willing to admit to me you had a duty to obey that regulation?"

"Yes, sir, I do."

"Do you believe you're guilty of the offense of violating that lawful general regulation by keeping this weapon in your car under the passenger seat without any lawful authority?"

"Yes, sir, I am."

The judge then moved to the more humiliating charge, adultery. Parrish read the elements of the charge to John, how being a married man and having sexual intercourse with a married woman amounted to conduct that was "prejudicial to good order and discipline," that tended to "harm the reputation of the service or lower it in public esteem."

As family and friends watched, Parrish read the United States military's legal definition of sexual intercourse: "Any penetration, however slight, of the female sex organ by the penis and ejaculation is not required."

The judge asked, "Any questions about those elements and their definitions?"

John, the former swinger, replied, "No, sir."

"Please tell me what happened," Parrish said.

John had no choice but to answer.

"Between February 2000 and February of 2001," he began, "I had sexual intercourse with Michelle Theer on several occasions in Fayetteville, North Carolina."

"OK, and were you married at the time?"

"Yes, sir, I was married," he said, but quickly added, "I was separated, but married," explaining that he wasn't married the entire time he was having sex with Michelle—that his marriage had ended in January 2001.

"And was Michelle Theer married during that period of time?"

"She was also married at that time, sir."

"Didn't she become a widow after seventeen December 2000?" the judge asked.

"Yes, sir."

"So, did the sexual intercourse between you and Michelle Theer occur between February 2000 and sixteen December 2000?"

"Yes, sir, it did."

"Did it occur more than once between February 2000 and sixteen December 2000?"

"Yes, sir, it did."

"Now, are you willing to admit to me that under the circumstances, your conduct was to the prejudice of good order and discipline in the armed forces or was of a nature to bring discredit upon the armed forces by having that sexual intercourse with Michelle Theer when both of you were married to another?"

"Yes, sir, it was."

But it didn't end there. The judge then asked John why he felt that this sex that had occurred more than once prejudiced good order and discipline in the United States armed forces.

"For two reasons, sir," said John. "One, because I had soldiers with whom I worked that knew of my affair with Michelle Theer. And, for the second reason, she was a civilian and she knew that I was in the armed forces, sir."

"Do you believe you're guilty of that offense of adultery with Michelle Theer?"

"Yes, sir, I do."

The judge then informed John that the maximum punishment for having a gun under his seat for a week and having sex with Michelle Theer in motels was a reduction in rank, a dishonorable discharge and three years in jail.

After once again asking John if he fully understood the ramifications of his pleas—and that he hadn't received any promises or threats to enter them—the judge said, "I find that your plea of guilty is made voluntarily and with full knowledge of its meaning and effect. I further find that you have knowingly, intelligently and consciously waived your rights against self-incrimination, to a trial of the facts by this court, and to be confronted by the witnesses against you.

"You may be seated," he said.

With three years of John's life promptly dispensed with, the trial began in earnest.

At 1:40 p.m., the government's opening statement was delivered by Captain Sean Summers, a just-the-facts-ma'am presentation that suggested the prosecution would save its rhetorical fireworks for summations.

"The murder, the getaway plan and a cover-up," Summers began, and then recited in military jargon the details of the case: that on 17 December 2000 at 2250 hours Captain Marty Theer had been shot dead with a 9 mm pistol at 2500 Raeford Road, the work address of his wife, Michelle Theer.

Summers told jurors about the Christmas dinner, the gas stop, the blood drops and shell casings found at the scene, the police interviews with Michelle and her boss, Dr. Tom Harbin, John's friend Peyton Donald, and John himself. He told them about John's post-murder trip to fire a gun at a pawn shop and the pre-murder meeting with Michelle at Zorba's. He told them about the phone calls between John and Michelle and their plans to move to the Caribbean island of Saba.

And he told them about the half-million-dollar life insurance policy on Marty, payable to his wife.

The murder, Summers said, was followed by a cover-up

planned and carried out by John and Michelle, featuring a car break-in that looked like no break-in at all.

It was a rapid-fire, staccato opening, scarce of inferences. Never did Summers say the prosecution believed John Diamond was a murderer.

"The murder, the getaway plan, followed by the cover-up," repeated Summers. "Thank you."

In contrast, Coy Brewer laid on the Southern lawyer charm. In his molasses-thick accent, he opened by saying, "On behalf of Sergeant Diamond and those of us involved in representing Sergeant Diamond in this case, I thank you for your attention, I thank you for your participation."

Brewer then previewed a traditional reasonable-doubt defense, telling the jury that there would be no eyewitnesses, no confession, no accomplice statement, no direct physical evidence—no footprints, hair, fingerprints—linking John to the murder or even the murder scene.

"All of the evidence will be that Sergeant Diamond has, from the very beginning that he was questioned, unequivocably denied any involvement in this crime," said Brewer.

All that was left, he said, was circumstantial evidence that calls for inferences to be drawn. "I simply ask you to listen carefully to the facts and then keep an open mind until we have a chance to make our argument to you about what inferences are really reasonable—what inferences are rational and are appropriate," he said.

Nodding to the defense's credibility-grabbing strategy, Brewer did concede that John and Michelle had had an affair. "He's pled guilty to that," the lawyer said. Brewer also conceded that both were suspects in Marty's murder, giving them "a unique commonality that no other two people in the world shared." John and Michelle "were under this intense law-enforcement scrutiny from the very beginning and their conduct had to be analyzed in that context."

Yet he told the panel that this didn't mean there was a murder conspiracy between John and Michelle.

"The defense contends," he said, "that not only will there be no direct evidence, not only will there be no eyewitness evidence, no physical evidence, no admissions, no accomplice testimony, not only will there be none of that, but it is the contention of the defense that when these circumstances are analyzed, and analyzed rationally, that scenarios equally consistent, or more consistent, with John Diamond's innocence will constitute a fair reading of the circumstantial evidence in the case. We simply ask for your fair and open-minded attention to all of the evidence and for the opportunity, at the appropriate time, for us to discuss with you what the circumstances of this case really show. Thank you very much."

Though the openings differed in style, they shared a caution that belied the uncertainty hanging over the trial. Several key decisions had yet to be made by the judge, including rulings on how much of the information that Michelle had given to police could be revealed to the jury. The defense geared up for a fight; they didn't want her statements to police presented unchallenged by cross-examination. The panel may know everything she'd said to Clinkscales—or it may know very little. Both sides wanted to be careful not to promise too much to the jury, so they wouldn't lose credibility at the end of the trial.

"Government," the judge said, "please call your first witness."

Starting with Video Hut employee Joyce Ann Smith, who described how a frantic and blood-covered Michelle Theer had burst into the store seeking to call 911 because her husband had been shot, and going through Dominique Ryan Peterson, who was with Michelle and Marty at the Fox and Hound restaurant, the prosecution opened its case by giving a vivid account of the events of the night of the murder, but presenting no evidence damaging to John Diamond. It wasn't until late in the afternoon that the prosecution got its case rolling, calling Detective Ralph Clinkscales.

The lead investigator described his initial activities at the crime scene, telling jurors about his inspection of the evidence and the extent of Marty's injuries, when prosecutor Summers prepared to ask him about his interview with Michelle in the patrol car. Anticipating a defense objection, Summers said, "Your Honor, at this time I'd offer the 'What happened?' statement as excited utterance."

This sparked the first mid-trial legal battle. The judge had deferred ruling on the defense's motion to suppress testimony about statements Michelle had made to Clinkscales in the patrol car and later at her house. These included her admissions about marital problems and her account of hearing the gunshots while in her office. The judge said he wanted to wait until the issue arose in the course of trial. That time had come.

Judge Parrish sent the jury out and convened a hearing. Generally, the law protects defendants against damaging statements made by others by allowing the defendants to bring those people into court and cross-examine them—the right-to-confrontation provision of the U.S. Constitution. But, as so often is the case in the law, this is not an absolute right. The law also provides certain exceptions, one of which the prosecution in John's court-martial was trying to raise.

Michelle's statements to Clinkscales, the prosecution was arguing, had come in the heat of excitement, with no time for reflection—excited utterances, as the law calls them. Such statements are admissible in court, without cross-examining the one who uttered them, on the theory they are more reliable than statements that are pondered in advance and made in calmer circumstances.

Defense attorney Ronnie Mitchell, a civilian colleage of Brewer's, argued against allowing the statements. He said there was nothing excited about them, that a long time had passed while Michelle hung out in the patrol car, and she had spoken to several officers already. What excitement had existed early on, after the 911 call, had passed, the defense said.

Summers countered that despite the length of time that had elapsed since the murder, Michelle was "still under that state of excitement," a state that had lasted until the next day. It was not unusual, he argued, for somebody to remain in such an excited state for up to thirty-six hours after something as traumatic as a spouse's murder. Summers noted that Michelle had been crying intermittently, and several times Clinkscales had had to stop to allow her to compose herself.

Mitchell accused the prosecution of trying to have it both ways: that under one prosecution theory, Michelle was traumatized by her husband's murder, yet under another, she had coldly plotted with John Diamond to commit that murder. "The government and its witness are both being a little disingenuous with this argument," said Mitchell.

The judge disagreed. In a major blow to John, he said Michelle was "still obviously under great distress and was distraught" and "there does not appear to be any time for reflection and fabrication." Rejecting the calm, cold killer idea for now, the judge said it was reasonable to believe she had been distraught because there was no evidence yet presented that Michelle was a murder co-conspirator, and even if she were, "It can still be startling by actually seeing a dead husband."

This cleared the way for Clinkscales to testify about Michelle's statements to him about going out to a Christmas dinner, about getting gas and returning to the office to get her books, about hearing the gunshots and coming outside to find her husband in a pool of blood, about running to the video store to get help after locking her keys in the office.

This would have been a bad enough ending to a long, trying day for John Diamond—a day that had begun hours earlier with him pleading guilty to two charges—but there was more. The prosecution wanted to interrupt Clinkscales' testimony to call a witness who had been waiting all day outside.

Michelle Theer.

26

Michelle had had no intention of testifying in John's trial. Her legal plan was to invoke her Fifth Amendment right against self-incrimination and stay in Colorado with her mother and sister. But under military law, it wasn't enough to simply assert one's constitutional right—it had to be done in open court to document before the judge her so-called unavailability to testify.

For the second time, Michelle took the stand as a hostile prosecution witness against John. The presence of her lawyer Gerald Beaver seated next to her did little to calm her. Her voice shook. She gripped her hands together. She knew that a room away, her dead husband's family and friends were watching her, as were John's parents and sister.

"State your name," prosecutor Sean Summers began.

"Michelle Catherine Theer."

"And home of residence?"

"I have no permanent residence at this time."

"Do you know Captain Frank Theer?"

"Yes," Michelle started to say, then caught herself. "I respectfully decline to answer the question based on the Army's decision to name me in these charges. My attorney has advised me to exercise my Fifth Amendment privilege and not make any statements, because they can be charged—used against me. I truly regret . . ."

The judge interrupted her.

No more patient with her than he'd been the last time, Colonel Parrish said, "Mrs. Theer, I don't want a speech from you. You either invoke or you don't invoke. No speeches, do you understand me?"

"Yes, sir."

"Make sure you understand me."

"Yes, sir," she said again.

Summers then asked, "Mrs. Theer, do you know the accused, Staff Sergeant Diamond in this case?"

"Sir," she said, "I respectfully decline to answer the question."

The judge grew frustrated. "First of all, counsel," he said, directing his remarks to Beaver. "I don't understand how whether or not Mrs. Theer knows her husband can incriminate herself. So I don't see there's basis to, whether or not she knew her husband."

"Your Honor," Beaver said, "I misunderstood. I thought the question was: Did she know Staff Sergeant Diamond?"

Beaver of course had not misunderstood. The judge had. Still, Parrish snapped, "The first question was whether or not she knew Captain Theer. So, please answer that question again. There's no basis for the witness to invoke on whether or not she knew her husband."

Summers replied with a soldierly "Yes, sir," and then asked, "Do you know the deceased, Captain Frank Theer?"

"Yes," Michelle said.

"How do you know him?"

"He was my husband."

"When did you get married?"

"June first, 1991."

"And were you married from June first, 1991, until December seventeenth, 2000?"

"Yes."

"Do you know the accused, Staff Sergeant John Diamond?"

"Sir," said Michelle, "I respectfully decline to answer the question."

"I want to refer your attention now to October of 2000," said Summers, plowing ahead. "Did you take a trip with the accused to the island of Saba?"

"Sir, my attorney has advised me to exercise my Fifth Amendment right to decline to answer the question."

"Did you apply for a job at Saba University?" Summers asked on.

"Sir, I decline to answer the question."

Over and over, she refused to answer any of his questions. He asked her about everything from the Christmas party to her interviews with Clinkscales to her activities with John after the murder. The only thing she would confirm was that she had worked at Harbin & Associates and that she'd attended her husband's funeral in Colorado.

Just to make it clear the extent to which she was invoking her rights, John's attorney questioned her in even more detail, and again she took the Fifth dozens of times.

After she was through, at about 5 p.m., the judge pointed out the obvious: that Michelle Theer wasn't going to testify in John's trial. She was, under the legal definition, unavailable.

The first day of trial was adjourned.

27

Most of the second day of John's court-martial consisted of the testimony of Clinkscales, who gave jurors a detailed description of the crime scene. The panel also saw graphic crime-scene photos of Marty's bloodied body sprawled on the parking lot; close-ups of his wounds, including the tiny red dots from where the bullets had entered his body, causing internal bleeding; and the nasty wound to his head that had caused most of the external blood flow. Clinkscales led jurors through the rest of the investigation: the search for John Diamond, the interview with John at the police station, and the family briefing about the case.

At this point, the trial came to another standstill over legalities. Prosecutor Summers now wanted Clinkscales to speak about another set of statements made by Michelle: her remarks in the station house after the family briefing, the most important of which was Michelle's admission that she had called John Diamond from the Fox and Hound. This was the statement investigators had elicited by telling Michelle that her cell phone records would be checked. She had originally said that the last time she'd spoken to John was at 4 p.m.—then she'd changed her statement to say she'd actually called him from the restaurant bathroom.

If admitted, this statement would be the only evidence at trial about the call. Nobody else knew about it and the phone records didn't reflect it. Lourdes Diamond could say that John had gotten *a* call—but she didn't know from whom. By linking Lourdes' testimony with Michelle's admission, prosecutors could make a strong case that this call was evidence of a murder conspiracy: Michelle's signal to lover John to go to the parking lot and kill Marty. Prosecutors could still try to make that suggestion with only Lourdes' testimony, but it would be much weaker.

Since Michelle had told the detective about the call so long after the murder, it would be implausible to suggest that the statement was an excited utterance. So prosecutors tried a different legal theory: Her remark was a so-called "statement against interest." Under the law, such a statement can be considered more reliable—and thus allowable.

"It's not a confession, but it implicates her," argued Summers. "It's against her interests. Clearly no one would admit to that if it weren't true."

But defense attorney Ronnie Mitchell argued that Michelle's statement wasn't against her interest—at the time she'd said it, she had not been told by Clinkscales that John was a suspect, nor had she been told that she was a suspect. If anything, Michelle believed John was innocent, having looked into his eyes and decided he hadn't killed Marty, Mitchell said. Therefore, she'd seen no harm in saying she'd talked to him the night of the murder, the attorney concluded.

As for why she hadn't mentioned it before being told about the check of phone records, Mitchell suggested Michelle may not have understood the question when originally asked. Clinkscales had asked when the last time was that she'd talked to John, and she'd said 4 p.m. that day. It wasn't a lie to leave out the Fox and Hound call, because she'd never actually spoken to him; the call had never been answered, the defense said.

Initially, the judge sided with the defense and barred Clinkscales from testifying about Michelle's phone-call statement. Then, later in the day, the prosecution tried a new tack, using Michelle's own writings against her. Prosecutors showed Parrish a section of the timeline memo. In it, Michelle said that she feared she was a suspect at the time she'd spoken to Clinkscales after the family briefing. That would then make her statement against her interests, the prosecutor argued.

The problem, legally, was that the timeline remained in legal limbo; the judge still had not ruled on whether it represented off-limits privileged communication between Michelle and her lawyer or was potentially admissible diary ruminations. The prosecution and defense reiterated their arguments from the pre-trial hearing, and the judge finally ruled.

"It is written in a very strange way, indeed," the judge

said. "This was not done for the purposes of attorney–client privilege, and therefore it's not privileged."

It was another blow to the defense—Michelle's timeline had a host of material the defense didn't want in—but not as bad as it could have been. In a mixed—some would later say mixed-up—ruling, the judge said he would let in the timeline, but he was still not convinced enough to let in the Fox and Hound phone-call statement.

"So the objection is sustained," he said.

The prosecution would still have much with which to work from Clinkscales' testimony—the detective was allowed to recount at length his interview with John that included the details of the sexual trysts with Michelle. That set the stage for the testimony from the Theers' neighbors, including Felicia Montgomery, about seeing John and his car in the neighborhood after Marty's murder.

The prosecution could then try to argue that the conspiracy between John and Michelle had existed before and after the murder. But without that restaurant phone call from Michelle, the conspiracy case was wobbly. At best, the defense could argue, John had used exceptionally bad judgment in his selection of sex partners.

The defense also scored points in cross-examination by Ronnie Mitchell showing shortcomings in Clinkscales' police work that raised questions about his reliability as a witness. Clinkscales acknowledged that he'd never seen any blood on Michelle the night of the murder, even though other witnesses said her face was covered in it. The detective had no explanation of where the blood had gone. He said police had never looked for fingerprints on the shell casings, on the stairwell, in Michelle's office or in the office bathroom that had the yellow liquid in the toilet, which he couldn't even say was urine, because that hadn't been tested, either. Mitchell also took issue with the way Clinkscales had memorialized John's statements during the interview.

"You had the capability of tape-recording the interview with Mr. Diamond, didn't you?" asked Mitchell.

"Yes, sir."

"But you did not tape-record it, did you?"

"No, sir," said Clinkscales. "I've never taped any interviews."

"You have difficulty in recalling what Mr. Diamond said to you during portions of this interview . . . haven't you?"

"Yes, sir," the detective acknowledged. "Not exactly what he said, but verbatim—I can't remember verbatim what he said."

After Clinkscales, forensic pathologist Dr. Robert Thompson described for the jury what was shown in graphic photographs of Marty's wounds. Thompson spoke of how Marty had been shot five times with a 9mm handgun in the legs, torso and forearm, and point-blank to the head. He estimated that the gun was four to six inches away, leaving a gunpowder abrasion.

"He would have been unconscious almost immediately and would have died very quickly," said Thompson.

Aside from the head shot being last, the coroner couldn't give the order of the other shots, or say how much time had elapsed between them. To provide a more detailed picture of how Marty had died, the prosecution called nearby resident Ramsey Lewis, the flu sufferer who'd heard the shooting while he was lying on the sofa watching a rap video on VH1. Ramsey recounted what he called the "deliberate" manner in which the shots had been fired, highly suggesting a calm, cool killer.

The defense took issue with Ramsey's testimony—the man admitted he'd never fired a gun before and knew little about firearms—but Ramsey stuck to his description.

"It was deliberate, it was not hurried, it was just focused," he said as the second day of the trial wound down. "It was just straight ahead."

The prosecution would no doubt argue that Lewis was describing the work of a trained killer, somebody like Army Ranger sniper Sergeant John Diamond.

The prosecution opened the third day of testimony on Wednesday, August 22, by calling witnesses to show that John and Michelle had had a relationship that went beyond mere casual sex.

David Fredrick of Saba University was the first of three witnesses from the tiny Caribbean island to provide evidence that John and Michelle had had plans for a life together after the murder. Fredrick recounted how Michelle had first shown interest in a teaching job at the Caribbean medical school in June 2000, and indicated on her application that she could start in early 2001—just weeks after the murder. Fredrick, the school's president, spoke of how she had been a promising candidate because she had no dependants who would have to carve out a life on the little island.

Fredrick said that Michelle did tell him she had a fiancé who would like to try to finish his bachelor's degree at Saba. She forwarded a list of his academic credentials.

"Is the fiancé named in this?" asked prosecutor Sean Summers.

"It does say 'John's Credentials,' " said Fredrick.

Under cross-examination, Fredrick said that after Michelle and John had visited the island in October, the university never heard from her again. He also had no record that John Diamond had ever applied to the school. He also said that the island, while remote, isn't so isolated that a person could disappear there.

"Any law-enforcement agencies that were interested in doing so can communicate with your school?" asked Brewer.

"Yes," said Fredrick.

After two more Saba witnesses appeared, testimony

shifted back to the mainland with John's former professor at Methodist College, Drake Johnson, saying how John had spoken openly in class of having a fiancée who was a psychologist. Also testifying were two of Michelle's neighbors, Jim Marshall and Norman Zaldivar, who recalled seeing John visiting Michelle after Marty's murder.

"It was just annoying to me," said Zaldivar. "The neighbors were coming to me and saying, who is the guy walking in front of my yard? [They were] thinking my wife was having an affair." He said that after he confronted Michelle, John's car had disappeared.

Next up was Heidi Mougey, the office manager at Harbin & Associates, who recalled meeting John for the first time in the spring of 2000 at a Bennigan's restaurant when she'd gone there with Michelle after work for beers. She then spoke of John's frantic phone call to the office in the days before Marty's murder.

"He called wanting to see if Dr. Harbin was there," recalled Mougey. "He started trying to ask me a bunch of cryptic questions that I didn't understand. I finally asked him to tell me straight out what he was wanting to know, and he told me that the night before Michelle had got home, her ex was there, and he abused her. So, I told him that we would just pretend that I didn't know about it, I would give Dr. Harbin his name and number to call, and I had Dr. Harbin call him."

Mougey said she'd never seen any bruises on Michelle, and the night of the Christmas party, Michelle had shown no signs of being in a hurry or under stress.

Dr. Thomas Harbin, Michelle's boss and onetime confidant, recounted how he'd never wanted Marty to attend the Christmas dinner, but had only consulted when Michelle said that Marty would be disappointed if left out. Harbin also saw nothing unusual between the Theers at dinner, even though he knew about their marital problems.

Harbin spoke of Michelle's private conversations with him about the couple's disagreement over whether to have children, and her suspicions that Marty was having an affair. He recounted how Michelle had pondered whether to stay married to Marty long enough to get a share of his reenlistment bonus.

It was through Harbin that the prosecution tried for a third time to get in evidence the fact that Michelle had phoned John from the restaurant. Michelle had told Harbin about the call, explaining that she was trying to reach John to get a ride to work while her car was in the shop. But once again the judge declined to allow the testimony, saying he wanted to privately consider this and other evidence presented to him in hearings away from the jury. "So," he told prosecutors, "if you lay a sufficient foundation to show that the conspiracy exists, then Dr. Harbin's testimony can come in front of the members," said Parrish.

To bolster the conspiracy case, the prosecution called two of John's Army buddies. A soldier named John Dash recalled his visit in the summer of 2000 to an apartment where it had appeared that John was living with Michelle. Dash hadn't known who Michelle was at the time, but recognized her picture in the paper later after the murder. John's barracks friend John Pickett then recounted overhearing John on the phone in the days before the murder trying to calm somebody down.

"I asked him if everything was OK," said Pickett. "And he said, yeah, that— something with Michelle's husband had hit her or something like that."

Seeking to show that the conspiracy had continued after the murder, the prosecution called a reluctant Deborah Dvorak to the stand to testify against her brother. After saying that John was not allowed to communicate directly with Michelle from the brig at Camp Lejeune, prosecutor Summers asked Deborah if Michelle had ever tried to get her to relay information to John.

"There's probably been a few times that she's told me something new that's happened," said Deborah. "So when she tells me something new, I may tell him."

She acknowledged that she was Michelle's friend and that they spoke about once a week, but she tried to downplay how close they were, claiming to not even know Michelle's phone number.

"Do you have to look up her number each time?" asked Summers.

"Yes."

"Do you have it written down somewhere?"

"Yes."

"Do you have it with you?"

"No."

"It's not in anything that you brought with you to court or on this trip?"

"No."

The prosecutor concluded the tense standoff by saying, "I don't have anything else for her at this time," and handed her off to the defense, which had no questions.

Despite Deborah's terse testimony, relations with Michelle were strained now to the breaking point. As the court-martial progressed, Deborah began to feel that Michelle wasn't as concerned about John as she had claimed—and now seemed to have no interest in his family. At one point, Michelle walked into the room where family members watched the court-martial over closed-circuit television, and she didn't even acknowledge Deborah. Another time, on a sidewalk near court, Deborah offered Michelle a ride to get away from news photographers. Michelle told her to go away and then ran in the opposite direction, Deborah would later say.

The trial was moving quickly. There had been three days of testimony, and prosecutors had just two more days planned.

By the start of day 4—one of the toughest days of the trial for John, as Lourdes was first up on the stand—Deborah and Michelle were no longer on speaking terms.

28

She'd kept his name and ditched his alibi.

Lourdes Diamond took the witness stand on the fourth day of John's court-martial, as independent and confident as she'd been at his Article 32 hearing. After giving a brief history of their relationship, from meeting in Panama in 1995 to their divorce in January 2001, Lourdes explained to jurors that John had been with her watching a movie the night of December 17, 2000—just not the entire night.

"Did anything happen during the movie that changed who was watching it?" asked Summers.

"Yes," said Lourdes, testifying in Spanish through an interpreter.

"What happened?"

"In the middle of the movie he received a call on his cellular phone," she said, then explained that he'd gone into their child's room. "When he came out of the baby's room, he got dressed and he left."

After lying in three police interviews, Lourdes said, she'd finally decided to tell the truth. She repeated her testimony from the Article 32 hearing about how she'd feared being deported or losing her son if she lied.

"Is the story you've told here today in court the truth?" asked Summers.

"Yes."

"Has anyone offered you anything or promised you anything to get you to change your story?"

"No one's offered me anything."

She had decided, she said, that John no longer loved her, that he had never stopped cheating on her and never would. Even after she'd testified at the Article 32 hearing, and John remained in jail, she got a reminder of her husband's betrayal. When she went through his things to give to his father, she'd come across a black briefcase she had never seen before. She opened it.

"It had some weird clothes in it, like flashy clothes, like blue, real bright silver," she said, "like it was club clothes."

To underscore John's duplicity, the prosecutor had Lourdes read to herself a trial exhibit: a note that John had written in the summer of 2000.

"There's something here that says 'his wife,' " she said.

"It refers in that exhibit to his wife moving to Saba," said Summers. "Do you know what Saba is?"

"No, I don't have any idea where that is."

"Has he ever talked to you about moving to a place called Saba?"

"No."

Defense attorney Coy Brewer did what he could under cross-examination, taking Lourdes through the events of December 17 again, but the damage was done. If anything, the cross hurt John's case more as Lourdes explained why she'd stayed with her husband despite his philandering and abuse.

"I don't know if he thought about it or if he didn't, but I always felt like that we were never going to separate, that we were always going to be together," she said. "I came all the way from my country with him. That was my husband—with a lot of illusions, you know, like when a person comes to a strange place, illusions that we were just going to have a family together."

In a civilian court, her testimony would have ended with the questioning of the lawyers. But in military court, the questioning can extend to the judge and jury.

One of the jurors, a sergeant major, had written a question.

"Ma'am, were you given any reasons why your husband was divorcing you?"

"He never admitted that he had ever had a relationship with any woman," she said. "He just told me that he wanted to be alone."

After a lunch break, the prosecution bolstered Lourdes' testimony with that of another woman who'd decided to stop lying for John: Lourdes' mother, Priscilla Solis.

Also testifying through an interpreter, Mrs. Solis said that late the night that John had left in the middle of *The Patriot*, she was awakened by the sound of a door opening. "He was returning," she said. "I could hear when he walked from the door to the kitchen. Then I heard the clothes washer come on later on."

She said that her daughter told her, when the police came, to tell them that John had been at home watching a movie.

"Why did you decide to tell the truth?" asked prosecutor Summers.

"Because they told us that they could send us to Panama," said Mrs. Solis, "that they could take the baby from Lourdes."

With John's alibi shattered, the prosecution moved on to the gun. Although it was never found, prosecutors called Sergeant Peyton Donald to show that John had had access to the same kind of 9mm used to murder Marty. Testifying against his old friend, Peyton said he'd loaned his gun to John just before the murder, gotten it back days later, then loaned it to him again six weeks later. That was the last time he'd thought about the gun until police contacted him, asking him to call John to find out what had happened to it.

Peyton recounted the dispiriting call to his former squad leader, who'd initially professed to have no idea where the weapon was. Peyton said that John had then called him back to say he was going to get it, only to call yet again, later that evening, to say that his car had been broken into and the gun was gone.

"Did you ever get your gun back?" asked Summers.

"No, I didn't," said Peyton.

"Have you gotten it back to this day?"

"No, I haven't."

To suggest to the jury what had actually happened to that gun, prosecutors called investigators who'd handled the car break-in report and taken John's statement that he had parked his Firebird on the base over the weekend and returned to find it burglarized. The prosecution then called OSI Special Agent Vince Bustillo to narrate the surveillance video showing John driving to and from Michelle's house in that same car shortly before the break-in report.

"So, essentially, he lied about the location of his car?" asked Major Bagwell.

"Yes," said Bustillo.

What's more, the video clearly showed that the passenger-side window wasn't broken. The video evidence was bolstered by the testimony of John's brother-in-law, Victor Dvorak, who recalled seeing John in a car looking very much like the Firebird John and Michelle had driven the weekend that they'd visited the Dvoraks in Florida.

With that testimony complete, the prosecution made another big push to introduce Michelle's statements to police, the most important being her admission that she had called John from the restaurant. The prosecution also wanted the jury to see an item pulled from Michelle's computer: the

Q&A purportedly transcribing conversations between her and John.

The judge had indicated that he would allow this evidence if the prosecution had shown through other evidence and testimony that a murder conspiracy had existed between John and Michelle. The legal burden for proving the conspiracy—and thus allowing Michelle's phone-call statements and the Q&A—was not high: the more-likely-than-not evidence standard.

"Sir," prosecutor Summers told the judge, "the government believes there's ample evidence of conspiracy. Actually, our position is, it's been proved beyond a reasonable doubt. That's above the standard."

Brewer countered that the only thing the prosecution had proven was that John Diamond and Michelle Theer had been sleeping together, something that John had already pleaded guilty to. "There is no evidence—no direct evidence—in this case of any discussion, agreement, meeting of minds," said Brewer. "So, there is no direct evidence of a conversation where any illegal act was discussed where there was any agreement between Michelle Theer and John Diamond."

After hearing the arguments, the judge took a fifteen-minute recess. He returned to the bench just after 5 p.m. with his ruling. He began by enumerating everything that he considered evidence of a conspiracy, from John and Michelle's motel trysts to John's efforts to remain in touch with Michelle after he had been jailed. Noting that the legal standard requires only a preponderance of evidence to allow it in, the judge said "a conspiracy existed between Michelle Theer and the accused to murder Captain Theer."

The statements, the timeline, the Q&A—everything—would be admitted. Clinkscales would be recalled to the stand to give the jury the lowdown on what Michelle had said about the phone call to John from the restaurant. It was the biggest blow to John since Lourdes had stopped providing an alibi. Prosecutors now had everything they wanted.

All the restraint they'd shown in opening statements would go out the window in summation.

29

The prosecution rested on the fifth and final day of testimony. It was time for the defense case.

To the surprise of John's own family, his lawyer Coy Brewer called just one witness: Fayetteville police K9 Officer Kurt Richter, who testified that Michelle had told him she thought she'd seen someone run away from her office building after Marty had been shot. Richter said his dog had tracked a scent across Raeford Road and through the golf course at Highland Country Club before losing the trail at a construction site in a cul-de-sac behind the course.

As they watched the trial on the closed-circuit TV, it wasn't clear to John's parents, who had depleted their bank account to hire Brewer, why there wasn't more of a defense case. But Brewer, then and to this day, was confident in his reasonable-doubt approach, that the prosecutors had failed to meet its burden and there was no cause to give them anything else to work with by presenting an affirmative defense case. It was a common defense strategy, and one that often succeeded if the summation was powerful enough.

Everything now hinged on closing arguments.

The opening of Major Randy Bagwell's summation was telling.

"It's been a fairly long week," he said.

Summations were presented on Monday, August 27, 2001—one week after John Diamond had pleaded guilty to adultery and weapons charges. There had been five days of testimony, one defense witness and a crushing ruling by the judge to allow Michelle's computer records and statements to police.

With military efficiency, justice moved swiftly for Staff Sergeant Diamond—too swiftly, he would later believe.

"We have proven," Bagwell continued, "through overwhelming evidence, that this accused is guilty of conspiring with Michelle Theer and committing the murder of Marty Theer."

Bagwell then presented a compelling story of passion, conspiracy, murder and cover-up. He illustrated this with a PowerPoint presentation to the jury that opened with pictures from the crime scene: the inside of Michelle's office, the steps where Marty had been shot, the bullet hole in the side of the building, the hedges behind which the prosecution said the shooter had hidden. He looked at the soldiers in the jury box and he spoke their language.

"Make no mistake about it: this was not a random shooting. It was never a random shooting. It was not a botched robbery and it was not some mugging," Bagwell said. "This was an ambush, and it was executed in military style with military precision."

This jury needed no expert witness to be convinced that the circumstances of the murder showed this killer had had military training; the jurors were their own witnesses.

John and Michelle—by John's own admission illegal lovers under military law—had extensively planned, and come up with the murder as the bloody solution to getting Marty out of the way, Bagwell argued, so the couple could live and love on an exotic Caribbean island, a dream life bankrolled by a half-million dollars in life insurance money starting on January 1, 2001.

It had taken great coordination and communication to come up with the plan, Bagwell said, and so, when they weren't sleeping together in motels, they were calling each other feverishly, up to fifteen times a day, planning, scheming, conspiring up to the night that Michelle had gone out for an office Christmas dinner at the Fox and Hound restaurant on December 18, 2000.

That night, Michelle had excused herself from her dinner party and made a critical call that was never answered. At that exact moment, fifty-some miles away, "Diamond's cell phone rings at exactly the same time in his apartment," said Bagwell, now exploiting the legal victory that had allowed Michelle's statements into evidence. "It's not answered that we know of. His wife says the phone rang, he picked it up, and he walked out of the room, and she never heard him say a word into it. Then he comes out, dressed warm."

Although they'd never spoken, the phone call, Bagwell argued, "is evidence of their agreement to do this, evidence of the agreement to go out and commit the murder, because it was a signal to get in place."

Under the prosecution scenario, Michelle and Marty had returned to the deserted office building after the gas run to Quick Stop around 11 p.m., Michelle had run upstairs to get the books she'd purposely left on her desk, then waited until Marty had run out of patience and gone up the stairs, perhaps knocking on the door.

Bagwell, given great leeway by the judge to speculate aloud, suggested a reason why a candy wrapper had been found in Michelle's office trash can. "Those seconds were ticking by like minutes. Minutes pass like hours. She's probably pacing around. She's probably dry-mouthed," said Bagwell. "All she's doing is waiting to hear the shots. Maybe she's counting all the money she's going to make. Maybe she's thinking about the weekend before, when she was having sex with the accused in Raleigh. Maybe she's thinking about anything she can to get this out of her mind."

Taking the speculation even further, Bagwell entered Marty Theer's mindset. "A minute passes, two minutes pass, three minutes pass," the prosecutor said. "He's got to be thinking, 'What is she doing up there?' He's already aggravated because they had to turn around from the gas station to come there. So what's he to do? He's going to go up and see what's keeping her. He gets out of the truck, locks it, puts the keys in his pocket and starts up the stairs."

Telling the jury, "this is something we're all more familiar with in the military" and "all of you have probably done that, where you do an ambush site selection on a map," Bagwell argued that trained Army sniper John Diamond and Michelle Theer had used 2500 Raeford Road as the best site for their own little operation. "You've got a kill zone that is perfect because, as many of you know, when you're setting up a kill zone for an ambush, you want the enemy to have absolutely no place to go," said Bagwell. "And that's what the accused left Captain Theer. Absolutely no place to go."

Firing from down below and through the railing—difficult for some, Bagwell said, but not for a Ranger—John had first hit Marty with a "glancing blow" shot to the left side while Marty was at the top of the stairs, sending the sequins from his red suspenders fluttering to the landing, Bagwell said. The second shot had nailed Marty in the abdomen, the third had gotten him in the buttocks and the fourth had hit his left leg, shattering the thigh bone, under the prosecutor's theory. Hobbled by the broken bone and bleeding inside, Marty had stumbled to the ground next to John, who'd finished him off with a close-up shot to the head behind the left ear.

"One can only imagine what goes through the mind of someone as they're leaning over them to put that shot behind the ear," said Bagwell. "Maybe he was thinking about the money. Maybe he was thinking about the life he was going to have with Michelle Theer in the future. Maybe he was already thinking about lying on the beach and doing diving down in Saba. Whatever he was thinking, he didn't let that get in the way of keeping up with his mission. He moved across the objective, and he executed Captain Theer."

Although no evidence directly placed John at the crime scene, there were clues that a person of his military training had been there, said the prosecutor. Among them was the fact that two of the five brass shell casings had been picked up after the shooting—Bagwell speculated that the three remaining ones had been under Marty's body. John "knew that the brass could come back and be tested by someone to link him," Bagwell said. Michelle, too, had had the smarts to know that they should get rid of as much potential evidence as possible.

"If she had run to the door when she said, she would've seen Sergeant Diamond picking up his brass and getting ready to move out," said Bagwell. "Maybe she did see it. Maybe she goes to the door and opens it up, probably cautiously, to make sure everything is still OK. Maybe she peeks out. Maybe they look up, nod at each other, she waits for him to clear out, and then she rushes down the stairs." Only then, Bagwell said, does she run for help at the video store down the street.

Following the shooting, the prosecutor said, was the cover-up—proof that this had been a conspiracy. "She couldn't have done it without him, and he couldn't have done it without her," said Bagwell. "Her part in this, for the cover-up, is, she has to talk to the police." Michelle, he said, was the "conduit of misinformation," while also trying to monitor the investigation and, even after John's arrest, relay information to him. As for John, the key evidence of his role in the cover-up was his trip to the pawn shop to fire the gun—and thus make it impossible to perform a gunshot residue test on his hand—and to dispose of the murder weapon, said Bagwell.

His best defense—an alibi from his estranged wife, Lourdes—had collapsed as the woman broke free of John's emotional grip, Bagwell said. "She wanted to believe him. She wanted to believe this was just a 'little investigation.' She wanted to believe that the guy she was married to, the father of her son, the person that she was gong to be linked to for the rest of her life was not a cold-blooded killer," said Bagwell. "She wanted to believe that really badly. She wanted to help him. She also knew she had to do the right thing. And that's what she did when she came forward."

John, meanwhile, hadn't done himself any favors by moving in with his co-conspirator Michelle after the murder—"not a real bright thing," the prosecutor said—angering the neighbors and triggering a video surveillance that had exposed the break-in as a fraud, leading to John's arrest and ultimate downfall.

"This whole case is about a conspiracy," said Bagwell. "These two are linked. The acts of one are the acts of the other. They're constantly communicating. They're in it together. They're up to their necks. In this case, they're over their heads. They conspired to commit murder for profit. And they did it."

At about 11:30 the jury was sent out for a one-hour lunch break. They returned to hear the defense summation. With the evidence and the judge's rulings against John, his defense had only one thing left to do.

Risk it all.

30

"Today, it is your duty to make a profoundly important decision," Coy Brewer drawled. "Today, what you do with that decision can give life and vitality to the Constitution, which you're sworn to protect and maintain."

Calling upon the soldiers on the panel to follow the many rules of military justice, Brewer asserted that the most important rule of all was obeying the burden-of-proof requirement: that John Diamond must be found guilty beyond a reasonable doubt. "It's really very rare that we're called upon to make a decision based upon that level of certainty," he said. "Most of the time, we make decisions based upon what we think may be true, probably true, more likely to be true or not."

In this case, as in all other criminal cases, the burden was higher, Brewer told the jury, and he went on to give the legal definition of reasonable doubt.

It was a traditional beginning of a summation for a criminal defense attorney, one used in every courtroom in every case, misdemeanors and felonies, throughout the country. Brewer went on to make the traditional argument of a defendant in a circumstantial case: that the circumstances didn't mesh together well enough to convict John beyond that reasonable doubt.

"During his closing statement to you, Major Bagwell, the trial counsel, drew—as he is permitted—a whole lot of inferences," said Brewer. "That is perfectly appropriate. He is permitted to do that. During his talk to you, he used the word 'maybe' over thirty times. He used the word 'probably' over sixteen times. The word 'might' about ten times. Because that's what he was doing; he was drawing inferences. He was taking facts and he was saying that from those circumstances, he could draw inferences. He may do that, and it's certainly appropriate.

"I am permitted—and it is appropriate for me—to do the same thing."

Here is where the summation veered from boilerplate.

"It is my contention," he said, "that the compelling circumstances and the compelling inferences establish that on the night of December 17, Michelle Theer shot and killed her husband, Captain Marty Theer."

Brewer said there were three possible scenarios in the murder of Marty Theer. The first was that a robber had done it. "I'm not going to insult your intelligence," Brewer said. "I'm not going to contend to you that that is a reasonable possibility."

The next was, as the prosecution alleged, that John and Michelle had conspired to kill Marty, and John had pulled the trigger. That, too, strained credibility, Brewer argued.

"If the prosecution's theory is true, then Michelle Theer, Ph.D. psychologist, and John Diamond would've had to have been two of the dumbest, most moronic people walking around Cumberland County. They would've had to have been full-time stupid," said Brewer. "There is a limit to how completely stupid two people can be."

Instead, there was a third alternative, he said.

When the pieces were put together, Brewer argued, they would paint a picture of a woman who was as smart as she was guilty. "Michelle Theer's decisions were not only cunning, but intelligent and ruthless, both before and after the night of December the seventeenth," said Brewer.

Beginning with a detailed timeline of the night of the

murder, Brewer laid out his reasons why John Diamond was suddenly and dramatically turning on Michelle Theer. With a window of just fifteen minutes from the Theers' gas purchase at Quick Stop at 10:42 p.m. to Michelle's 911 call at 10:57 p.m., Brewer suggested that there simply wasn't enough time for the shooting to play out the way prosecutors theorized. In that fifteen minutes, the Theers would have needed to have driven three miles down Raeford, through numerous traffic lights, park at the office building, have Marty wait three or four minutes in the car until he got impatient, leave the car, get shot and be discovered by Michelle, who would spend a moment cradling his head before running down the street to call 911.

"Let's look at what the timeline would be if she is the shooter," Brewer said, then presented a scenario in which Michelle asks Marty to go up the stairs to get her book, gets the gun out from under the seat and "comes out of the car firing."

"He comes down the stairs," Brewer continued. "She shoots him in the head."

Under the defense theory, Michelle then picked up the keys, ran up the stairs, set the keys down on the books, took a piece of candy, put the wrapper in the trash, and only then rushed back downstairs to call police. "She runs to the Video Hut just as hard as she can, because she wants, when she gets there, to sound like a hysterical, frantic woman," said Brewer.

This scenario, the lawyer argued, explained why Marty had been at the top of the stairs when he was shot instead of while sitting still and alone in his car. "I would contend to you that at that moment when the target is stationary . . . that is the moment to act, particularly if you've been out there in the cold for thirty or forty minutes," said Brewer. "Why wouldn't a trained shooter simply come up and take a head shot through the window?"

Rather, firing on Marty at the top of the stairs, with the shot partially blocked by the railing, pointed more to somebody like Michelle, said Brewer. "It's consistent with an inexperienced—determined, but inexperienced—shooter," he said. This is bolstered, he said, by the shot sequence, when "the first shot essentially missed," and the others looked like "an inexperienced shooter trying to aim."

After the shooting, Michelle could have hidden the gun quickly anywhere; police had never searched any of the other offices, the area around the building next door or even a nearby Dumpster, said Brewer.

This murder, the lawyer argued, was in fact part of a plot—only John wasn't in on it.

"It is my contention that not only was Dr. Theer the shooter, but that it was her plan from the very beginning to kill her husband and lay it all on Sergeant Diamond," said Brewer. "If you look at the evidence rationally, that plan comes across loud and clear."

To draw John into her web, Michelle had concocted the story that she was abused by Marty, prompting John's frantic call to the office in the days before the murder. "As a psychologist, she knew that John Diamond would call somebody and tell somebody about it and talk about it," Brewer said. "It [also] provided an innocuous means of her asking him if she could borrow a gun: 'My husband—I'm scared of him, he's abusing me. John, get me a gun. I want to borrow a gun.' Sergeant Diamond loaned it to her."

He did this, Brewer said, out of love. "John Diamond loved Michelle Theer before December seventeenth for a whole long time, and he still loved her after December seventeen," Brewer said. "He may very well still love her."

The defense lawyer contended that if this were a conspiracy, and John were the shooter, then they never would have chosen that stairwell as a kill zone. "It is a horrible choice," said Brewer. "It is well lit, it's on a well-traveled street. . . . Diamond has to hide from neighbors, people driving up and down the street. He's got to hide from patrons of the commercial establishments that might be there. He's got to hide from people making their late rush to the Video Hut to get the movies back in on Sunday night. He's got to do this for a substantial period of time."

But if Michelle were the shooter, "this place makes every bit of sense," said Brewer. It gives her a place to which she can lure Marty, where she can hide the gun, where she can make a credible case to police that somebody stalked them, the lawyer said.

"Dr. Theer did not have the choice to commit this crime in a private place; then it would've been just her and her husband," said Brewer. "There's no one else it could've been laid off on. She had to choose a public place. So she did. The public place that she chose was the very best public place, the safest for her."

The choice of weapon also was smart for her, Brewer said, contending that it made no sense, if John were the killer, to borrow the murder weapon from a friend who could easily talk to police. Brewer called that scenario "dumb to the point of almost not having words to describe." John, he said, could have gotten a gun anywhere else—"This country is lousy with guns," said Brewer. What's more, he said, John had returned the gun to Peyton Donald in the days after the murder, leaving it accessible for any law enforcement agency to easily test it.

"There is only one conceivable, plausible, articulable [cq] explanation, and that is, during the period that Sergeant Diamond had the gun, John Diamond did not realize or believe that this was the murder weapon," said Brewer. "If Michelle Theer is the shooter, everything about the gun falls into place. Using the 'my husband abused me' lie, she persuades John Diamond to loan her the gun. . . . She had no reason to want an untraceable gun, because when she asked John Diamond for the gun, it is her plan and intent [that] he's going to take the fall with the gun."

Brewer theorized that Michelle had gotten the gun from John on Saturday when they'd met for lunch at Zorba's and then, perhaps wearing latex gloves, stashed it under the seat of the Explorer. After dinner Sunday night, when they'd arrived at the parking lot, Michelle watched her husband go up the stairs and "starts firing, not particularly skillfully, but with determination," said Brewer. After the last shot, she had cradled his head to explain the gunshot residue on her hands.

Even John's seeming lack of an alibi proves that he wasn't part of a murder conspiracy, said Brewer. If he had been planning to murder Marty that night, he never would have gone to Lourdes' apartment, only to have to leave abruptly when signaled by Michelle. It made even less sense for him to rely on Lourdes for an alibi when he'd served her with divorce papers the day after the murder, on December 18, said Brewer. She'd only changed her story, the lawyer suggested, out of fear of the government. "She had to know the government didn't believe her story," he said. "So if she testified consistent with her story, if there was going to be any retribution, if there's any rational fear of retribution, it is from the government."

After the shooting, Brewer contended, Michelle had stepped up her efforts to frame John. By telling police about the phone call from the restaurant, she'd anticipated that they would search John's apartment and find the gun that she knew he'd borrowed, he said. The problem, he said, was that Michelle didn't know that John had returned the weapon to Peyton Donald.

"She is playing this whole thing," Brewer said. "She needs to know what he knows. She needs to know what the police know. She needs to know who is being suspected." As part of this, she had drafted the Q&A with John, never intending for anybody to see it, said Brewer.

John was so clueless about what was going on that it was only when Peyton Donald asked about getting the gun back that it had all come together in his head, said Brewer. That was when John had made a very bad decision about reporting the break-in, the lawyer said.

"I'm not going to insult your intelligence by saying that the factual scenario"—the break-in—"did not occur," said Brewer. "But I would contend that what makes sense is that indicative of, yes, a moment of unprepared-for panic, that it is consistent with Sergeant Diamond acting irrationally and impulsively . . . and possibly acting at Michelle Theer's suggestion."

When Michelle had later called Donald saying she had something for him, "She was still kicking around the idea of laying it off on Sergeant Diamond," said Brewer.

In the end, the lawyer said, all the evidence pointed to Michelle Theer as the killer, who was "playing a delicate game" to keep John Diamond close to her, while at the same time setting him up.

"All of it makes sense if it was her and not him," Brewer said. "She had the stomach to do this. . . . She's hard, she's cold, she's ruthless."

Concluding his summation, the lawyer said, "If Michelle Theer being the shooter is fairly and rationally possible under circumstances, if the evidence does not eliminate that as an evidentiary certainty, then it is your duty, as to these charges, to return a verdict of not guilty."

31

After a twelve-minute break, the jury was brought back into the courtroom to hear the prosecution's final remarks. Like civilian court, the government has both the burden of proof and the last word.

In his rebuttal, prosecutor Sean Summers called Brewer's summation "a classic co-conspirator defense"—that when there's overwhelming evidence that two people have committed a crime, one fingers the other.

"The stuff you heard today from the defense counsel—the statements you heard, the story you heard—has not been supported by one witness that came in here to testify," said Summers. "It is his comments, his imagination, on what might've happened. And imagination is not reasonable doubt."

Going through the defense summation point by point, Summers said that John and Michelle had had plenty of time to commit the crime with John as shooter, and that their actions and statements after the murder—from John going to the shooting range to the car break-in—pointed squarely to his guilt. As for Lourdes Diamond's credibility, "If you believe the defense theory, if it has any merit at all, Lourdes Diamond came in here and gave an Oscar-winning performance to you." She was, he contended, a "one hundred percent believable, honest witness."

John, on the other hand, clearly showed a consciousness of guilt, a legal concept that can be considered by the jury in deciding whether to convict him, the prosecutor said. "He lied about his alibi, where he was that night," said Summers. "Why would an innocent person need to do that? He lied, in part, about his relationship with Michelle Theer. An innocent person wouldn't need to lie about that. He lied about his car being broken into. He lied about a weapon being stolen. . . . Innocent people don't tell lies to the police. That's the whole consciousness of guilt. They know they're guilty, so they're lying to cover it up."

Summers finished his rebuttal by saying that, "The defense has tried to use a magic trick on you. You all know how magic works. It doesn't really work with genies or lamps. That's what they tried to do with this. Look over here at Michelle, look at what she's doing, hoping you won't notice everything John Diamond has done on the other side.

"He is guilty of the murder," Summers said. "He shot Captain Theer himself. He's guilty of the conspiracy. He planned and executed it with Michelle. And he's guilty of obstruction of justice."

After the five hours of summations, the judge handed the case to the jury, delivering his final instructions. Colonel Parrish told jurors that their deliberation should include a "full and free discussion" of the evidence, and that, "The influence of rank shall not be employed in any manner in an attempt to control the independence of the members in the exercise of their own personal judgment."

When the deliberations were complete, the panel was instructed, the members would take a secret vote by written ballot. The president of the panel, the military equivalent of a foreman, was empowered to determine the order in which the specifications on the counts could be considered. If two-thirds of the panel found John guilty, then that would be the verdict.

On a panel of six, then, four people would determine John's fate.

Jurors retired in private at 3:29 p.m. on August 24, 2001.

Three hours and fifteen minutes later, they had a verdict.

32

Just before 7 p.m., Colonel Parrish called the court to order.

"Have you reached your findings?" the judge asked the president of the jury, a colonel.

"Yes, Your Honor, we have," the colonel said.

"Fold your findings in half, please," the judge said. "Bailiff, please hand that to me."

The judge read the verdict to himself, giving away nothing in his face. He handed the sheet back to the bailiff, who gave it to the jury president.

"Accused and counsel, please stand," the judge said.

John stood military straight.

The jury president read the verdict.

Guilty on all counts: obstruction of justice, conspiracy and murder.

"You may be seated," the judge told John.

John showed no emotion.

33

Marty Theer's mother, Linda Gettler, watched the reading of the verdict on a TV screen from the viewing room upstairs. Beside her at the long conference table were Marty's grandmother, Ruth Dunbar, and Sherri Carlson, one of Marty's oldest friends. John's mother, Kris Diamond, also sat at the table.

The women trembled as the verdict was announced. They cried when it was over, each consumed with her own emotions: relief and sadness for Linda, white-hot anger for Kris.

The next day, the two mothers had their own day in court.

At the sentencing hearing for John Diamond on August 28, prosecutors called Linda Gettler as their only witness. After taking the stand, Major Bagwell asked her, "Please tell the members how you know Captain Marty Theer."

Linda said simply, "He was my son."

With that, she gave a heart-breaking presentation to the jury about her only son, showing the panelists photos of a young Marty with her and his grandparents. She spoke of camping and fishing trips, and of how close Marty had been to his grandfather—her father, a World War II vet in the Air Corps whose health now was so bad he couldn't attend the trial.

"They spent a great deal of time together," she said. "They had long talks, they took long walks. They built a doghouse for our dog. My dad was the father for Marty."

She showed the jury a picture of a young Marty with model rockets he'd built. "He was always interested in space and rockets and flying and things like that," she said, telling the jury that when he was 8 or 9 years old he'd written an essay about where he saw himself in twenty years. "His essay had him on a space station, circling Pluto."

She showed the jury a photo of an older Marty, trying to make that dream a reality by attending the Air Force Academy. Another picture showed Marty on the Fourth of July, with a flag in the background. She spoke of how they'd raised the flag while playing a *Songs of Liberty* album of patriotic songs. "Marty would say the Pledge of Allegiance, and a lot of times when he was a lot younger, he'd have a cap gun that he'd give a salute with. It just meant a great deal to him."

She spoke of his high school years, his military service, his dreams of having children. And she spoke of the pain his death had caused.

"It's been absolutely devastating," she said. "For me, it's the fact that every time the phone rings, I know when I pick it up, I'm not going to hear, 'Hi, Mom.' I'm never going to hear, 'I love you, Mom.' "

It had been especially hard on Marty's grandfather, she said.

"My dad has been through many things the past twenty years, surgeries, things like this. Marty was always the reason to keep going," she said.

And she spoke of how he'd never wanted to go to that Christmas dinner with Michelle and her co-workers. He'd wanted to stay home and watch football. He'd only gone, she said, because Michelle and her boss had invited him.

The prosecutor gave Linda one last chance to speak. He asked her if there was anything else she wanted to say.

"There's a lot of things, I don't know," she said. "I couldn't possibly say all the things I would like to say. What I can say is, I was extremely proud of my son. Not only did I love him devotedly as a mother, but he turned into a person that I really like and respected. He brought joy to all of our lives. I never heard Marty say an uncharitable word about anybody. If he couldn't say anything good, he didn't say anything. I learned a lot from Marty, his direct approach to life, the fact that he never backed down from challenges and went straight ahead, the way he dealt with people—made friends wherever he went. He'd do anything for anybody at any time. He never put himself first."

She concluded by saying, "The people who did this will probably have the chance of living out the rest of their natural lives, maybe not the way they would want to live them, but they'll be alive. . . . Marty's voice has been forever silenced. Anything he might've done or accomplished is gone."

The defense was also allowed to call witnesses on John's behalf, beginning with Army Captain Marcus Carter, who'd once served under John in Panama and described him as a soldier's soldier, one of the top 10 percent of squad leaders. "He was the guy I could depend on," he said. "His overall knowledge—bottom line, he knew his job."

He was followed by John's mother, who spoke of her own little boy who would grow up to become a soldier. As a boy, she said, he had been "bull-headed, strong, opinionated, caring." He'd joined the Army right out of high school. "He wanted to be part of a team that was highly respected, that had pride in themselves," she said.

The last few months, she said, had been an ordeal. "We're close-knit," she said, "and we feel what he feels. He's gone through all the emotions that you can go through. As a family, it's brought us closer together."

"The court members are going to be considering your son's case," Brewer said. "Is there anything that you wanted to say to them?"

"That I respect their decision, and I ask them for mercy

and compassion," she said—but she didn't completely mean it. In her heart, she would say years later, she'd felt nothing but hate. "I never knew I could hate that much," she recalled.

John's sister went next to the stand, describing him as a "wonderful" older brother. Fighting tears, she spoke of how close they had been growing up. "We moved around a lot because my dad was a construction worker," she said. "Every six months to a year, we were moving from school to school. I think that we depended on each other to get through that. Being in a new school and not having any friends, we were together."

As a youngster, she said, "He was always trusting and naïve and gullible." And protective. "I remember when we were in school. At one school we went to, I was getting picked on by somebody. He was just always there," she said. "I couldn't walk home with him, I couldn't stand too close to him, of course. But he was just always there."

While he was in jail, she said, she had tried to be there for him. "He calls me every day," she said. "You get a ten-minute phone call, collect, and then we would hang up and he would call me again, maybe two or three times a day for the last six months." When she visited him, he always smiled. "That's how he is," she said. "He covers everything with his smile."

"Is there anything you'd like to say?" the lawyer asked.

"Just that I understand your decision, I do," she said to the jury. "But I just want you to look at him as a human being, because he is. I love him very much, and that I'm sorry for their loss."

The defense called its last sentencing witness.

John Diamond.

No longer as emotionless as the day before, John's voice cracked as he stood before the judge. But he still stood tall, still very much the Ranger.

"Sir," John said to the judge, "it's my understanding that I can say what I need to say?"

"Your understanding is correct," said Colonel Parrish.

John then spoke.

"Panel members, sir, I have a statement prepared by Captain McKnelley"—John's military-appointed lawyer for the sentencing hearing—"but in all good conscience, I cannot read this statement," he said. "I will look you in the eyes and I will tell you I'm not a perfect person. But I'll also tell you that I did not—"

John stopped himself. "I know you've made your decision, and that's fine. I can respect that," he said. "I didn't kill anyone. And I did not conspire to do it with anyone."

He paused to take a breath.

"My whole life—honor, integrity and discipline have meant more to me than anything else, because no matter what happens to me, no one can take those things from me," he said. "Maybe what's happened to me, something good will come out of it. Maybe someday, people will find out what actually happened. I can't tell you. I can't tell them, because I wasn't there that night. If I had known what was going on, in good conscience, I would have told someone. I have a son and a daughter, so I know what would be going through their minds. I'd do anything to protect them."

He said that he knew he would never be released from prison on parole. "You have to admit that you did something wrong to see parole," he said. "I cannot admit to something I did not do, because that's more wrong to me. At least in my heart, and my honor, I know I was right, and I know I'm innocent. I know, in no way, what I say can change any of that, because it's done. I know that."

He spoke of how sometimes perceptions become reality, "but it doesn't lead to the truth," and for this reason he wasn't angry at those who had put him away for life.

"I have no animosity towards the family. I don't even have animosity towards the prosecutor or the judge or you, because you have a job to do," he said. "In some way, I know that you all thought what you did was right. I had faith in the system that's supposed to be just. Now I know that sometimes, justice is just how you look at it."

After he was finished, lawyers on both sides got to make their final arguments. "The victim," Bagwell told jurors, "was Marty. You get to decide what punishment is fair and just. You have to take into consideration that Marty is no longer with us because of his"—John Diamond's—"actions."

The prosecutor showed no compassion for John's statement. "He got up there and cried and whined," said Bagwell. "We cannot force him to produce that gun at trial, but do you think for one second that if he was holding the only piece of evidence that could set him free, he wouldn't just give it to you? He's guilty. He got up here and lied to you."

In urging the panel to vote for life without the possibility of parole, Bagwell speculated on how terrifying Marty's final moments must have been.

"Captain Theer was at the top of those stairs, nowhere to go. The accused steps out, starts shooting at him," the prosecutor said. "Marty—at that point, who knows what he was yelling? Maybe he was yelling, 'Michelle, get down!' Maybe he was yelling, 'Michelle, let me in!' She's a coward just like [Diamond], she's hiding underneath the sofa in her office so she doesn't take any rounds herself.

"The coward behind me," said Bagwell, pointing to John in the courtroom, "is shooting the man in the back. He's shooting him in the back. An unarmed man, trapped at the top of those stairs, getting shot in the back." Only when Marty was down on the ground, still alive, does John deliver the final shot, said Bagwell.

"He was probably still conscious, looking up at the accused," he said. "What do you think he was thinking at that point? Do you think he was begging for mercy? Do you think he was crying like the accused did when he got up here? What mercy did he show him? He put that ninety-millimeter handgun a few inches from his head and ended his life."

Marty had been killed for money, said Bagwell, "nothing more than money."

Marty, he said, was the real soldier in this case, a patriot since he was a young boy, who'd understood the meaning of the honor and discipline about which John had spoken. "What kind of honor is it to go to another man's house every time he's [gone] or in the field and sleep with his wife?" Bagwell asked. "Is that honor and discipline? That is ridiculous.

"For the actions that happened that day, life without parole is the only option," said Bagwell. "You should definitely not feel sorry whatsoever for him, because he made that cold, calculated decision, and knew the consequences. Maybe it even crossed his mind, it couldn't have been worse. He made the decision, he took the chances, he rolled the dice. He knew the consequences when he put the gun to his head and shot him. . . . For that, life without parole should be the consequence."

Later that afternoon, the panel made its sentencing decision. John was knocked down from sergeant to private. He was given a dishonorable discharge.

And he was ordered to spend the rest of his life in prison, never to be paroled.

After the sentencing, as he was being led out of the building for jail, the guards allowed John a few moments alone in an office with his mother while they waited outside.

"Mom," he said, "I didn't do it. If I did, I would tell you."

His mother said, "I know."

34

He told people it was only about sex. But it wasn't.

Within about two months of meeting Michelle Theer, he was talking about a future with her.

"Hey, babe, I had a wonderful weekend, as if I ever didn't when I'm with you. Although the more time we spend together, I realize the harder it is to be away from you," he wrote to her in a May 20, 2000, email. "But I also know that some day we will be together. That's the day I live for. I love you."

Even as a swinger, he was respectful of her feelings. "I'm looking forward to this weekend with you in Charlotte—or should I say the experience of seeing everything," he wrote of an upcoming Carolina Friends event. "Just remember, if you're uncomfortable, then so am I, and vice versa. You mean the world to me and I don't want to jeopardize it or ruin it."

In another email, he said he couldn't get enough of her. "Always thinking about the next time I get to see you, even after we just leave one another," he wrote. "You are sexy, gorgeous, intelligent, sassy, bitchish—the good kind. And thank God, you're mine. I love you."

Both emails were signed in his usual way, "Love always, John."

The emails—John's love letters, some of Michelle's replies—were pulled off Michelle's computer after John's trial. The correspondence was soaked in the passion that Michelle had so craved, and betrayed a level of commitment that both would deny—to others, and sometimes to themselves.

Michelle gave John more than a good time. She nurtured him, encouraged him, helped him with his studies at Methodist College, prepared him for a life outside the military.

"Thanks for asking about my test," he wrote in an email one day. "I'm pretty sure I aced it. I have another one tomorrow. Man, this stuff is easy. I'll be glad when it gets harder or at least the classes get more interesting."

This was more than just bravado. He did well at Methodist, his report card from the summer 1999–2000 term showing an A in intro to college math, a B-plus in college algebra, a B-minus in survey of the New Testament, a B in English composition. He would also do well in the autumn term 2000–01, with an A-plus in introduction to literature and an A in general psychology. His cumulative GPA was 3.55.

To be sure, John was smitten. He couldn't do enough for Michelle. He brought her Corvette to the shop when it needed rear shocks and work done on the exhaust system. He helped her move furniture at her office. "I love making your life easier. That's my function in life, you know," he wrote in June.

The only bad times for John were when Michelle wasn't around. One twelve-day trip she took in mid-June sent him into an emotional tailspin, leaving him with no outlet for his sex drive:

> I don't know how I can get through these next 12 days. I've never missed anyone before, but now I'm missing you and you haven't left yet. I hate this emotional stuff. I can't wait until you come back so we can take care of each other. You know, sex, sex, sex, and, of course, more sex. I'm really looking forward to spending every night with you. If you can put up with my unending sexual urges. And, of course, my normal every day strange behavior. I'll make sure I stay in the gym and at the pool so I can stay sexy for you. I love you very much. I'm definitely looking for-

> ward to our future, every minute of it.
> Love you always,
> John.
>
> PS: Looking forward to our meeting at the airport parking lot, a little mutual pleasure.

He quickly followed this up with another email making it clear that it wasn't just the sex he craved.

> There's an ache or void in my heart when you're not with me. I know that we are meant to be together and that we are kindred soul mates. It took us awhile [sic] to find each other in this not-so-perfect world but through our union, we've created our own little piece of perfect, our love. I've never been one to say very much about what I feel, and maybe that's because of the mother thing. But I do know that I'm not worried about letting you in close to me.

He loved her so much, he said, that, "I'm scared." He obsessed about losing her, and every moment she was away, he thought about her.

As a postscript, he noted that he'd gone to a club that evening and had an interesting conversation with a woman named Lisa, who told him she used to be a dominatrix.

> Wow, never would have guessed it. You know, she's the quiet type. I guess those are the ones you have to watch. Isn't that right, my bedroom porn star? Laugh. That's the way I like you though: Sweet in life and slutty in the bedroom. Laugh.

About a week-and-a-half into her trip, John sent a note telling her about his daughter from his first marriage, a girl he had barely seen. From the context of the email, Michelle had told John the same about her Air Force father, who was away for months at a time. It touched a nerve with John.

"I'm always there for her momentarily, but I want to be more," John said. "It's hard because I was so self-absorbed with my career at the time, she took a backseat [sic]. I never want and will never allow that to happen again with her or you." He said he was eager to have his daughter meet Michelle. "She's just like you. She's strong-willed, very intelligent, beautiful and of course very sexy at times. Laugh. If I had someone I wanted her to end up like, it would definitely and without a doubt be you."

He closed by saying, "I want to spent the rest of my life with you and whatever exists after that."

As Michelle's affair with John flourished—and his feelings for her deepened—her marriage to Marty grew worse. Michelle never attributed the troubles to her relationship with John, or to her swinging escapades. Rather, she blamed her husband. "She was initially generally unhappy with Marty," recalled Michelle's boss, Tom Harbin, who served as a confidant during this period, listening to Michelle speak of her marital woes. "The reason seemed to be he was not a lot of fun and didn't like to do things."

Complicating matters was Marty's growing desire to have children. "Marty wanted them NOW," Michelle wrote to his mother after his death. "His biological clock was ticking. I had a great deal of concern about: (a) being a single parent six months out of the year when he was deployed, (b) his completely unpredictable schedule (from day-to-day), and (c) the absence of any family support in the local area."

At the same time, Marty was undergoing a career crisis. Michelle told Marty's mother that he had been unhappy with the Air Force for some time, and could have opted out in December 2000, though it would have meant losing a lucrative bonus the military offered to try to keep people in the service. Michelle told his mother he could have easily turned down the cash—as much as $200,000—and gone anywhere they wanted. Michelle saw moving back to Denver as an "obvious choice," she wrote, "because of my willingness to have a child with family support nearby."

"But Marty was uncertain about what he wanted to do when he got out and what he was prepared for in a civilian job," wrote Michelle. "Relocation would also necessitate me getting a new job."

They discussed this for months, getting nowhere. Michelle said the final decision was up to Marty and she would support him, but he had to be comfortable with it. She didn't want him blaming her years later. "He continued to waffle," Michelle wrote to his mother. Marty considered signing up for another three to five years in the Air Force, or just getting out. At one point, Michelle said she even suggested that Marty could put off looking for another job and be a stay-at-home dad while she earned the income as a psychologist.

Their problems reached a breaking point, Michelle would claim, when she found something suspicious on Marty's computer in the spring or summer of 2000. She said it was a personal ad on the Internet from a man who seemed to be Marty Theer. This was similar to what she had seen about a year before in Florida.

While Michelle's detractors would later question whether she'd concocted the story—there was never any independent evidence that Marty had anything more than an unhealthy obsession with online porn—Michelle would always insist that she'd known her husband was straying.

"It was not until I discovered his affair that things reached a head," she would later write. "I did not confront him immediately (as I had done three years earlier in FL), but took off my wedding rings and told him he must go to couple's counseling or our marriage was over. I gave him an ultimatum."

Marty resisted. That was the summer and fall of 2000, when Michelle moved out, when Marty relented, when they went to Dr. Kastleman, when they moved back in together, when Michelle and John traveled secretly to the island of Saba where Michelle was thinking of teaching psychology and John was thinking of teaching scuba diving and martial arts, dreams that would never become reality.

About a month after Michelle moved back in with Marty, their landlord decided to sell their rental house and the couple was evicted. They soon found a new home, on English Saddle Road, and moved in November. At the same time, Marty resolved the long festering issue of whether to stay in the Air Force by deciding to re-enlist. That month, he bought Michelle a ruby-and-diamond heart pendant from Gordon's Jewelers at Cross Creek Mall in Fayetteville.

"All the hustle and bustle of finding a new place, moving, and the holidays seemed to distract us from our problems," Michelle later wrote to Marty's mother. "Once we stopped talking about them and Marty signed on for three more years, the immediacy of our problems receded. We both felt relief at not having to confront all these issues all at once."

Michelle acknowledged that "Marty and I had some rough times recently," from Michelle's depression to the "huge decisions" they struggled with. "But we came through all that," she beamed. "We found happiness again. Moving to the new house was like having a new start."

In fact, behind this positive exterior lurked mounting problems and pressures for Michelle. She continued to take a cocktail of medication for depression, anxiety and insomnia. Not long after she and Marty moved into the new house, Marty's mother, Linda Gettler, came out for a visit, the first extended stay she had ever had with them, and Michelle would later characterize having her mother-in-law around as a "stress."

Marty's mother sensed it, too. Although Linda Gettler described the marriage overall as "pleasant," she saw signs of strain. When the three took a car trip to Washington DC, Marty's mother watched Michelle shrug off Marty's attempt to hug her. Then over dinner, Michelle called Marty "stupid." Her son had always spoken highly of Michelle, and on the way home from Washington, his mother recalled, "He told me they had had some problems they were working out and everything was going to be OK."

In fact, apparently unknown to Marty, Michelle was thinking as seriously as ever about divorce. Always a great maker of lists, Michelle sat at her computer and compiled a detailed accounting of the couple's assets and debts, spelling out how it would all be divvied up. The list was only found after John's trial.

1) Student loan debt, community property. Marty may buy out his portion, 50 percent equals $29,000 with cash or continue to make 50 percent of the payment over the next ten years, $325 a month;

2) Ford Explorer debt. Marty will maintain possession of vehicle and be solely responsible for remaining payments.

3) Support based on current 5K month net pay equals $1,500 a month for 54 months, one half length of marriage.

4) Retirement forfeiture options. Michelle agrees to waive all claims to the 23 percent of his retirement to which she is legally entitled in exchange for

FM's share of current investment assets after student loan debt valued at $12,000;

5) Request maintenance of current insurance coverage on 'Vette until date of final divorce granted';

6) Marty will be removed as user from CitiBank Visa;

7) Michelle will be removed as user from First USA, MBNA and NationsBank Visa;

8) No further joint debt will be accrued.

Another document she titled "Student Loans: Why I feel he should pay half," listing the reasons:

1) My choice of graduate school, i.e. private, was due to geographical limitations. This prevented me from going to a state school or one where I could have received more assistantships.

2) Portions of the money were used for non-school related items (vacations, car, furniture, etc.)

3) It is a community debt and should be considered as part of our marital debt just as our assets.

In Michelle's other relationship—with John Diamond—there were no assets. But it was hitting the skids in the same way as her marriage with Marty. Even when their affair burned the hottest, Michelle found some aspects of John's personality irritating. The flip side to his effusive love was a dark moodiness.

Back in mid-August, for instance, one of her swinger contacts invited her and her partner for a weekend rendezvous at a Marriott in Research Triangle Park, asking for just $40 to cover the room and food. Michelle replied by email on August 17 that, "Things are getting tense."

She noted it was 1 a.m. and she was still at work—and contemplating spending the night rather than go home to John.

> I didn't even say anything about this weekend to John. He gets so moody sometimes and tells me nothing is wrong, but I know it is because he won't touch me. He withdraws affection etc. Right now, I want to go home and tell him to get his ass out, back off and leave me alone. So what is stopping me? Who knows? But I refuse to tell you that is what I am going to do because we both know it's 50/50. Just bitching.

She concluded by saying, "Frankly, I don't want to see him at all right now."

She ultimately did, over and over again, and his flowery emails continued for weeks—as did the swinging good times. John's love notes became even more obsessive. He spoke of being unable to sleep when she wasn't with him. He talked of marriage and having children. He spoke more frequently of being jealous about Marty. He was also nearing the end of his military service, and reality was threatening to barge in on their fantasy affair. John was considering continuing his college education in Texas or Colorado, and wanted Michelle to come with him. All of a sudden, he was making the same demands that Marty did: demands that sent Michelle into the arms—and bed—of men like John Diamond.

Tired and medicated, Michelle was growing weary of it. Just days after she and John returned from the Saba/Club Orient trip in October 2000, Michelle told him that they couldn't spend Halloween together. She began to distance herself from him, communicating less, shutting herself off emotionally.

In an October 28 email, John expressed his hurt—and jealousy. "I just hate to think that he gets you in ways I don't," he told Michelle. "I'm scared and tired. I just don't want to lose you. I have never loved anyone or anything for that matter as much as I love you." Her cancellation of Halloween "makes me think maybe other things won't happen either," he wrote. "You know I put up a good front but sometimes things get to me and I need that little reassurance from you that things will be OK. Baby, I can't offer much right now but one thing that I promise to always give you is my love."

John was especially hurt over what, from the context of the email, appeared to be her spurning him sexually. "My heart hurts so much right now," he wrote. "And now that I won't even talk to you is just cruel, especially knowing that at least that bastard gets to see you, talk to you and even sleep with you in a manner of speaking."

He concluded by saying, "I want to give you a beautiful child and hopefully a wonderful life with me. I need you. I love you always. Love, always, John." Almost as soon as he'd sent the email, John appeared to have regrets. "Baby, I'm sorry. I should realize that you have a lot more to lose than me," he wrote in a follow-up. "Last night, I didn't sleep. I was worried about you and your feelings all night. Sometimes, when I lose control of the situation, I guess I can strike out. So, I'm sorry."

Acknowledging that being with him doesn't make things "simple and easier," he said, "I hope you'll still want to see me." He pleaded with her that they could take a trip to Durham. "Look forward to hearing from your angelic voice, kissing you. Love always, if you'll have me, John."

Michelle wouldn't have him. On November 19, she finally spelled it out, fully, clearly, without any room for misinterpretation, a long, detailed email:

John, no words can ever begin to express how destroyed I feel inside right now, nor can I ever help you understand how giving up on us will somehow make me feel better in the short term, but somehow I have to make one last attempt to try.

I wish I was as strong and confident as you, but inside I am a scared weak link. I have loved you from the moment I set eyes on you. You showed me love and happiness like I have never known or felt before. You opened my eyes and I saw a world I never thought was real.

But now I feel as if it is a cruel joke, that in order to really have it, I have to try at it. I have to give up every bit of security I have and put complete faith in you. And if things don't work out or it is all an illusion, then I am left with everything I have ever feared most of in my life: alone without a home, rejected, unloved.

Some of my insecurities about our relationship come from the fact that I have never felt this way before, that it is truly too good to be true. Some of it comes from my childhood—parents, father, and all the fucked-up things they said and did.

Although I recognize that about a billion people have it worse than me and I have no room to complain.

Some of it comes from you and the secrets you kept from me for the first two-thirds of our relationship. Some of it comes from the things that I feel like you continue to hide from me or mislead me about, things that should not matter, that do not matter to me, except that I wonder what the motivation is to hide them.

This lack of honesty and truthfulness has created a tear in our relationship that I cannot ignore. It prevents me from taking that leap of faith into eternity with you. It is the real barrier in our relationship, even more so than my health, your ex, your career path or financial issues.

And as much as I adore your spirit and adventure, and although I have one too, I cannot bounce from one place to another every hour. From the depths of my soul, I need stability, and running from my problems in search of a fantasy life will not make me better.

It makes me physically ill in my brain, not my head. My brain hurts to think of moving to Texas or Utah or Florida. To think about moving somewhere without a job lined up, to think about doing the work to get re-licensed and search for a job, to think about moving, looking for a place to live, coordinating with your job/school needs, I just cannot do it.

I truly mean it when I say I do not have the physical, emotional, spiritual or mental energy to consider any such plan of action. And as hard as I say it, and you listen to it, you just do not hear because it is not in you. It is contrary to your nature.

I've moved around my whole life, never lived anywhere longer than a few years. Right now, I just need rest and peace, at any cost. So right now, I am giving up on us because it is torture to me to think about paradise glimpsed and not believe it can really happen, yet have it dangled in front of me every day.

I would rather return to my world of blind numb ignorance than to endure gut-wrenching agony day after day.

There is a terrible sense of relief that comes from finally succumbing to the demons that haunt us. I pray to the goddess that I am a positive experience in your life, that you will believe in love and find it again, that you will continue to follow your destiny and make it happen.

I love you,
Michelle.

John treated the break-up like a death. His emotions followed the familiar stages: denial, anger, bargaining, depression—everything but acceptance. Her letter had this big tall tough Army Ranger blubbering like a child.

"I broke down, literally. I've never cried like I am now," he bemoaned in an email. "I will never understand why you forsake us. I would never leave you and I would never not love you, but it must be easy not to care and want to live a life without love. I just wish that I had never fallen in love with you. It would have been so much easier."

Turning maudlin, John lamented, "I think sometimes I was meant to be alone. Love isn't for me, and this had made that painfully clear. I will always love you no matter how you have hurt me. And, yes, you have destroyed my faith in love and destiny, because I never realized destiny could be so cruel."

Just as quickly as he drifted into the fog of depression, John found a way out. He pulled himself together and fired off a follow-up email sounding more like the old John Diamond.

"Hey baby," he wrote, the swagger returning, "I just wanted you to know that no matter what, I will always be here for you. I've never been in love and I thank you for allowing me to fall in love with you. I also thank you for letting me know what a broken heart feels like. I don't mean that badly, either."

He said he was leaving for Texas—"There is just no reason for me to stay here anymore." His mother was forwarding him the paperwork for a college there; he was thinking about going to medical school one day.

"I think I'll immerse myself in work," he said. "It's the only way I know that I cannot have to deal with my emotions."

He signed it, "Goodbye, John."

Faced with this, Michelle just couldn't leave it at goodbye—hers or his:

> It is clear from the tone of the two letters you sent me that the one I wrote was damaging, and I apologize. That was not my intent. I hope to make you understand, not hurt you. I hope you do not mean some of the things you say here. I think you know that this is not easy for me. This is the hardest decision I have ever made. I know you will succeed as whatever you choose in the future.
>
> Forever in my heart,
> Michelle.

This was all the opening that John needed. From sad to resolved, he now found room for negotiating his way back into her heart, an emotional journey all in one day. Writing to his "dearest Michelle," he asked her whether, if he could come up with "another option"—say continuing his studies at Methodist College or at Durham so she wouldn't have to move—she would still be interested in staying with him. They might, he said, be able to come up with "something workable."

Of course that still left the inconvenient existence of Marty Theer. "You also said that you were leaving your husband, granted not now, but later. Was that really true?" he asked. "If it is, then I would wait. I wouldn't see you if that would make things easier for you, but I would wait. And when you were ready to begin a new life, I would be there."

"Well," he said, "hope you call. Love, John."

• • •

She did.

Michelle took him back, barely. She seemed reluctant, tentative, talking to him less, but still sleeping with him.

John, on the other hand, plunged into a romantic free-fall. Apparently sensing the tenuous nature of the renewed relationship, he was wracked with insecurity, calling Michelle dozens of times a day, every day, mostly to her cell phone, but sometimes to her home and office. Some of the calls were only five seconds long—quick messages or hang-ups when he got her voice mail. She returned very few of the calls. He sent her emails spilling out his feelings. When they were together, he was prone to his moodiest behavior.

"I got a little weird," he said, without elaboration in a November 30 email about his behavior, but blamed it on not being able to see her enough. He sent a second email that day—what he called his "daily reminder that I love you"—in which he gushed, "You're quite angelic when you want to be and quite the little devil at other times. Laugh. I think I love this other side more. Laugh."

As November turned to December, he said he couldn't wait to see her—that this night would be ideal because he didn't have a class. A third email that day apologized yet again, this time for "overreacting," something he blamed on his hectic work duties. He told her that he'd bid on her Christmas present on eBay—two items that are "very unique"—and that, "I still haven't forgot about my present either. Remember, a nice, long, romantic letter. Plus, I'd like a nice, long erotic one, too. Don't leave out any details, even the small ones. I love you. I'll be writing you a nice love letter for your birthday."

He told her that he was looking forward to "tomorrow around 12:00 at your office" and to going with her to Raleigh for the weekend to celebrate her 30th birthday and to see her friend Rafael Harris.

Ending the email on a steamy note, he said, "Bring a towel to clean up with. I'm feeling very sexual. I love you forever and always, John."

Two days later, John told her his horoscope that day was "right on," saying that the "gears are in motion to begin a new commitment. And don't chance fate and lose out on love."

Michelle was now apparently claiming to him to have some sort of looming health problem. He reminded her to take her pills—"and that means iron supplements and birth control. Although I do want you pregnant, now would be a little difficult to explain. Laugh." On a serious note, he said that if she needed blood, he'd be happy to donate some of his own. "I would do anything for you, especially donate something that you need."

He said that if she were feeling OK, they could get dinner and see a movie.

"PS: had a wonderful dream, quite wet, about us last night. Kiss Kramer and Topaz for me."

John's appeals to Michelle's erotic side were not as effective as they'd once been, her mind drifting elsewhere, away from him, away from Fayetteville. On December 7, 2000, her college friend from Florida, Donna Miller-Brown, emailed to say that Michelle's car license plate had arrived in the mail from the Florida Department of Motor Vehicles. Donna said she would send the plate to Michelle's office because she didn't know her new home address.

She ended the email asking, "What are your Christmas holiday plans?"

Perhaps a testament to how she felt about her home, Michelle had been living in North Carolina for more than a year, and never changed her tags, nor applied for a North Carolina driver's license, instead driving with Florida plates and a Colorado license. She explained to Donna in a reply email that, "I'm resisting identifying myself as a North Carolinian and trying to hang on to my Florida identity."

She said that she planned to spend the weekend with Rafael Harris, who was sweating out whether he had passed his state psychology licensing exam. "It's really weighing down on him. I hope he can have a good time this weekend," Michelle said, making no mention of John. As for the holidays, "Marty and I have no real plans," she said, "just staying around F'vill."

Despite the mystery illness about which she'd complained to John—and her ambivalence about staying with him—the weekend went ahead as planned. Michelle told Marty that she was going to meet Rafael; Marty had no problem with the trip. He knew and trusted Rafael, and didn't want to leave town anyway.

On Saturday, December 9, 2000, Michelle and John met Rafael in a restaurant. Rafael was taken aback to see John; he was under the impression he would just be meeting with Michelle. But it was a great night. He had just found out he'd passed the state's psychology exam and could now practice. The three celebrated over dinner at a restaurant and then hit a club called the Warehouse, with the night becoming increasingly awkward. "I felt somewhat the third wheel," Rafael recalled.

Late at night, the three retired to a motel in downtown Raleigh; Rafael had one room, John and Michelle shared another. Michelle paid for both rooms. That night, John and Michelle had sex.

But the glow from the weekend was extinguished almost the second John and Michelle got back to Fayetteville. The day after their Raleigh trip, on December 10, John called Michelle in the morning and made plans to meet at a cafe called The Coffee Scene. For two hours he sat there, and she never showed up. She never called. He was as angry as he was confused.

When he got to his computer, he sent her a firmly worded email. Under the subject line, "What's up?" he wrote:

> Baby, I get the distinct feeling I've done something wrong, so please let me know what I've done. I'm exercising patience with the sarcastic comments, seeing how they'll do no good anyway.
>
> No call, no nothing. I'm not used to being stood up. . . . Baby, I understand you are busy, but at least you could have called really quick to let me know something.
>
> I can only assume the worst. This morning, you probably wouldn't have called, but since I called you, I think you felt obligated to talk to me or something. Baby, I'm here for you and no one else, but I can't help if you want talk to me. Don't shut me out, please. Talk to me. Call me as soon as you get a chance.
>
> Love you forever and always.
>
> Eternal love and devotion,
>
> your love,
>
> John.

Whether Michelle spoke to him after this email—or continued to torture him with her silence—isn't known. But records showed that he sent a second, darker email the next day:

> I'm sorry you have forsaken us. I really do love you, but I guess your love just wasn't there. You lied quite well. You fooled me.

Ominously, he said,

> I signed my life insurance over to you two weeks ago. I'll make it look like an accident so there's no problem with the money.

> I wanted to spend my life with you but since I'm so easily thrown away by you, I guess I am not worth that much. So, oh well. It was a hell of a ride.
>
> A friend is squaring me away with something. I'll take a few hours to think about life and maybe write something. I will always love you and hopefully see you in another life.
>
> I love you,
>
> John.

He didn't say what the friend had given him. But it was at almost this exact time John asked his friend Army Sergeant First Class Peyton Donald about borrowing a gun. It was a 9mm semiautomatic, Smith & Wesson Model 5906 that Donald had bought in Panama because he felt his wife might need protection. John told Peyton he wanted to use the gun for target practice on a Fayetteville range.

As suicide threats go, this one didn't last long. A day after telling Michelle he was going to end it all, John sent her an email, addressed to "My dearest Michelle," saying that he was sorry he'd worried her.

"I did drive to someplace secluded," he said in the Tuesday, December 12, note, "and three times I tried to pull the trigger, and I realized two things. One was that I was giving up. And two, it would have hurt you."

He said he "cried long and hard" to find an answer, but couldn't. "I know that we were meant to be, no matter what. I can't believe that you would give up. I know things are tough."

It was here that he made reference to a serious allegation she'd made about her husband. "He makes you miserable and even tried to kill you. Yet you still want to be with him. Why?"

The letter didn't elaborate, but on the same day he wrote the email, an upset John Diamond called Michelle's office.

Office manager Heidi Mougey took the call. John told her that he urgently needed to talk to Michelle's boss, Tom Harbin. John kept asking Heidi what she called "cryptic questions I didn't understand."

Finally, Heidi asked John straight out what he wanted to know. He said that the night before, on December 11—the night that John had tried and failed to commit suicide—Michelle's ex-husband had been at their home and abused her.

The statement didn't make any sense to Heidi. For one, Michelle wasn't divorced, and as far as Heidi knew, Michelle was still living with her husband. Also, Michelle had never mentioned anything about being abused by her husband, and Heidi had never seen any marks or bruises.

In his email to Michelle that day, John said that the night before he "went back to the ex"—his estranged wife, Lourdes. "Why?" John said. "Well, I figured if you could live the rest of your life unhappy and married to someone who you don't love the way you love me, then why couldn't I do the same?"

In fact, John had been spending more time with Lourdes than he was admitting. Although legally separated, he had moved back into the apartment three months earlier, in September, about the same time that Michelle had returned to the house with Marty. John wasn't there full-time and he didn't stay in the same bedroom as Lourdes, usually sleeping in their son's bed or on the sofa. He continued to take off for days at a time without explanation. But Lourdes put up with the arrangement. John still paid most of the bills.

In his "What's up?" email to Michelle, John had mentioned none of this. It was her marriage about which he was most concerned, not his. "Maybe you should leave him now and give us our chance," John said, urging her to overcome her fears. He even said he'd considered proposing to her just the night before, and still would if he thought she had been serious when she'd once told him she wanted to marry him.

"You told me that you don't think he told his parents about the divorce, but now I wonder if you ever told him about the divorce," he said. "All I know is that I make you happy and he doesn't. Yet, you always choose him over me. Why? I want to give you your time to think. I guess I was right. In order to prove our love to someone, you must be willing to lose everything."

Saying, "I wait painfully for your call," John signed the email, "I love you forever and always. Eternal love and devotion, hopefully yours, John."

The next day, Tom Harbin spoke to Michelle about plans for the office Christmas dinner. He wanted to have it at the Fox and Hound restaurant in Cary, near Raleigh, that Sunday night, December 17. He was planning on a small dinner, inviting only Michelle and the office manager Heidi. Spouses wouldn't come.

Michelle didn't like the plans. She said Marty would be "disappointed" if he wasn't invited. Harbin acquiesced, expanding the dinner to include his wife, Heidi's boyfriend, Dominque Peterson and Marty.

In fact, Marty had had other ideas for that night. Always the homebody, he'd wanted to go to bed early because he had to fly the next morning. But Michelle insisted. She said her boss wanted Marty to be there to get to know him better.

On Saturday, the day before the party, John was a wreck. That was the day he was in Rickie Bizon's barracks room frantically calling Michelle, trying to find out why she was avoiding him, but she wasn't answering. John's cell phone records showed that he had received an eight-minute call from Michelle's house at 11:10 a.m. Usually, when John finished a phone call with Michelle, he would just get up and leave. This time he told his friends about Michelle's claim that Marty had raped her and how she was thinking of finding somebody to kill him.

Within an hour of that phone call, John met with Michelle

at Zorba's restaurant in Fayetteville. The only thing John would say about the lunch meeting was that they'd discussed the office Christmas dinner Michelle planned to attend the next night. It wasn't known what they did the rest of Saturday, though the phone calls continued, with John's cell phone showing four more calls from Michelle's house that evening, lasting from twenty-eight seconds to nearly six minutes. The last call he received from her home was just before 10 p.m. and lasted two minutes and eighteen seconds.

The next day, Sunday, December 17, John called Jim's Pawn Shop at 12:32 p.m. It wasn't yet open. He then received a call from Michelle's cell phone at 12:32. At 1:36 p.m., he called the pawn shop again, this time for a minute and a half.

Later that afternoon, around 4 p.m., John called Lourdes from the video store asking what movie she wanted to get. He suggested a Mel Gibson film that she hadn't seen.

"Well," she said in agreement, "let's rent *The Patriot*."

35

Her first panic attack happened when she was backing out of a parking space in a bank lot. She rammed into another car.

Her second came at night, at home. The only damage was to her pride. Her sister and father were there, and when she calmed down, she was embarrassed, and afraid.

Fear, paranoia and loneliness gripped Michelle Theer in the late summer and fall of 2001. During John's court-martial in August, she'd moved from the Florida house she was watching for a former professor into her grandmother's home in New Orleans. "I think she was just lonely in Florida," her sister—Angela Forcier, recalled. "When she lived there before, she had had lots of friends, and I think she was hoping to find that again and she just didn't."

Michelle also was still reeling from an incident involving a man named Nelson King whom she'd met in June 2001 when she was dating his friend Darren. Something about Michelle struck Nelson as, in his words, "shady," and so he looked her up on the Internet, finding stories about the murder case. Nelson warned his friend about Michelle, but Darren refused to listen. Nelson then called Fayetteville police.

When Michelle found out and confronted Nelson, he promised not to call police again. When he did anyway, he tried to deny it.

"So you want to play mind games with me?" Michelle said, according to Nelson. "Go ahead. I'm the fucking master."

When this didn't scare him off, and he later warned Darren's parents about Michelle, she confronted Nelson again when they ran into each other in a nightclub. According to Nelson, she got in his face and said, "I'll have you killed, too."

Michelle would later deny to her family that this had happened, saying that she'd felt betrayed by Nelson, and was now all the wiser. One of the reasons she went back to her maiden name, her sister said, was so people wouldn't recognize her. Michelle told her sister that Marty would have wanted it that way, and, anyway, Marty had never really liked the name, having inherited it from a father he'd never known.

Michelle lived with her grandmother for six weeks, from mid-August to the end of September 2001. Her sister joined her there, taking a semester off from school at the University of Colorado at Boulder. "The whole thing was causing a lot of depression and stress for me and it was affecting my school work," she recalled. Most of the time, Angela said, Michelle was sad and withdrawn, depressed by the loss of her husband and wracked by anxiety from the court-martial and the ongoing police investigation. She was tired of the media calling her and weary of seeing what was written in the newspapers and hearing what was said on television. "Michelle was very scared and fearful the whole time we were in New Orleans," said Angela. "She acted like she was afraid somebody was going to jump out of the bushes and attack her, or that somebody was stalking her."

About a month after Michelle had moved in with her grandmother, shortly after John was convicted, he started calling the house collect from jail. Michelle's hard-of-hearing grandmother didn't understand the recorded message saying there was a collect call from prison, and would hang up without accepting the charges. John would then call back, and the process would be repeated. Only when the phone rang incessantly would Michelle speak briefly with John, "to save my grandma from that torture," said Angela.

In early October, Michelle moved from her grandmother's house into an apartment on St. Charles Avenue in an old refurbished building that had once been a New Orleans orphanage. She had her cell phone bill address changed, and opened a new bank account. She also rented a storage unit.

Unable to work—Detective Clinkscales' letter to the Florida Department of Health had stalled the process for her to get a psychology license—Michelle was living off of savings and credit cards. She thought about making money decorating old cigar boxes and antique luggage and selling them in boutiques, or working as a waitress, but never got around to it. Still anxious and paranoid, she bought a big female German shepherd for protection. Michelle named the dog Athena, after the goddess of wisdom.

While Michelle was described by her sister as emotionally reeling in New Orleans, Michelle's lawyer presented a calm and confident front in North Carolina. After John's lawyers had pinned the murder on Michelle, her attorney Gerald Beaver told the local paper, "We were somewhat taken aback." He told *The Fayetteville Observer* that Michelle looked forward to the investigation's completion and that he continued to believe there would be insufficient evidence to charge her. "Of all the mistakes in judgment Dr. Theer made," Beaver said, the worst "was her choice of a male companion."

On that front, Michelle didn't stop. After the relationship with the man in June went south, she dated another man in New Orleans, who gave her a diamond ring with the stone cut in the shape of a heart. When they broke up, Michelle said she'd tried to give him back the ring, but he'd refused it. "She was under so much stress and very unstable, and they ended up breaking up," Angela said.

Michelle also met another man and had a brief relationship. Angela claimed he was scared off by a phone call from the 910 area code—Fayetteville, North Carolina—"threatening that if he continued to associate himself with Michelle that he would involve himself in a murder case," she said. Authorities would suggest another reason: Andrew was engaged to another woman at the time he was seeing Michelle.

In December 2001, Michelle's sister moved from New Orleans back to Colorado to get a job and prepare for the winter semester of college. Authorities in North Carolina seemed to be in no hurry to charge Michelle. "We have not forgotten and if anyone thinks we have, they are wrong," police Captain Bill Simons told the *Observer* in mid-December. "We're waiting on certain things to take place." John was transferred from Camp Lejeune to Leavenworth, the military prison, where he received occasional visits from Deborah Dvorak. Three families—Marty's, Michelle's and John's—all would endure a second cheerless Christmas.

For Michelle, the new year was difficult. In January 2002, her biggest source of support, her sister, was to set sail for the Semester at Sea program, living and studying aboard a ship for three-and-a-half months. Although Angela had mixed feelings about leaving her sister, Michelle had encouraged her and helped pay for the trip. Michelle and her mother went to the Bahamas to send off Angela. Before she boarded the boat, Angela gave Michelle a poster she had drawn with a globe and flags from all the countries she would visit. On it she had written, "I owe you the world."

During the trip, Angela kept in touch with her sister by writing letters, telling of her experiences in each port. She tried to phone, but Michelle was screening her calls and Angela often didn't get through.

"I was desperate to talk to her, but she was just so scared, that she wouldn't pick up the phone," Angela said. "She was very lost. She had lost everything. She had lost her husband. She lost all of their dreams. She lost her practice and everything that she enjoyed doing and had worked so hard for. She lost so many friends. She lost all sense of security and safety and stability. She just really felt like she had nothing."

Contacted by the *Observer*, Michelle's lawyer, Gerald Beaver, was unimpressed. "It's a rather amazing story he tells," said Beaver, "and one should consider the source when hearing it."

John's sister ratcheted up the pressure on Michelle by publicly blasting her, again in the local paper, revealing details of Michelle's efforts to communicate with the jailed John via Deborah. In a February 7 interview, she said that Michelle had skillfully manipulated her and John. "She would call me crying and say she didn't have anybody and I was the only one she could trust and I was the only one she could talk to," Deborah said. She told the paper about rewriting Michelle's letters to John, the locks of hair Michelle had wanted John to have and the silver wedding bands that Deborah had worn into the jail to show John.

From his prison cell at Leavenworth, Kansas, John began telling his relatives that he had been "stupid" and fallen under Michelle's "spell." He said that he was willing to serve time for his portion of the crime, but not to take the whole fall—that Michelle needed to be arrested, too. He filed a complaint against Michelle with the North Carolina Psychology Board alleging unethical behavior for sleeping with him while she was his therapist. Michelle, in turn, "went off the deep end," according to John's father, George, making bizarre phone calls to John's family, who refused to talk to her. Once, Michelle called Deborah trying to disguise her voice with an English accent and then asking her about the case.

"Michelle, why are you doing this to me?" Deborah asked. "I'm not stupid. I know that it's you." The phone then went dead.

Despite John's overtures to the military, nobody was interested in talking to him. The Army already had its conviction and had no use for John's belated statement. Police in Fayetteville also were confident that it was only a matter of time before they had enough evidence to arrest Michelle without any assistance from John. Her lawyer, Gerald Beaver, monitored the investigation and gave reports to her.

The news wasn't good.

By late April 2002, the word around Cumberland County law-enforcement circles was that a murder indictment was imminent. Beaver called Michelle and told her to brace for the worst.

It came on Tuesday, May 21, 2002.

Eighteen months after Marty Theer's murder, a grand jury indicted Michelle on first-degree murder charges. Authorities told the local media that they'd waited so long because they wanted to prepare the strongest possible case. Marty's relatives expressed relief, but it was premature to celebrate. John's sister, on the other hand, was ecstatic. She told reporters she couldn't wait to call John in prison to give him the good news. This time, Deborah Dvorak said, she would be an enthusiastic trial witness. She had a lot to say on the stand.

With the indictment handed up and the case against her solidified, the next step was to arrest Michelle.

But first they had to find her.

Michelle had disappeared.

36

It read very much like something she had once written about herself in her personal ad:

> Name: Michelle Catherine Theer.
>
> Age: 31.
>
> Height: 5-foot-4.
>
> Weight: 130 pounds.
>
> Hair: Brown, though could be dyed another color.
>
> Eyes: Brown.
>
> Skin: Fair.
>
> Vehicle: Burgundy 1999 Ford Explorer.

This time, Michelle's vital stats weren't posted on the Internet, but entered into the National Crime Information Center computer. Law-enforcement agencies across the nation were put on the lookout for Michelle, wanted in the murder of her husband. Her lawyer, Gerald Beaver, said he didn't know where she was. "My anticipation is, she would do the responsible thing and come here and surrender," he told reporters. "She's always made herself available in the past with the court-martial hearing, and I anticipate her coming here and turning herself in."

As she was believed to have crossed state lines, US Marshals were called in. They traced Michelle's last known address to a little house in New Orleans and knocked on the door. Her grandmother answered. Asked where Michelle was, all she knew was that the last time she and her granddaughter had spoken, Michelle was on the road. That was on Wednesday, May 22—the day after her indictment. Her grandmother thought she'd said she was in Texas.

In fact, Michelle was still in New Orleans. "I kept thinking of MawMaw"—Michelle's pet name for her grandmother—"and wondered what she would think if—when—she finds the truth that I stayed in town another day in a hotel," Michelle wrote a week after she'd fled, in a letter to an anonymous relative.

In the letter, which authorities would extract from the hard drive of her computer, Michelle provided a detailed account of her flight from New Orleans. "It was really hard leaving MawMaw, especially on such short notice and in the middle of the night," she wrote. "But I couldn't take the chance, not knowing what the morning would bring."

In early May, with Michelle knowing the indictment was coming any day, she told her grandmother that she was planning to leave New Orleans for Colorado and then go to Los Angeles, where Michelle's maternal grandmother lived. Michelle's grandmother in New Orleans had expected to have a day or two notice before Michelle left, not the sudden late-night departure, taking along her three pets, Topaz, the Macaw, and sheepdogs Kramer and Athena.

"She was tearing up and her voice was shaking when she said goodbye," Michelle wrote.

> By the way she hugged me, I felt like she knew she might not ever see me again. I know she is worried and that nothing either of you can ever say will make it easier for her. My father will certainly never say a word to her, helpful or otherwise. He'll probably never mention me again unless she asks, and he will just say: I don't know.

Michelle lamented that she would never again see her Los Angeles grandmother, who was seriously ill. Michelle had wanted to fly her out to New Orleans for a visit, but her health prevented her from traveling. Michelle didn't think it would be any easier on her New Orleans grandmother. "I hope they can at least find some comfort in the thought that I am finally finding some peace and hope to live my life to the fullest again," she wrote.

Michelle spent her last day in New Orleans running errands and preparing for life on the lam. She loaded most of her possessions into a moving truck and drove to a hotel, where she unloaded some items into the room. In the middle of the night, she returned to her grandmother's house to retrieve more boxes stored in her Corvette, placing them in a storage facility she had rented under the name Elizabeth Pendragon.

She returned to her New Orleans hotel and "had the joyous task of reloading the truck for the move," she wrote. "Somehow I couldn't fit everything I wanted to take with me. Mostly it was because I didn't want the truck loaded down, piled to the roof, not being able to see out the windows and looking like I was making a big move."

It was still a tight fit. The cage for her bird Topaz took up a fifth of the cargo space, something she hadn't counted on.

It was a sleepless first night on the run. Michelle's hands were cut and sore from moving. Her mind raced with all the errands to run the next day:

> I finally went to sleep around 5 a.m. and although I was going to head out at 7 to get an early start, I decided to sleep until 10 so I wouldn't be starting off so empty.

Her worries were for naught. She completed her final errands, including two hours spent packing the truck. She spoke to her mother on the phone. Her mother suggested that she leave New Orleans that night, Michelle wrote.

> I had just eaten, and I was so exhausted. It really didn't hit me until I got on the highway and out of the city. Then my body felt like lead.

Authorities would claim that Michelle had left New Orleans with her sister, who'd finished Semester at Sea two weeks earlier. But Angela Forcier said that she was actually in Los Angeles with her grandmother, who was recently out of the hospital, when Michelle called and "said that she essentially wanted to disappear."

"She had tried for almost a year to live in New Orleans and she did not feel like she could continue to live a life of fear and paranoia and despair," said her sister. "The deal was that I didn't know how to contact her and I knew that she was leaving and I did not know if she would attempt to contact me again."

Michelle traveled only thirty miles on Thursday night, getting as far as a town called Slidell. She checked into a motel but again couldn't fall asleep. Checkout was 11 a.m. and she knew that would be too early, so she booked the room for a second night and slept until lunchtime Friday. She spent the day re-organizing the packing, making lists and forming "a loose plan of action." She called relatives and got to bed at a decent hour, checking out in time Saturday morning. She spent most of the day in Slidell, sending letters, talking to her mother on the phone "one last time." With Memorial Day weekend traffic snarling the highways, Michelle only drove for a couple of hours Saturday night before stopping to look for a room.

Most hotels were booked, but she found a Holiday Inn with only one room left, what was described to her as the Presidential Suite, at $145 a night. "I figured, what the hell," Michelle wrote.

> It was only 7:30. So I figured I would have time to enjoy the room, and I couldn't imagine driving around for hours looking for a hotel or sleeping in the car trying to rest.

Upon checking in a she found a room that was "nice but not really anything presidential," with a bedroom, living room and two bathrooms. The bedroom had a double Jacuzzi tub and the bathroom had an extra-large handicapped-access shower enclosure. As soon as Michelle turned on the shower, Topaz started squawking, "so I put her in there."

> She spent 30 minutes throwing a washrag around, playing in the puddle, hanging on the drain in the middle, flapping her wings and rolling over on her back. What a sight. Athena kept sticking her head in and looking at Topaz like she was crazy and then coming over to me and grunting. She didn't like it when Topaz splashed her, but she kept going back to look. She was fascinated at the spectacle but very confused by it. She still does not understand play, much less playing along like that.

Michelle then stripped off her clothes and put her already wet dog in the shower.

> I got in there with her, struggled and had a few near escapes, but got her soaped up with Pantene and rinsed out. Goodness, her hair is so thick, it took forever. I had handfuls of her hair coming out, and I kept slinging them against the wall so they wouldn't block the drain.
>
> What was really bad, though, is when I got out of the shower to go get a towel for her and saw myself in that big huge mirror they always have along the back of the vanity, I looked like Bigfoot. Athena's hair had splattered, rubbed and oozed all over my body, and I hadn't even noticed. It was so gross. It took me 30 minutes to clear off the mess.

She thought about giving her other dog a bath, but didn't have the energy.

> That is when I took my jacuzzi and read my book. The last of Athena's hair was left in the tub when I got out. I tell you, you have not really lived life dangerously until you wrestled on a slick floor in the shower with a soapy shepherd for 30 minutes naked. Kramer was the one sticking his nose in and looking at us like we were crazy that time. ☺ It was great.

The next day, after a good night's sleep, Michelle and her animals checked out, and again only made it a few miles down the road because holiday traffic was so heavy. She stopped in a town she didn't identify, looked in the Automobile Association of America book for a motel and located an AmeriSuites that had an affordable rate and allowed dogs. She spent two nights there, Sunday and Monday. The first night, she went to the mall and got her hair cut, then returned to the room.

"Getting my hair cut was definitely an emotional experience," she wrote.

> I've never had my hair so short. I thought I would be nervous or sad about losing it, but I didn't at all, not even a twinge. I don't know if I like the way it looks a lot (I think I look like a lesbian with short hair), but I can style it a lot of different ways. I can curl it around my face and it is very easy to manage. I can run my fingers through my hair, and it is almost shaved in the back. I like the feel of the hair on my neck and head, of being able to shake my head back and forth and have the locks swish across my face. It enhances my feeling of liberation and freedom and also of a fresh start, change, a new life, a new me.

She slept in late Sunday and relaxed by the pool. She tried to start reading again—until now she had been unable to concentrate on a book. She fell asleep at 11 p.m. and woke up at 3:30 a.m. Unable to go back to sleep, she did financial planning, called her mother later in the morning, and treated herself to the motel's complimentary breakfast of doughnut, cereal, fruit, juice and coffee before checking out Monday morning.

"The final leg of my drive was the worst," she wrote.

> The traffic was horrendous. And I was bored of driving. Stopping for tolls is a real pain in the butt, too. Sometimes I would have to sit for 15 minutes to get to a booth there was so much traffic. I listened to my Spanish lesson Cds for awhile, and that passed some time. I was looking forward to learning a new language and doing some of the other things I have al-

> ways wanted to try. I also found my old favorite talk radio station and listened to them for awhile, which was great. But I was very glad to get home.

To be back in Florida.

Michelle checked into another AmeriSuites for two nights, Monday and Tuesday, unloaded boxes, "got some paperwork stuff done" and combed the Yellow Pages "for lists of all the various places I need to go to or use."

As she wrote this letter on her computer, it was 3:30 a.m. Tuesday, May 28, 2002—a week after she had been indicted for murder. She had a busy Tuesday planned. If her energy held, she would look for a place to live. She planned to check the local paper for a furnished apartment that could be rented by the week.

"I passed one today and stopped in, but the wife is the manager and the husband was an oaf," she wrote.

> It was decorated horribly—total garage sale. But it was very spacious. There were only 12 units or so, arranged in a U shape facing towards a garden area in the middle. It was right off one of the main roads, and I am going back tomorrow to see the wife. Of course, the pets will be my primary limiting factor. For now, I just want to find a place to settle in and get comfortable and look around for a job.

The rent on the place she saw that day was $140, less than what she was paying in New Orleans, though still steep considering that she had no income. Since it was a small complex, Michelle expected the landlord wouldn't request a photo ID or a Social Security number.

"As I get ready for bed, I think of all of you and wonder what everyone is doing, planning, thinking, now that they are living their life," she wrote to the anonymous relative.

> I feel a lot of guilt about being a burden on others, about abandoning my family, about leaving all the pressure and stress on all of you. I love you all so much, and all these hard times have brought me closer to . . . you. I know that even though we may be separated physically we can continue to grow closer.

Michelle mused about the other families who had been split in American history, and how she might fit into that heritage.

> Many of the legacies of our country that we have are from the correspondence of relations who spent their entire lives apart, with only letters delivered by stagecoach to keep them in touch. I know that in today's world, we can do the same. In some ways it will be easier (I can type a hell of lot faster than I can write), but in others harder (everything electronic can be traced, court orders can get phones tapped and email accounts accessed, which limits our ability to make use of this technology).
>
> And I am, oh, so tempted to use it, I want to call every day. I want to send an email every night. I want to mail letters all the time. But I know I have to restrain myself, so I will pour my thoughts into this journal and send you weekly mailings. And I will imagine you unobtrusively slipping an envelope in a public mailbox as you go about your daily routine and making its way to my lonely heart.

It was, after just a week on the run, the loneliness that hurt Michelle the most.

> I am a social creature and am happier when I have a social group. I have not had that in the last 18 months

> or so because I was too paranoid, too edgy, too angry. Now I feel I can let some of that go because I am not that person anymore, but I know I will still have to be cautious. I don't even know where to begin to make friends, but this is a very social city and it won't be hard. I just have to get out there slowly, choose carefully and be selective.

She concluded the letter by writing,

> Good night for now. I've spent most of these pages documenting my journal without really expressing all the emotions and thought I have had. There have been so many things. But they will all surface as they are worked out. And I will do that here. Hugs and kisses.

She signed it, "Just me."

Two days later, on Saturday, June 1, Michelle signed a six-month lease at the Regal Apartments in Lauderdale-by-the-Sea, a town on the east coast of Florida about 40 miles northeast of Miami. Giving the name Liza Pendragon, she took one of the seven one-bedroom cottages in the pink-and-white complex, paying $950 a month. She moved in with her parrot and two dogs. "She was very pleasant," landlady Cindy Geesey recalled in an interview with The Associated Press. "She was very considerate, even putting a sheet over the sofa to keep from getting dog hair on it."

The new tenant kept a low profile, never parking in front of the complex and asking the landlady not to tell anybody she was there. She explained that she had fled an abusive husband in California who was a policeman and had ways of tracking her down.

One of the first people Michelle befriended was a man,

who moved into the apartments the same day she did. She introduced herself as "Eliza," but never gave a second name. Over dinner dates, she said she was a first-grade teacher fleeing an abusive boyfriend—a federal agent—who'd threatened to kill her. She told another man in the complex that she knew an Egyptian prince who had given her jewelry.

In the privacy of her apartment, Michelle spent her first week plotting out her future. At the time, she was down to little money, listing $29,000 in cash stored in a Fort Lauderdale safety deposit box, broken down into one packet of $10,000 and another of $3,000 in hundred-dollar bills, a packet of $2,000 in fifties, and one packet of $4,000 and another of $10,000 in twenties. To survive much longer, she had to obtain new identities and get a job and credit cards.

On her computer, she drafted a "Plan of Action," spelled out in a list:

1. Create second stage ID, Alex Solomon (contaminated by medical/phone connection)
   a. Have Florida driver's license;
   b. Change driver's license to another state ASAP;
   c. Have residential lease;
   d. Have auto registration and insurance card as pieces of ID;
   e. Get prepaid cell phone in false name;
   f. Get Voicestream mobile service for every day use;
   g. Get mail drop;
   h. Get voter registration card;
   i. Open bank accounts?? Temporary only.

2. Create third stage ID, Maia Branwen
   a. Have fake ID from PTRC to use for mail drop only;

b. Print lease, Toyota Camry auto registration and auto insurance as ID;
c. Create Baptismal certificate;
d. Get driver's license (use original TX birth certificate);
e. BCC for student ID;
f. May need GED;
g. After one year, apply for new SSN;
h. Get voter registration card;
i. Open bank account;
j. After two years apply for passport.

3. Create fourth stage ID (escape back-up), Ashford Tierney
   a. Finished TX birth certificate for temporary use only, no copies;
   b. Maybe recreated AK birth certificate ???
   c. Ordered fake Alaska ID and international driver's license, PTRC
   d. Print Florida lease, auto registration and auto insurance Ford Taurus as ID;
   e. Create Baptismal certificate;
   f. Get mail drop in Miami;
   g. Get FL driver's license in Miami;
   h. Get GED in Miami;
   i. Enroll in U of Miami;
   j. Wait one year
   k. Get prepaid Miami cell phone (for birth certificate request and SSN application);
   l. Request official birth certificate to mail drop address;
   m. File for report of delayed birth in AK (create brand new identity from scratch);
   n. Get new mail drop for SSN application;

o. Apply for new SSN in Miami (need FL DL, school records and BC);
p. Get final mail drop in Miami using new ID and real SSN;
q. Get voter registration card;
r. Open bank account in Miami with mail to newest mail drop;
s. Move to new city, no forwarding, new phone;
t. After three years apply for passport;
u. Consider women's shelter as source for assistance getting documents.

Shortly after writing this, she started putting the plan in action. In mid-June, Michelle got a PO box at Mail Boxes Plus. She identified herself as Eliza Pendragon, showing a Connecticut driver's license with her picture. She also sent a letter to her father in New Orleans.

Then she made a major decision.

She planned to change more about herself than her hair and name.

37

Robert Ashley, a British-born carpenter, lived in the same apartment complex as Michelle. One day in late June 2002, he saw a taxi parked out front. Then he saw the woman he knew as Liza Pendragon walking up the pathway toward her apartment, directly across from his. Her swollen face was covered in bandages and stitches. A sling held her arm.

She walked slowly, deliberately, as if every step was painful. She wore loose clothing: sweat pants and a baggy T-shirt or sweatshirt.

"Are you OK?" he asked in his English accent, just as she approached her door. "Can I help you with anything?"

She didn't reply.

She had her keys in her hand and struggled to get the key into the lock. He helped her open the door, unlocking the deadbolt and knob lock for her, and eased her onto the sofa.

She had stitches under each eye, under her nose and on her chin. A splint was on her nose.

She said, "Thank God I'm safe."

She explained that she had been in a car accident.

"Do you have any family?" he asked. "Do you have anyone I can call?"

She said no.

He looked more closely at her face. It was covered in stitches, with bandages under her eyes and nose and lower chin. Her face was swollen.

He asked her if he could get her anything. She said water. He put some ice in a glass and filled it up with water. He handed her the glass.

She seemed to drift in and out of consciousness.

"I'll come back and check on you later," he told her. "It looks like you need to rest."

And then he left.

He returned later that morning before leaving for work. She was in the same position on the sofa. Her face was still swollen. He asked her what she wanted, and again she said a cold drink. He got her a cold drink and made her soup that he got from his house. He walked her two dogs.

Talking to her further, she said she had been in a car accident in Orlando. She said she had been with school friends and was thrown from the back seat through the windshield.

It was her car, a maroon or crimson Eddie Bauer Ford Explorer, which Ashley had seen parked at the apartments in front of his kitchen window.

He pulled off her bandages and dabbed Vaseline on the stitched-up areas with Q-tips under the eyes, under the nose, under the chin.

He returned that night after work. He got grapes, ice cream, ice—she was using a lot of ice packs for the swelling. She was getting better. She was up and around the apartment. He made her soup and ice cream.

For the next few days, he helped her, making meals and walking the dogs, and the two spoke. She said her friends were in critical condition in Orlando two to three hours away and the hospital had sent her home in a taxi.

"It did seem odd," he recalled later, of such a long cab ride. "But with the condition she was in, I didn't think about that."

She said she had packed up her pets and belongings and run away from an abusive husband in San Diego, California, and was seeking a teaching job and trying to learn Spanish. There were Spanish books and tapes in the cottage. She said she some day wanted to visit Mexico.

He asked her if she had made contact with her family.

"Not yet," she told him. "Not yet."

She slowly peeled the bandages off. He dabbed the wounds with Vaseline and put the bandages back.

After three or four days, he asked her if there was anyone who could help her. She then said he didn't have to come by anymore—someone else was going to take care of her.

"I didn't go back," he recalled. "I figured I was through. I was set free."

He later saw a man in a white pickup visiting the woman. He didn't know the man's name, but the truck was there frequently. Authorities believe the man was Dana Horton, whom Michelle had been dating.

They had met outside a Mulligan's Neighborhood Grill & Raw Bar in Lauderdale-by-the-Sea, where he was celebrating his 25th birthday. His friends saw Michelle walking down the sidewalk and invited her to join the party. Introducing herself as Liza, she left the party with Dana. They took a walk on the beach, talked, kissed and went back to her cottage apartment for a night of sex. As they started spending more time together, she told Dana her last name was Pendragon and she had fled an abusive boyfriend in California. The boyfriend worked for the federal government and knew how to track down people, she told Dana.

Over the Independence Day weekend, Dana visited his family in Nebraska, leaving behind his new girlfriend, who told him she was going to Orlando to meet with a friend helping her deal with the ex-boyfriend. She had said her birthday was July 4, so Dana called her. That's when she said she had been in a car accident.

When he returned to Florida, Dana was shocked at seeing her face bandaged and bruised.

"I felt real bad for her," he later told ABC11 television.

In fact, Michelle had not been in a car accident. About a week before she hobbled down the path at the apartments, she had visited the Fort Lauderdale offices of plastic surgeon Peter Simon for a consultation. Identifying herself as Alexandra Solomon, she told him and the staff that she was a teacher from San Diego wanting major work on her face.

She wanted to address her saggy eyelids; acne scars near her mouth, temples and cheeks; and skin blotches near her eyes from old laser treatments. She also wanted a better nose and jaw line. The goal, Simon would recall, wasn't to change her appearance, but to improve upon it, to make her look more attractive and less tired.

Simon suggested both surgery and laser treatment and

quoted her a price. She paid upfront with money orders: $11,397 for the surgery and $3,375 for the laser work.

Nine days later, on July 3, 2000, Michelle underwent six hours of surgery. Simon trimmed away skin over her eyelids and removed fat under the eyes to get rid of the bags, placing ointment on the wounds to help them heal. He added a small implant in her chin to make it stick out more, then bandaged it. He removed a small ugly vein inside her right nostril and went to work on the rest of the nose, breaking bones and grafting cartilage onto the tip to give it a straighter, more defined look. A splint held the nose together.

Dr. Simon told Michelle to return in about a month to complete the procedures, including work to smooth over her acne scars and to remove the blotches near her eyes.

It was in this condition—eye area cut and covered in ointment, chin containing a new implant and bandaged, nose broken, rebuilt and splinted—that Michelle had arrived at her apartment and run into Rob Ashley.

While recovering from the surgery, Michelle continued to tie up loose ends in her personal life. On July 15, she wrote a letter to her father on her computer.

"I still love you and think of you every day," she began.

> I am sorry I have not been able to contact you until now. I am fairly sure you are being watched and listened to, but frankly even if you weren't, I can't trust your significant other.

Michelle explained that she had no reason to distrust her father's second wife:

> You know how she likes to talk, tell stories and voice her opinion. It is one of the things I actually liked about her because, in many ways, I am the same. But

> it could really hurt me if she had any knowledge of my doings. Besides, we all know she can't keep a secret to save her life (or mine.)

Michelle then sought to heal emotional wounds.

> I am sorry we fought and things ended on such a bad note. That is one thing I wanted to never, ever do for the rest of my life. I regret we did not have a chance to see each other to talk and patch things up, but I was very hurt because the last shreds of what was left of my life had been ripped apart. I was a throbbing mass of pain and probably would have just fought with you more. I don't think anyone knows as well as I do how fragile our world is and that one may never have another chance to make things better and say, I love you, again.

She said that she was "taking a chance and writing you"—Michelle had already seen what could happen in court with things left on her computer—but had a "couple of important things" to discuss with him.

The first was that she wanted him to sell her beloved yellow Corvette.

> I know that I love it and if I could take it with me, I would. But I can't. Besides, there are too many memories, too much emotion in the car. I wouldn't be able to be in it again. Corvettes are a part of my past now, just another one of many loves I have lost.

Michelle said that she had left behind, in a yellow file folder, the title and maintenance records and power of attorney. She noted that if he couldn't find it, her mother also had a power-of-attorney form.

> She will not argue about signing the title over to you. She knows it will be easier for you to take care of it since the car is there, and you have a better chance of selling it in the south than she does up north.

Giving her father explicit instructions, she told him to put the car title in his name "ASAP so no one else can claim it." She said this would cost only about $100. "Please do this soon, if you have not already," she wrote. He should then sell it as soon as possible and give the money to her sister, Angela. Michelle didn't want Angela to have the car because it wasn't safe to drive in the Colorado winters.

"She is a student and in a lot of debt, and I will never be able to help her again," Michelle said. "Whatever she does with the money is her choice."

Michelle then said that she hoped that by now Angela had the Ford Explorer.

> I have no way of knowing if she received the letter (although I know it was mailed), if my voice mail was received, if the car was picked up or if it made it back to Colorado. I want her to have it. Her and her mother both need new cars, and I figure they can trade it in, sell it, and put the money towards something else to keep it and refinance what is left on the payments as they choose. They have my blessings to do whatever is best for them. Please help in any way you can to make it happen for them.

She did suggest that if her mother and sister kept the Explorer, they should have the title changed to their names "so no one else can claim it."

In fact, the letter about the Explorer had arrived at her father's house in New Orleans. Her sister, Angela, found it when visiting over July Fourth weekend. Following the instructions in the letter, Angela and her father went to a parking garage in Biloxi, Mississippi, where they found the truck. They opened the door with the electronic keypad lock—Michelle had given them the code—and inside were the ignition keys.

Michelle then noted that there was probably something else in the car: $10,000 in cash.

> It would have been either banded and/or in an envelope from the bank. I didn't have a chance to contact my friends before they left the car to see if they could look for it, but they tell me now they did not find it while they had the car. I believe my friends. They are honest, love me and would never hurt me.

While cleaning the car, Angela did find $5,000 under the seat in a Hibernia bank of New Orleans envelope; the other $5,000 was never accounted for.

"Angela should have the money," Michelle wrote, concluding the letter.

> It is from my stock sales and, again, mine to give as I see fit. I don't want some bozo to buy a used car and find ten grand hidden when he goes to clean it. What Angela does with the money and the money from the sale of the Corvette is her business, and you should tell that to anyone who asks you what she is using it for. As far as I am concerned, she should use it to party the summer away so they can never take it away from her. I love you.
>
> Michelle.

Although she signed it, this was not the end of the entire message to her father.

> I am signing the previous pages as if they were the end of the letter in case you are showing the letter to anyone or feel obligated to reveal that information. I am continuing the letter here and hoping that you can at least keep this part private between the two of us.

Having taken care of her logistical concerns, Michelle now addressed her emotional pain over fleeing the murder charges—and trying to make right the wreckage she'd left behind.

> I have been so violated and felt I had no privacy for the last two years, but have some things I need to write to you; however, if you choose to share it with others and betray my confidence then at least I will have my answer about how you feel about me and whether or not you are supportive of me and my hopes for finding happiness. I truly hope you have not abandoned me. I also hope that you can support me in my decisions to leave, even though you probably do not agree with it. It would kill me to know that you view helping me as losing and/or chose not to help me for my own good.

Saying, "I love you, and I would do anything to protect you," Michelle pleaded with her father that she hoped he, too, would protect her, believe her and not judge her.

> You have always told me to do what I believe in, to do what I think is best for me and to do what I think will make me happy. I am doing that now. Whether I succeed or fail in the long run, I will know that I took up for myself and tried to make a new life for myself.
>
> I only wish I had found the courage to walk away from the hell I was living in before and done this

> sooner. My life the last 18 months has been toxic. This is the first time in a long time that I feel control over my life, and despite some fears, I finally have a sense of control, belonging only to myself, and a fragile but precious sense of freedom. I know I am giving up a lot and losing my life, but I can live with that choice.

She wrote that just knowing that he loved her and was willing to help her "means more to me than you can know." She said she had "lost everything and everyone.

"Please don't let me lose you, too," she said.

With that, she reminded him to sell the Corvette, give Angela the Explorer, look for the missing $10,000 and do everything possible to help Michelle to help her sister.

> Even if you are showing this letter to anyone or leaking any information (and in the deepest corners of my heart, I hope you are not because that fear is the one thing that still makes my heart weep), and you do not care about me or helping me, I hope you will fight for Angela's rights to the car and money. I cannot emphasize enough how important it is that everyone who asks should be told that what Angela does with the money is her business, and no one, including you, should ask what she is doing, account for it, or make assumptions about what she is using it for. Whether or not she has a way to get it to me or how or when is only for her to know.

As for Michelle's own debts, including student loans, she told her father that those would simply go unpaid.

> The government destroyed me. The government will have to bite it on the student loans for the education I

> lost. That may sound cold, callous and criminal, but it is what I believe. I was robbed of the insurance money and VA pension that should have taken care of me when I had to quit work, when I was destroyed by my husband's death, raped by the police and stoned to death in the media.

She complained that she'd had to cash out her retirement funds and will never collect the Social Security she is due.

> They maliciously twisted the rules of the system against me, and I don't feel any obligation to follow the rules of the system. They can all go to hell before I ever pay back any debt to big business.

That also went for her former landlord. Angered by newspaper reports that she still owed rent in New Orleans, Michelle wrote,

> I don't know what that bullshit was about. . . . They had already tried to kick me out because of the dogs, anyway, so they didn't exactly lose out.

After her debt rant, Michelle said,

> I love you and miss you. I wish we could talk. I just want everything taken care of before I am gone forever, and saying how sorry I am to you is something I had to do. Please take care of yourself. Please make the most of your life and be happy. I want that so much for you. You truly deserve it.
>
> Remember that the way to happiness is not always the easiest route. Some times you cannot just go with the flow. If I had been more assertive about

> making changes in my life and figuring out what would make me happy and follow through with it sooner, things might have turned out differently for me and all of you.

She signed it, "Forever."

As Michelle wrote this in her Florida apartment, federal marshals were on her trail, interviewing her mother, father and sister. Her mother told the marshals that she had received a package from Michelle with her college diplomas and other personal items, but had no idea where she was. WANTED posters went up with Michelle's photo and description. The marshals' website also put out the word to find her. They had found Michelle's storage unit in New Orleans, with $190 rent past due, and spoken to the facility's owners, who agreed to alert authorities if Michelle tried to contact them.

On July 28, while Dana Horton was traveling to Nebraska for his grandfather's funeral, he spoke to Michelle on the telephone from the airport during a layover. She asked him if he could take care of some cloak-and-dagger business for her. He agreed.

She asked him to call a man named Tom on his cell phone and to give him this cryptic message: "I met your doctor in a bar last night." The call had to be made from a public phone using a prepaid calling card so it couldn't be traced.

She also asked Dana to inquire if Tom had received a letter from her, then tell Tom to "empty the trash" from a storage unit as quickly as possible because somebody was after the stuff.

If Tom had any questions, he was not to talk to her directly; rather, if he wanted to contact her, he would have to send a letter and give the time and date to expect a call from her, Dana was instructed.

Several times, Dana tried calling Tom from airport payphones on July 28, but Tom never answered. When Dana arrived in Nebraska the next day, he deviated from the instructions and called from his mother's house on her regular phone.

The number that Dana dialed connected him to Michelle's father, Tom Forcier, who would later confirm that he had gotten a call from a man who didn't identify himself and who gave strange statements about a doctor and a storage facility. Tom claimed he wanted to have nothing to do with the caller, fearing it was somebody trying to find his daughter, and hung up.

Six days later, Michelle paid her August rent and went back to her plastic surgeon, Dr. Simon, to complete her treatment. This time, Simon used a laser to remove the top layer of skin around the acne scars and blotches, allowing a new layer to grow back without the imperfections. Additional laser treatments would likely be necessary. Simon placed ointment on Michelle's skin and sent her home.

That night, after work, Dana Horton bought dinner at Wendy's, a hamburger and fries for himself and a Frosty for his girlfriend—she had told him that she thought she could only eat something soft and cold because of her sore face—then drove toward her apartment.

On the way, he looked in the rearview mirror.

Following him were men in a dark car.

38

Dana Horton's fear was that it was the man whom Liza was running away from, the law-enforcement guy in California. Dana drove past her apartment, keeping watch in the mirror on the dark Ford Crown Victoria. The car remained behind him, then drove past. Dana breathed a sigh of relief. He told himself he was just being as paranoid as his girlfriend.

But as he approached his girlfriend's apartment complex, a green sport utility vehicle now appeared in the rearview. Dana drove past the apartments and pulled into the parking lot of another complex, but couldn't shake the SUV. He drove out of the parking lot, turned left, then right, and still the SUV was on his tail. Finally, he drove back to his girlfriend's complex and pulled into her parking space.

When he saw men rushing toward him from the SUV, Dana said to himself, Holy crap, what have I just done?

The men were on him instantly.

"Where is she?" one demanded.

"Where is who?" replied Dana. "What are you talking about?"

"Don't fuck with me!" he shouted. "Where's your girlfriend?"

"I don't have a girlfriend."

"Look," the man said, "the person you're dating is not who you think she is."

The man told Dana the woman he knew as Liza was really Michelle Theer.

And she was wanted for murder in North Carolina.

At this point, Dana thought that this was an incredible story—that Liza's ex-boyfriend was really outdoing himself.

That's when the men identified themselves as federal agents. They asked Dana again where the woman was.

He pointed to one of the cottages.

"She's right over there," he said, "in Apartment One."

Through the window, Deputy US Marshal Walter Reilly saw Michelle Theer lying on a living room sofa. He knocked, shouting that he was police, and when she opened the door, he saw a woman with a reddened, swollen face covered with ointment. It looked like she had been burned. She had blonde hair that had been cut shorter than the style in her WANTED pictures.

"Michelle Theer, you're under arrest," he said, handcuffing her. She had a look of shock, followed by resignation.

She told him they had the wrong woman. She said her name was Liza and, "That's all I've got to say." On her wrist was a hospital-style bracelet with the name ALEX SOLOMON.

"Well, you know why we're here," Reilly told her. She looked down and said nothing.

As she was led out of the cottage, her two dogs barked incessantly.

"Dana," she said as she was led out, "please take care of the animals."

Dana watched, dumfounded.

They had found her through phone records. Deputy US Marshal David Kingsbury discovered that a number of calls had been made on the same calling card from three Fort Lauderdale payphones to Michelle's New Orleans storage facility. Marshals in Florida checked motels and weekly-rental apartment houses around three of the phones where those calls had been made. Local sheriff's deputies had photos and a description of Michelle.

Then Kingsbury discovered a call made on that same calling card to the cell phone of Michelle's father, Tom Forcier. That call had originated from the Nebraska home of a middle-aged woman with no known connection to Michelle Theer. But records showed that a former occupant of the home was a younger man named Dana Horton, who had a work address in Fort Lauderdale, next to Lauderdale-by-the-Sea.

Guessing this might be a new boyfriend, marshals staked out Dana's work and apartment and ran a vehicle check, finding that he drove a black Ford Ranger pickup. On the day of the arrest, marshals saw that pick-up pull out of Dana's workplace around 7 p.m., going first to his house, where he changed clothes, then to a Wendy's. After that, they followed the pickup to the Lauderdale-by-the-Sea apartment cottages, where they confronted Horton and were led to Michelle's unit. The apartment was within ten blocks of the three payphones. Horton himself was never suspected of any wrongdoing by authorities.

Upon her arrest on Monday, August 5, 2002, under a federal warrant accusing her of unlawful flight to avoid prosecution, Michelle had been on the run for 2 1/2 months, and had made it 800 miles from New Orleans.

Inside her cluttered apartment were books on how to avoid paper trails and make false IDs. They had titles like *ID By Mail* and *How to Disappear in America.* There were a birth certificate for an Elizabeth Tierney born in Lubbock, Texas, and applications from an Internet company called PT Resource Center, whose website hawks "custom-made identification cards for people who are tired of being tracked and monitored within government databases and want to regain their privacy." One application sought a card in the name of Ashford Elizabeth Tierney of "Juno" Alaska. One of her IDs was valid: a real Florida driver's license in the name of Alexandra Solomon with a fake Miami address.

Also in the apartment were a stun gun, two cell phones, computer equipment, books about Mexico and learning Spanish and a book about witchcraft. Inside a deck of playing cards was a photo from her wedding day. She also had copy of Marty's obituary with a large picture of him in full military dress; somebody had torn out the paragraph listing his name and those of his relatives.

There were two dogs, a German shepherd and a black schipperke, and a parrot. The dogs' toys and leashes were in a pink bag.

Michelle didn't resist arrest, but she didn't make things easy on the marshals, either. When Reilly brought her to the city jail, Michelle was in a foul mood. Asked by the jail staff if she had any personal possessions, she screamed at Reilly, "What about my sweater and my hair scrunchie?"

When Reilly remarked she had more to worry about than a sweater and a scrunchie, Michelle yelled, "You sure know how to push my fucking buttons! You're sure a motherfucker! You're a motherfucker!"

The jail turned Michelle away because of her medical condition, and Reilly took her to the local hospital, where he handcuffed her to the bed while a doctor examined her. When the doctor asked Michelle what medications she was taking, she gave such a long list that the doctor snipped that it would be easier if she just said what pills she wasn't taking.

"I'm a fucking doctor," Michelle snapped back, "and I know what I'm talking about."

News of Michelle's arrest hit the local media, bringing tears of joy from John Diamond's sister, Deborah, who told *The Fayetteville Observer*, "They finally arrested the real murderer." Marty Theer's mother, Linda Gettler, added, "It couldn't have happened to a nicer person." And John's former lawyer, Coy Brewer, told WRAL-TV in Raleigh–Durham,

"It remains my hope that the truth will eventually come out. I still believe she pulled the trigger and the evidence shows that."

For the next week, Dana Horton tried to make sense of it all. He logged on to the Internet and found the truth—that the woman he knew and had been falling in love with was actually Michelle Theer, wanted in the 2000 love-triangle murder of her husband.

"She'd talk to me as I'd fall asleep and say, 'Nothing's going to happen to you while I'm around,' " he told the local television station, ABC11. "Stuff like that made me feel real comfortable, so to read just how evil this person is, I felt stupid, because I was played," he said. She'd never told him she had a Ph.D. in psychology.

"She was the most caring, the most considerate. You take a perfect relationship, that's what I had: the most perfect relationship for eight weeks. . . . That's all taken away from you and then you find out all of it was fake."

Michelle's landlady spent the day after Michelle's arrest looking for a home for the dogs and parrot until the woman's father came by to get them. "She would have been one of the last people I would have expected," Geesey told *The Fayetteville Observer*, saying she thought that the woman had been fleeing an abusive relationship. "I feel dumb as a stick."

In a Florida courtroom, Michelle, her hair slicked back, clad in a jail uniform, didn't fight extradition to North Carolina. Escorted by two Cumberland County fugitive division deputies, she was taken on a ten-hour drive to Fayetteville, sleeping most of the way in handcuffs and leg shackles and saying nothing. She was admitted to the female infirmary at the Cumberland County Jail to recover from her plastic surgery. She conferred with her court-appointed lawyer, Matthew Cockman, who would only handle the early pre-trial matters. She would later get state-funded counsel for a trial. In an affidavit, she said she was broke, owing $8,000 for her car and another $16,000 in credit card debt. Authorities would later determine her credit debt to be much higher, around $82,000.

While she was in jail, Detective Ralph Clinkscales joined two US Marshals in New Orleans in searching two storage facilities that Michelle had rented, one under her real name and one under the name Liza Pendragon. They found a day planner for the years 2000 and 2001, medical records, letters and other papers.

Nine days after her arrest, she made her first appearance in a Cumberland County court. Her face still swollen and covered in ointment, she stood before Superior Court Judge Jack Thompson on Thursday, August 15, 2002, and heard the charges against her: conspiracy to commit murder and first-degree murder.

"Miss Theer, do you understand that you have the right to remain silent, that anything you say may be used against you?" Thompson asked.

"Yes, sir," said Michelle.

She also said that she understood the charges and the potential penalties: life without the possibility of parole—or worse.

For on the day that Michelle appeared in court, District Attorney Ed Grannis said he would seek the death penalty.

39

Just as John Diamond's father had done, Michelle's father, Tom Forcier, defended his child. In an interview with *The Fayetteville Observer* published on August 25, he said that his eldest daughter was not a murderer. "It's not in her nature," he said. "She doesn't have a violent nature." Echoing George Diamond's contentions, Tom claimed his child had been set up by vindictive, incompetent authorities. "The Fayetteville Police Department couldn't find any evidence at all other than the fact that she was there when it happened," Forcier said. "It doesn't matter if she's innocent. . . . The police department in Fayetteville did everything they could. They should have let the case die and left her alone."

And like John's father, Tom spoke of the emotional pain. "It's tearing my life apart, and all of my family's lives apart," he said, "and there's nothing we can do," said Forcier, who was never charged in the case.

But this is where the relatives agreed. John's sister, Deborah Dvorak, told ABC11 in November that her brother was innocent. In his daily phone calls from Leavenworth to his sister, he still talked about Michelle. "He's sorry he ever met her," Deborah told the station. "He was involved with the wrong woman at the wrong time."

Over the next year, Michelle would remain in jail without bail, while she prepared for trial. Through the assistance of the state, she was appointed one of North Carolina's top defense lawyers, Kirk Obsorn of Chapel Hill, a passionate attorney who specialized in death penalty cases. Osborn filed a flurry of motions seeking evidence from the military and police that he thought would help Michelle. Among the requests were statements from Marty's former commander, Lieutenant Colonel Michael Sweeney of Patrick Air Force Base in Florida, about Marty's alleged obsession with Internet pornography. Strongly opposed by prosecutors on the grounds that the information was irrelevant and private, Osborn insisted in his motion that the statements were relevant to Michelle's defense. "It is exculpatory and essential to a fair determination of the defendant's innocence or guilt, and therefore not privileged," the motion said.

In the summer of 2004, both sides were ready to talk plea bargain. Prosecutors had already agreed to drop the death penalty and were now seeking life in prison. Kirk Osborn wanted a bigger concession. He proposed that Michelle plead guilty to accessory after the fact of murder, a charge that would get her 93 months in prison. At the time, Michelle was 33 years old. If she behaved herself, she could be out shortly after her 40th birthday, with a lot of life left to live.

Prosecutors wanted her to plead guilty to a more serious offense, either conspiracy to commit first-degree murder or second-degree murder. The sentencing range was 94 months to 120 months. If all went well in court, and there were enough mitigating factors found and Michelle got the lower end of the scale, she'd be spending the same amount of time in prison as if she had gotten the deal Osborn proposed.

Osborn went back to his client and recommended she take it.

Michelle rejected the deal.

From day one, she had stated, adamantly, in public and in private, that she was innocent.

She would let a jury decide.

40

"Do not let her deceive you as she deceived her own husband."

The Cumberland County District Attorney, Edward Grannis, was standing before jurors on September 27, 2004. It was nearly four years after police had pulled into the parking lot to find Michelle cradling her dying husband's bloody head.

But that was not the image the prosecution wanted to leave with jurors. The DA and his deputies, Margaret "Buntie" Russ and Gregory Butler, made it clear from the outset that they weren't just going to portray Michelle Theer as a murder conspirator. They wanted jurors to think she was also a lying, cheating, greedy, cold-blooded, manipulative slut.

Aided by a series of favorable rulings by Superior Court Judge E. Lynn Johnson, character evidence would flood Michelle's trial in a way that it never had in John's court-martial, even though Michelle—unlike John—never faced a morals charge like adultery.

It is one reason why the case of the *State of North Carolina* vs. *Michelle Catherine Theer* would not be resolved in a fast march like John's was before Colonel Parrish, but rather in three slow months. Michelle also had a different defense than John. Rather than concede many of the facts and try to win the case in summation, defense lawyer Kirk Osborn fought everything and everybody, filing and arguing motions to limit evidence, engaging in long cross-examinations, putting on a number of his own witnesses, calling for mistrials at least four times—even shedding tears at critical moments.

The courtroom drama added to what already promised to

be a sensational trial, full of sex and violence and betrayal, but one conducted outside the national spotlight. Michelle's arrest garnered some attention outside the Southeast—*People* magazine ran a comprehensive article—but the story had no legs. The trial drew only local coverage; Court TV lost interest when Judge Johnson banned cameras from his courtroom. A gag order on lawyers dampened media buzz further.

The lack of national press did little to quell the excitement inside the courtroom, however. No sooner had the trial begun than the defense came out swinging, as Osborn sought to bar evidence about Whiskey, the police dog who, on the night of the murder, had followed a scent across the street and down a golf course fairway before losing it near a construction site. Lambasting Whiskey as no Lassie, Osborn said the dog had a bad record of finding people, only novice level certification for tracking on a trail and no certification at all to work with his new handler, Officer Kurt Richter. "There's no data to show that this dog is reliable to do what he does," said Osborn.

In one of a series of rulings against the defense, Judge Johnson on September 28 allowed the Whiskey evidence, and Osborn did what he could in cross-examination, eliciting from Richter that the officer hadn't been able to learn from the dog how old the scent was, who it was from or even which direction, to or from the construction site, the person had been going. For all Whiskey knew, it could have been a jogger running toward the office building a week earlier, his handler testified.

It was a minor point for the defense, only to be offset by Richter's testimony about Michelle Theer's "blank face" and lack of emotion while talking about her husband to police just minutes after finding the body. "I expected more emotion," he said.

Richter's description of an apparently cold and unfeeling wife was accompanied by the testimony of one of the first rescuers on the scene, who said that he'd looked at Marty, finding him dead, then checked Michelle's vitals. Her pulse and blood pressure were normal. Jurors were shown a picture of Michelle that night, her face grim.

Police witnesses testifying in the early days of the trial said that Michelle had spent much of the night looking "blankly" out of the patrol car, that the only tears were brief and far between, and that she had become most animated—"hateful," one witness said, prompting a defense objection—when told she could return to her office to retrieve her things. Another witness said Michelle had grown testy when told that her dead husband's commanding officer and his wife had arrived at the scene, telling police, "Fuck them"—an account that Michelle had bitterly disputed from day one.

This picture of Michelle contrasted with her courtroom demeanor. She wept as prosecutors displayed crime-scene photos showing close-ups of Marty's wounds. She also sniffled when the pathologist, Dr. Robert Thompson, described Marty's injuries in more detail. When jurors left for a break, Michelle burst into tears.

As the parade of law-enforcement witnesses continued the first week of trial, describing a grisly crime scene, a gunshot-ravaged victim and a defendant whose behavior was odd at best, defense attorney Osborn sought to poke holes in the prosecution case.

When blood analysis expert Jed Taub described the blood on Michelle's sweater, turtleneck and tights, which might have come from wiping her hands on her clothes and kneeling in blood, he acknowledged that none of the blood was tested for DNA—a small point, but one the defense hoped to add to others to show a pattern of shoddy police work. Timothy Luper Jr., who'd analyzed the gunshot residue tests at the state crime lab, said he'd found evidence of residue on the palms and backs of the hands of both Michelle and Marty.

But he said Michelle could have gotten it from touching Marty's head, which would have been covered in the residue from the close-range shot.

Osborn used the testimony of the law-enforcement witnesses to press the point that the crime scene had been improperly processed and preserved, drawing out testimony on cross-examination that the cigarette butts had never been tested for DNA, that the blood on the stairs had never been tested to see if it was from Marty or an unknown assailant, that neither the brass shell casings nor Michelle's office had been dusted for fingerprints, that the yellow liquid in her office toilet had never been tested, that the other offices on her floor had never been searched and that the entire crime scene had been hosed down and treated with bleach before sun-up. The celebrated candy wrapper wasn't even collected.

And yet, the damaging testimony continued, large and small. Photos of Michelle's impeccably neat office showed her keys sitting atop the two books on her desk and a candy wrapper in the trash, conjuring the image of Michelle calmly sitting there, sucking on candy, as her husband was gunned down on the stairs outside for reasons that had nothing to do with a robbery. Photos displayed to the jury showed the $66 in cash and credit cards left in Marty's wallet.

As provocative as this evidence was, the first round of really damaging testimony came a week into the trial, when Michelle's former boss and onetime confidant Dr. Thomas Harbin took the stand. Harbin told jurors on October 5 about the Theers' marital strife, the disputes over children, Michelle's suspicions that Marty had been cheating on her and her ultimate admission that she herself had been having an affair with an Army sniper named John. Harbin said that the night of the murder, Michelle had seemed normal—no rushing, no looking at her watch—and that the couple had "seemed to be getting along and having fun."

During cross-examination, Osborn attacked Harbin's credibility. It turned out that Harbin wasn't just talking to police about his private conversations with Michelle; he was also planning to write a book about the case with former *Fayetteville Observer* reporter Missy Stoddard, who'd covered the case through John Diamond's court-martial before moving to another newspaper.

This was, again, a minor defense point coming after heavily damaging testimony, a pattern in the trial. When Marty's mother, Linda Gettler, testified, she told the jury that Marty hadn't even wanted to go out with Michelle to the Christmas dinner, preferring instead to stay home and watch a Broncos game, then go to bed early because he had to fly the next morning. The defense would later show that there was no Broncos game that evening—it was in the afternoon.

It barely made a dent in the prosecution case. The jury saw the gut-wrenching spectacle of the victim's brave mother testifying for her son, telling them about his calls to her every Sunday, his love of his country and his family. Jurors leafed through Linda Gettler's scrapbook of Marty's pictures, many of them the same ones that John Diamond's jury had seen before putting him away for life without parole. Jurors were rapt. As she talked about that tense trip with her son and Michelle to Washington DC shortly before his murder, they leaned forward and looked at her with an intensity denied the other witnesses.

The pressure never relenting, each day brought more damaging testimony for Michelle. After her neighbors spoke of John's visits to the house before and after Marty's murder, Lourdes Diamond came to testify about the phone call and abrupt departure by John the night Marty had died.

Lourdes also provided character testimony, recounting a night she'd confronted Michelle at the It'z nightclub as Michelle was dancing with John in the fall of 2000. When Lourdes had asked Michelle if she knew that John was married and had a child, John snapped, "She knows!" according to Lourdes.

And on the dance floor the weekend before the murder, John and Michelle had acted like a couple, Michelle's friend Rafael Harris told the jury, recalling that he'd felt like a "third wheel" while the other two hung out together in clubs and spent the night in the same room the night of December 9, 2000.

About two weeks into the proceedings, the incriminating evidence mounting—Peyton Donald had just testified about loaning John the 9mm and then calling him at police's request to get it back after the murder—the trial mysteriously halted. Judge Johnson told jurors to hold tight, and for the next two hours on October 12, he met with attorneys behind closed doors.

A gag order during the trial prevented attorneys from saying what had happened, but later they explained that Michelle's lawyer had called for a mistrial. Kirk Osborn said that Peyton's account of his phone call to John had been improper testimony because it revealed some of John's alleged remarks, hearsay that couldn't be subject to cross-examination.

Judge Johnson refused to grant the mistrial, and ordered the proceedings to continue, with lead investigator Detective Ralph Clinkscales taking the stand, going through the case in detail, from the moment he'd arrived at the crime scene, to Michelle's remarks to him during interviews, to her behavior after the crime.

Under a fierce cross-examination, Clinkscales defended his investigative techniques. He said, for instance, that he hadn't dusted Michelle's office for prints because Michelle had said she'd been the only one in there. He didn't have the blood on the stairwell tested because Marty had been shot on the stairs and it only made sense that it was his blood. Cigarette butts hadn't been tested for DNA evidence, he said, because there was no evidence they had any link to the murder.

The next day, the defense lodged another legal challenge, this time seeking to bar the testimony of Charles McLendon, the Internet lover of Michelle from late 1999 to early 2000. "This is nothing more than a character assassination," Osborn complained on October 13, arguing that the testimony had nothing to do with the murder charge. But Johnson rebuffed Osborn again, finding that in a circumstantial case, the defendant's relationship with her husband and her state of mind at the time of the murder were relevant.

And so McLendon came to court to reveal the inner workings of online dating.

"There are a lot of dating services that are easy to get on to and just do searches on for whatever you're looking for—you know, single females," he said under questioning from prosecutor Gregory Butler. "Hopefully something local will pop up that sounds interesting."

Which is what happened, he said, in late 1999 when he'd found an ad for somebody using the screen ID lookn4unow and going by the name Susan.

"We just started emailing back and forth for about, I guess, a week or two, and then decided to meet in person," McLendon said. "We decided on the Barnes and Noble in Fayetteville on Friday or Saturday night."

He told her to look for a tall guy. She told him to look for a woman in business clothes sitting by herself.

"Did you check out the person before you walked over there?" asked Butler.

"Of course," said McLendon.

"What was the purpose of that? If you didn't like them, you were going to leave?"

"Probably," he said, drawing laughter in the courtroom.

McLendon then described their courtship and subsequent encounters, first at his house, then at hers, leading up to their breakup when he'd cracked into her email and found the names of other men.

"What was her password?" asked Butler.

"It was CHEATER," said McLendon.

When the next witness—psychologist Kenneth Kastleman—took the stand a day later, Michelle's lawyer tried to show that Michelle hadn't been the only one messing around. After Kastleman spoke of the sessions in which Michelle had lamented that Marty needed to respect her privacy, and Marty had professed befuddlement at Michelle's unhappiness, Osborn asked on cross-examination, "Was there any discussions of Marty's affair in 1997?"

Both prosecutors leaped to their feet.

"Objection," said Butler.

"Objection," added Buntie Russ.

"It didn't even exist," complained Butler.

But the judge said, "I'll let him answer if that was discussed."

Kastleman then answered, "To the best of my knowledge, no, that was not discussed."

"What about his trip with another woman to Virginia?" asked Osborn.

Again, both prosecutors objected, and heated words flew in front of the jury. There had been no evidence of that at all.

"Mr. Osborn, come on up," the judge ordered the defense attorney to the bench. He was joined by the prosecutors, and intense—though whispered—conversation ensued, ending with the judge saying aloud to Osborn to "Sit down."

"Sustained," the judge said, and that ended the line of questioning about Marty's possible affair.

The only infidelities to be addressed at the trial would be those of Michelle, and the prosecution painted a devastatingly tawdry portrait of her with the testimony of a Fayetteville police computer expert named C. T. Williams. He spent three days on the stand—nearly as long as John Diamond's entire trial—revealing for the jury the dark secrets found on Michelle's computers, from her "marriedbrunette" personal ad seeking a "rendezvous man," to the intimate email exchanges between her and John Diamond. Defense attorney Osborn repeatedly objected, saying, "This is nothing more than an attempt to smear Michelle," then reciting several constitutional amendments being violated by the evidence.

But Judge Johnson, who had privately reviewed thousands of the computer records, ruled that they were as relevant as Charles McLendon's testimony, showing Michelle's state of mind and the nature of her relationship with her husband. Osborn then called again for a mistrial, and was again denied. Williams read on and on, about swinger sex and obsessive love, and by the time he was done, Michelle's character was decimated. Recovery would be nearly impossible.

By late October, the trial jolted back and forth in time, with prosecutors calling Michelle's neighbors to talk about John's visits to the house after the murder, and her plastic surgeon to talk about the work on her eyes, nose and chin in July 2002. A Sprint phone company rep spoke of the incessant phone-calling between John and Michelle in the days leading up to the murder. And military investigators spoke of John's car break-in report, which was shown to be a fake by the surveillance video—played for the jury—of John being with Michelle after the trip to Florida.

The trial observed the one-month-long mark with the defense making its third call for a mistrial on October 28. This time Osborn cited the recently wrapped testimony of Air Force investigator Vince Bustillo, who'd recounted the phone call by Peyton Donald to John Diamond seeking the return of the gun. The testimony, Osborn argued, was rife with improper hearsay, and this time Judge Johnson agreed—to a point. He ruled that the testimony shouldn't have been given, that prosecutor Butler had known that what Bustillo was about to say was improper, and asked him anyway. Still, the judge found that the damage wasn't fatal, and told prosecutors they couldn't use any of the inadmissible hearsay material in their closing statements.

As the trial entered the second month, John's sister Deborah Dvorak, so reluctant a witness at John's court-martial, now held nothing back, recounting Michelle's often bizarre efforts to communicate with John in jail—the locks of hair and the rings and the secret messages. The officials from the Caribbean medical school recounted Michelle's and John's overtures to live and work there—and the dinner meeting that had turned ice cold when one of the school administrators revealed that he had once been a prosecutor.

Michelle's former Florida apartment neighbor Rob Ashley identified her as the woman he'd known as Liza, and spoke of the day she'd come back with her face bandaged, claiming to have been in a car accident. Her Florida acquaintance Nelson King recalled Michelle as having been "shady." And Marty's commanding officer at Pope Air Force Base said that Marty had been considering re-enlisting for twenty years—giving him a $100,000 bonus and the $12,000-a-year raise that would go with it—but that he'd suggested Marty first take a short-term enlistment to see whether he would get a promotion. When Michelle had found out about that advice, the commanding officer said, she'd called him personally to complain.

With the evidence against Michelle mounting, so too were the animosities in the courtroom. Michelle's lawyer Kirk Osborn tangled with prosecutor Buntie Russ over whether a jailhouse informant could testify that Michelle had admitted to killing Marty. Osborn claimed that prosecutors had coached the informant and promised leniency on her case.

"We have not coached her," Russ snapped. "He just keeps making bald-faced accusations."

"You want me to call you as a witness?" Osborn replied. "I'd be glad to call you as a witness."

It didn't come to that. In another victory for the prosecution, Judge Johnson allowed the testimony of Rosaida Rivera who, on November 4, 2004, denied having been promised any gifts from the prosecution, but did hold out hope that her cooperation would help her.

Rivera, eight months into a 20-month sentence for burglary, larceny and forgery, claimed to have spent time with Michelle in 2003 in the Cumberland County Jail's day room, where inmates could mingle, watch television and play games. Rivera said Michelle had confided that she had a married lover who was so smitten with her that he'd do anything for her. Michelle had wanted to end the relationship, according to Rivera, and had given the lover an ultimatum.

"The only way her and her lover could be together was if her husband was gone," Rivera said. "Her husband would have to be out of the picture."

Rivera also claimed Michelle had had a female lover in jail until wardens broke them up, and that Michelle had claimed that she and her attorney had an inappropriate relationship when he visited her in jail, a claim that had Osborn incensed for weeks.

On cross-examination, Rivera acknowledged that there was a big window in the jail visiting room through which guards watched. She also said she had received no special treatment for her testimony in the Theer case, but acknowledged that she had recently been moved from solitary confinement and now had access to phones and visitors.

Osborn called for a mistrial—his fourth such request—on the grounds that Rivera's testimony discredited him with jurors. Judge Johnson denied the mistrial, saying that the inmate obviously hated Michelle, had a criminal record and had asked for a favor from prosecutors. The judge said Osborn could call witnesses to challenge Rivera, which the lawyer decided against doing.

With this legal skirmish completed, the prosecution's case drew near a close. Within days, the state would call its final witnesses—marshals to describe Michelle's arrest in Florida and the phone call that had tripped her up. At 10:50 a.m. on November 10, 2004, the people rested their case after six weeks of testimony.

The defense began with another legal setback. The first witness was an expert in extra-marital affairs, who intended to testify that an affair by one spouse can influence whether the other spouse has one. In this case, Michelle had claimed in letters that she'd started messing around after she found out Marty was possibly seeing another woman. Yet Judge Johnson refused to let the expert, psychologist Debbie Layton-Tholl, who had spoken with Michelle in jail, say anything about Michelle's suspicions about Marty. She also was barred from repeating anything else Michelle had said during their ten hours of meetings unless Michelle testified.

And so Layton-Tholl spoke on November 15 in more general terms than she had intended, saying her research showed that 45 to 60 percent of marriages have affairs and that it was not unusual for people to be ambivalent about continuing with affairs, as Michelle had been with John—spending a weekend with him in December, then rejecting him, as their emails showed. Although Michelle was portrayed as toying with John, Layton-Tholl said that it was the other way around when John reacted to the rejection by threatening to kill himself. "He's very manipulative," the psychologist said.

Also barred from talking about Marty's personal life away from Michelle was Dr. Donald Stewart, a Cocoa Beach therapist the couple had seen while they were still living in

Florida. Stewart was able to testify about a letter he'd written to Marty's commander saying that the Theers' marriage in 1997 was being torn apart by Marty's absences because of deployments. The therapist had urged the commander to postpone Marty's next transfer to save the marriage. The testimony ended there, the judge ruling that under Florida law, Stewart couldn't reveal anything Marty had said during counseling.

The lack of love between judge and defense counsel permeated the courtroom. When Osborn challenged prosecution witness contentions that Michelle's office had been in a low-crime area—and asked for the city to provide statistics—the judge took it upon himself to illuminate the big city lawyer. Johnson said that if crime plagued the area, "I wouldn't live there." Not only did Judge Johnson reside near the crime scene, so too did a number of the Fayetteville elite, including a county commissioner, a state representative, a supreme court justice and the man trying to convict Michelle Theer, District Attorney Ed Grannis.

What's more, the country club across the street where the police dog had tracked the scent down a fairway the night of the murder was one of the most prestigious in the area, built by Grannis' father, Ed Grannis Sr., the judge said.

The defense trudged on. Seeking next to counter prosecution evidence that Michelle had shown a lack of emotion after her husband was killed, Osborn called Jenny Johnson, the crisis counselor assigned by the military to help Michelle and her family.

"She would go from zombie mode into complete hysterical crying," said Johnson, who also recounted the day that she'd brought Michelle to the police station for the family briefing and been chastised by Clinkscales. "Quite frankly, I thought it was unprofessional and it hurt my feelings," said Johnson. Another witness, Michelle's former professor,

Richard Elmore, described her as one of his best students, and said that when he'd called her several days after Marty's murder she was "overwhelmed with emotion."

The defense also tried to blunt the testimony of Lourdes Diamond, calling John Diamond's former military lawyer, Captain Katy Martin, who told the jury on November 22 that Lourdes had grown frightened and anxious over investigators' tough tactics. Lourdes thought she was being followed and was constantly being questioned. When she finally did change her story, Lourdes told Martin that John had actually spoken into the phone before going into the bedroom, suggesting that the call had in fact gone through—and wasn't the unanswered call that Michelle had spoken of.

The biggest push by the defense was to rehabilitate Michelle's image. On November 18, the defense called her now 23-year-old little sister to the stand. Angela Forcier was accompanied by her own lawyer, who, the judge explained to the jury, was on hand "to protect any Fifth Amendment rights" the witness may have.

"Would you please tell the jury who you are?" began Kirk Osborn.

"My name is Angela Forcier. I'm Michelle's sister."

After she'd stated her age and home town, Osborn asked: "Are you being threatened with prosecution in this case?"

The prosecution objected, but was overruled.

"Well, I was threatened with prosecution for accessory after the fact of murder," said Angela.

The judge now stopped the proceedings on his own, explaining that "I simply advised Ms. Forcier of her potential liability in this case"—for allegedly helping Michelle after she'd fled—but that it was not his responsibility to prosecute.

Very carefully watching her words, Angela proceeded with her testimony, giving jurors an alternative picture of Michelle: loving sister, devoted wife, patriotic reservist, and the first in the family to get a college degree. Displaying family photographs, Angela portrayed her sister's marriage as a fairy tale, and spoke of Marty as being like a brother.

Refuting the police testimony, Angela said that after Marty's murder, Michelle had been "completely devastated." The weekend of the funeral, said Angela, Michelle "cried a lot. She couldn't sleep. . . . She would lay awake and cry and she just couldn't sleep."

After John's court-martial, Michelle had still been a wreck. "She was very sad and withdrawn, very depressed," said Angela, "but I really began to think that her grief was hindered by all of the stress and anxiety and fears that she was experiencing as a result of being a suspect in the case." Michelle had also felt betrayed by friends and fed up with John, who'd kept calling her when she moved to New Orleans.

Finally, after her indictment, Michelle had called Angela—she said she had been in Los Angeles at the time with their ailing grandmother—and said she was taking off. Angela hadn't tried to talk her out of it.

"She was very lost," said Angela.

"What had she lost?" asked Osborn.

"She had lost everything," she said. "She had lost her husband. She lost all of their dreams. She lost her practice and everything that she enjoyed doing and worked so hard for. She lost so many friends. She lost all sense of security and safety and stability. She—she just really felt like she had nothing."

Under cross-examination, Angela acknowledged that as close as she felt to her sister, she didn't know everything about Michelle's life. She hadn't known about John Diamond until well into their relationship, or any thing about her online dating or swinging. She didn't know that Michelle had inquired about teaching in Saba. And she had no first-hand knowledge of anything that had happened around the time of the murder because she was in Colorado taking final exams.

"Now, Ms. Forcier, you love your sister very much, don't you?" asked prosecutor Buntie Russ.

"Of course I do."

"And you want to help her any way you can, right?"

"Yeah," said Angela.

With Angela saying she'd known nothing about Michelle's darker side, the defense called a witness who did. Dr. Moira Artigues, a Cary, North Carolina, psychiatrist, had interviewed Michelle for sixteen hours, and also spoken to her mother and sister, reviewed her school records and medical charts and read the emails pulled from her computer.

As they'd talked in jail, Michelle's emotions had fluctuated, the doctor testified. "When we would talk about her deceased husband, she would tear up and get really sad," said Artigues. "I noticed that the difficulties that she's been through in the last few years had caused her to really shut herself down emotionally. What I mean by that is to be a little guarded and protected at first, but seemed to warm up as we continued the interview and also seemed to warm up over time."

Obviously fond of her incarcerated patient, Artigues said Michelle seemed to show no envy or resentment toward her. "We were both young professional women with some very big differences—in that I was able to go home to my family at the end of the interview and I was leaving Michelle in the jail," she said. "A lot of times when I deal with criminal defendants, there's a lot of envy. There's a lot of bitterness. They can sort of treat me like I'm a Coca-Cola can, not having much feelings for me during the interviews. I never had any of that from Michelle."

What she found, Artigues said, was a woman whose life had changed radically after obtaining her psychology degree. "When Michelle was in school and there were lots of structure around her and there's a lot of demands on her, she did really well," said Artigues. "But then, when she moved to

Fayetteville, she was really left to her own devices. Her husband was frequently gone. They were having marital conflicts. . . . She really had no friends. She was socially isolated. She was starting a new job. So this was the first time in her life where she really didn't have the structure in place that she had had previously."

This is when Michelle had started taking sleeping pills and anti-depressants as she struggled to hold herself together. She was "emotionally fragile" and was "starting to fall apart."

"I think one of the ways that she held herself together was getting a lot of male attention," said Artigues. "This is a young woman who doesn't feel too hot about herself if she thinks her sexuality is the only thing she has to offer someone. . . . So I saw it as a self-esteem issue for her."

As the year 2000 wore on, the stresses had become worse, when the Theers moved to a new home, Marty's mother visited, Michelle's drug intake continued, and the affair with John was going badly, said Artigues. "It was very difficult for Michelle to break it off with John Diamond, because he would up the ante," the psychiatrist said. "He would not take no for an answer."

As for Michelle's behavior after Marty's murder, Artigues said it was clear she was suffering post-traumatic stress, becoming numb to the world, shutting down emotionally, losing perspective about money and feeling lonely and afraid. "Essentially everything had been stripped away from her at that point," said Artigues.

Osborn then asked the biggest question of the examination, perhaps of the trial. "Do you have an opinion as to a reasonable degree of medical certainty as to whether or not Michelle had the ability to plan and carry out Marty's murder?"

The question prompted twin objections from prosecutors Butler and Russ, which were sustained. After several attempts to get the question answered—all receiving sustained objections—trial adjourned for lunch, during which the judge pondered whether to allow Artigues to give her opinion about Michelle's ability to plan to kill Marty.

After reviewing the law, the judge announced, "You may ask the opinion question." The jury was brought into the courtroom, and Osborn asked the question again.

"My opinion," Artigues said, "is that Michelle Theer doesn't have the emotional wherewithal to plan and to sit with the plan of a planned murder. That's my opinion."

"What do you base that on?"

"I base that on the emotional fragility that I talked about earlier," she said. "That would take a great amount of emotional fortitude and steel nerves, and I don't believe that she had that capacity."

Taking the issue a step further, Osborn asked her why she felt Michelle had run from authorities.

"Her running was self-preservation," she said. "She had been stripped of everything. Her spouse was gone. Her profession was gone. Her house was gone. She felt she couldn't make friends because those relationships got interfered with in a significant way. Her future was gone, because whether or not she was going to be prosecuted was still a question."

Under a fierce cross-examination by Butler, Artigues was first hammered on how much she was making for her evaluation and testimony. She said $10,000 to $13,000. She said she charged $125 an hour in travel time to drive down from Durham, giving her $325 for making the 2 1/2-hour drive.

The prosecutor then challenged her findings. After Artigues rattled off the reasons for Michelle's emotional fragility, Butler said, "So everybody's got an excuse for everything, don't they?"

"There's a difference between making an excuse and having compassion and understanding and clarifying things for oneself to try and make sense," she said.

Reading Michelle's personal ad on the Internet about

seeking fun and adventure, Butler said: "Don't sound like she is looking for a relationship there, does it?"

"No," Artigues said, "it sounds like a young woman who thinks her sexuality is all she has to offer."

"Did you just pull that out of the air somewhere?"

"I'm a young woman," she said. "I know what it's like. I know lots of young women, and unfortunately women tend to devalue themselves in that way."

"Let me ask you," Butler said, "are you testifying about that based on all your education or because you are a woman?"

"Well, listen," she snapped back, "I don't abandon my common sense at the door when I'm using my education. I think you have to use your common sense too."

After Butler had read Michelle's ad, in which she described herself as fit, attractive, intelligent, he asked, "you're saying she's fragile?"

"It's not simple just to say she's a bad person or she's a she-devil," said Artigues. "It doesn't make sense just to smear her and be done with it. That would not be satisfying to me. I would like to know more about this. What led to this young woman feeling the need to do this?"

Turning to the relationship with John, he asked, "He loved her, didn't he?"

"I think he was infatuated with her."

"What's the difference between infatuation and love?"

"I think love is a choice you make to devote yourself to someone, to nurture them, surpport them, be by their side, walk through life with them," she said. "But the emails that I saw from John Diamond really were over the top, were idealizing, were clingy, were demanding. That to me is not genuine love."

"Don't some people love that way though?"

"People love that kind of attention."

"I'm sorry, ma'am," said Butler, "don't some people love that way?"

"I call that infatuation," Artigues said, "and I think it generally tends to burn out, that kind of love. The sustaining love is the love you decide every day to give to someone else."

As for Michelle's swinging with other couples, Artigues called it an example of "acting out"—a kind of incessant stimulation to avoid the complexities and pains of life, comparable to drinking or using drugs.

"You came here to say that because she acts this way, that this justifies or explains her behavior, didn't you?" asked Butler.

"I am in no way justifying her behavior."

"You're not?"

"I'm trying to understand it," she said. "I'm not saying it's good. I'm saying I'm trying to understand it."

After Artigues reiterated, firmly, her opinion that Michelle had lacked the wherewithal to plan and commit the murder—"In my opinion it would be impossible," she said—the prosecutor returned to the issue of money.

"Ma'am," he said, concluding his cross-examination, "it's been about almost two hours since we began talking, and at that time I think we figured up today you had already earned $1,650. Would it be fair to say that if we stop pretty soon right now, that you would have made $2,200 for your testimony here today? Would that be fair to say?"

"That would be fair to say," she said.

"I've got no further questions, Your Honor."

The defense called a handful of witnesses over the next two days to show both mistakes and heavy-handed tactics by police, to suggest that Michelle had been ambivalent about leaving Marty in the weeks before the murder and to refute the suggestion that Michelle had planned to run off with John after murdering Marty.

Michelle's other defense attorney, Elsie Miller, read to the jury emails in which Michelle had told her mother in the fall of 2000 that she'd turned down the teaching job in Saba. Testimony ended with a dispute over the license plate on Michelle's yellow Corvette. In the prosecution's rebuttal, a police witness said the plate had read "GODDE5S," with a "5" substituted for one of the "S's." But Osborn introduced evidence that the plate had actually read "TDX 29T."

It was, like so many issues, one that would have to be addressed in closing arguments. After thirteen weeks of testimony, both sides were finished presenting evidence. Closing arguments were to begin.

41

For a prosecutor, closing arguments are no time for understatement, a philosophy Gregory Butler embraced with zeal.

"This is a tale of two hearts," the Cumberland County prosecutor began in his summation. "One heart was that of Marty Theer, a loving, caring, energetic young man, a man who was forgiving, who was full of life. A heart of Marty Theer. The other heart is the heart of the defendant, a dark, deceitful, manipulative, even sinful, cold, evil heart."

Not a murderer, but a sinner. Butler would take his time bringing jurors to the reason for his oration—convincing them that Michelle had orchestrated her husband's murder. He first had to glorify Marty and condemn Michelle.

Taking jurors back to the night of December 17, 2000, the prosecutor painted a picture of a doomed man, unaware of the sinfulness that lurked in the passenger seat of his Ford

Explorer. Marty Theer, according to Butler, "had no way of knowing that, just moments after he pulled into the rear of 2500 Raeford Road, that the very lifeblood that sustained his heart would be flowing on the asphalt. He had no way of knowing that in just moments he would be lying dead on the asphalt on the ground beneath the stairwell."

Holding up a photo of a young Marty, the prosecutor spared no gory imagery in describing what would come next. "Look at the contrast of a young man with his whole life in front of him, his whole future," Butler said, then he displayed a picture of Marty at the crime scene, "and a young man, basically, whose brains came out. His blood lying on the ground. Marty Theer never got a chance to call his mother and say goodbye. Marty Theer never got a chance to fly the airplanes he loved to fly so well and so much. Never once again got to sit back in his recliner and have a drink beside him and something to eat and lean back and watch his beloved Denver Broncos play a game of football. He had no way of knowing what was about to happen to him."

Pointing to Michelle, he said dramatically, "In contrast to that—to the heart of the defendant, *her* heart, I contend to you, ladies and gentlemen of the jury, is one of the strongest pieces of evidence that the state has in this case, one of the many pieces, one of the many strong pieces. Her heart lied. Her heart manipulated people. . . . It was her heart that led a wicked life-style. It was a cold-blooded heart.

"It's hard to look over there and see a person, a woman, and think: Nobody can be that cold. Nobody can be that mean or that evil. Surely can't be. But you sat through weeks and weeks of evidence and it has painted the picture of what kind of heart and what kind of person the defendant is."

He said that on the night of the murder, as her husband lay in his blood on the ground after being brutally murdered, "Her heart spoke to us."

It did not beat fast enough.

"Your heart would be racing," he told jurors. "Your blood pressure would be up. Your whole system would be screaming out. You're not going to just sit there flat-lining," he said. "Isn't that the most telling evidence? . . . The tale was her heart. It wasn't racing. It wasn't elevated blood pressure. It tells you right there she was cold and she wasn't traumatized by what had happened."

In fact, this was not the prosecution's best evidence—that would come out in the rebuttal argument when Buntie Russ would go over the crime scene, witness statements and Michelle's own post-murder actions. It was hardly evidence at all. As defense attorney Kirk Osborn would note in his summation, nobody testified that a calm heart rate after a traumatic event was evidence of anything sinister. The only testimony about her heart rate had come from the defense witness, psychiatrist—and medical doctor—Moira Artigues, who said that a calm heart rate and normal blood pressure could actually be evidence of mental anguish: the body shutting down.

But the inference by Greg Butler was more than permissible legally, and the imagery was so vivid, the argument so poetic and brilliantly convincing, that it was what would most resonate with jurors. Although he would leave his scripted metaphor and begin to ramble into areas that weren't permissible—the judge sustained an objection when Butler tried, as the court-martial prosecutor had, to enter Marty's mind at the moment of the final shot—the "tale of two hearts" theme both tied up the case neatly and positioned the prosecution case perfectly for the rest of summations.

When Kirk Osborn stood before the jury, he had to not only make a convincing legal argument, but a moral one as well. Whether it was the difficult burden, the long trial, the fact that his own fidelity was in question, or whether it was just a case of old-fashioned courtroom theatrics, Osborn did something one doesn't much see during summations.

He cried.

"I want to start with a few things, just to clear the air," he said. "When we talk about Marty, we do not mean to demean him at all. . . . Nobody should die the way Marty did. Nobody.

"And," he continued, "I want to comment about my relationship with Michelle. It has been said by a state's witness that my relationship with her was too close, was so close—"

Osborn's voice began to break. "Well, I've been practicing for thirty years," he said, tears now coming down, "and I have represented hundreds of people charged with murder, and I have never had an inappropriate relationship with a person, ever. I'm happily married. I've got two beautiful daughters and a beautiful wife."

It was getting to be too much for the prosecution, drawing a tag-team objection from both Butler and Russ.

"I'm going to let him respond to the accusation as an officer of the court," Judge Johnson said. "Go ahead, Mr. Osborn."

"And I'll tell you now," Osborn continued, "she has been an incredible client, incredible. And she doesn't have me under her spell, and she's not manipulating me."

Shaking off the tears, Osborn got to the heart of the defense. "Let's clear the air about what she's not on trial for," he said. "She's not on trial for adultery. She's not on trial for having numerous affairs. She's not on trial for having sex with numerous men. She's not on trial for having a sexual addiction, if that's what you believe she has. That's not what she's on trial for. But, you know, most of the state's case has been throwing as much mud at Michelle as they possibly could. Because, you know what? They don't have facts to prove her guilty."

With that, Osborn argued, as John's attorneys had in the court-martial, that the prosecution had failed to meet its legal burden of proving her guilty beyond a reasonable doubt. He started by saying that Michelle could never be so stupid as to have committed this crime, to have thrown away her education and career and life by murdering her husband when she could have easily gone to divorce court. And yet, he said, an overzealous police force and a take-no-prisoners prosecution had twisted facts and harassed witnesses to fit a preconceived notion that Michelle was the evil black widow who'd manipulated John Diamond into doing her dirty work.

In fact, he said, there were doubts that John was guilty, too. "We felt it important to tell you jurors that he had been convicted," he said. "But how much justice do you get when your jury is selected, you are tried and you are sentenced to life without parole in one week?"

"Objection, Judge," Russ said.

"Sustained," said Judge Johnson, "as to the underpinnings of that trial."

Going to the night of the murder, Osborn said of police, "It's clear that they treated Michelle as a suspect immediately, and that colored everything they did from there on out." Police, he said, had conducted a shoddy investigation and the prosecution hadn't even fact-checked its own witnesses.

Even Marty's mother, as sympathetic as Linda Gettler was, actually was incorrect when she'd recounted Marty wanting to watch a Broncos/Seattle Seahawks game the night of the Christmas party. In fact, he said, that game had been played a week earlier, on December 10—the Broncos had actually played the Kansas City Chiefs in a day game on December 17.

And while Gettler was probably just mistaken, other witnesses had darker motives to be wrong, including Michelle's former boss, Tom Harbin, who admitted to writing a book about the case. "Now, this is a man who supervised Michelle for a year and found nothing that would cause him any concern. Nothing," said Osborn. "And yet, he betrayed her confidence, wanted to write a book about her."

The physical evidence also was suspect, he said. The cartridges found at the scene had come from the same gun, Osborn said, but the prosecution's own expert had said that they weren't necessarily from a 9 mm pistol—they could have also come from a Beretta 92F, an Army-issued weapon that no witness could place in John Diamond's hands. This, combined with the five bullet holes in the wall, raised the possibility, he claimed, of two shooters.

The gunshot residue on Michelle's palms and the backs of her hands was in the same concentration, suggesting strongly that she wasn't the second shooter. So who was it? "They have molded a theory of what happened and they have failed to do the proper investigation to see whether or not there was other evidence that may have helped Michelle," Osborn said.

Going through the trial testimony, Osborn hit the defense themes: that Michelle never would have been dumb enough to plan a crime in such a public area, that Michelle had decided long before the murder not to go to Saba. At the Fox and Hound, Michelle and Marty had acted normally. "She couldn't have acted the way she did if she had planned Marty's death," said Osborn.

As he spoke, Osborn noted that the jurors' attention was waning. They weren't making eye contact. They were yawning. He tried to keep them. "I know you're getting tired," he said. "I know you are. But I have things I want to tell you, because I won't be able to tell you them again. I won't be able to talk to you anymore, so please bear with me."

But it was a struggle, competing with the "tale of two hearts" case. He tried to counter the evidence about the normal blood pressure, noting that no prosecution witness had testified that it was unusual for that to occur. Instead, witness after witness had testified about Michelle's grief and confusion and depression after the murder. He went into the Theers' relationship, saying there had been problems with both Marty and Michelle. The summation was losing focus—and Osborn continued to lose jurors.

Finally, the judge said, "You have five minutes, Mr. Osborn," until the afternoon break.

The attorney spoke some more, but the jury by now was gone. "I know you're tired," he said again at 12:45 p.m. "This is probably a good time to stop."

When the jury returned, rested and refreshed from a 1 1/2-hour lunch break, Osborn focused on the relationship between Michelle and John, trying to show that John had been as needy and assertive as Michelle. "It was a back-and-forth thing," he said.

He sought to show that Michelle had had reasons for having an affair. "Michelle got involved with Marty"—Osborn paused at the error, the fatigue showing—"I mean with John Diamond, basically because Marty wasn't available. He was gone. And, you know, whether she was looking for male companionship, whether she was looking for sex . . . it's pretty clear that Michelle was a woman who needed a man in her life."

Rather than looking at Michelle as the manipulator, he suggested that John Diamond had been the driving force in the relationship. "He was a person that thrived on the pursuit," he said. "In this case, it was Michelle, who I think turned him on intellectually, probably for the first time. It was something that was irresistible. And, of course, being slightly unavailable, as Michelle was married, made it even more of a challenge."

Either way, he said, "Michelle had an affair with John Diamond for nine months," said Osborn. "She didn't have to kill Marty to continue the affair at all."

Turning to the timeline, Osborn sought to challenge one

of the strongest pieces of prosecution evidence: that John Diamond had received a signal call from Michelle summoning him to commit murder.

Based on phone records and other evidence, Osborn suggested that John may have returned to the apartment with the rental video much earlier than prosecutors claimed. According to Lourdes, John had returned when it was still light out. Based on weather data, that would have been shortly after 5 p.m.—not closer to 7 p.m. as Lourdes had eventually told authorities.

What's more, records showed that John had received a call at 5:44 p.m. from a friend named Eldridge. That, Osborn argued, could have been the call that John had received during *The Patriot*—not the unanswered call from Michelle.

Osborn suggested that Lourdes may have been wrong—or been coerced into being wrong by police and the military prosecutors—about the time the video had started. If it had begun at 5:30, not long after John returned as the sun was going down, then a 5:44 p.m. call made sense, the lawyer claimed.

"Now, I know this is confusing," said Osborn, again seeing the jurors' eyes drift. But he insisted that one reading of the phone records was that the call had come in much earlier than Lourdes ultimately believed, but that authorities "hounded [her] long enough to get her to testify to match the time."

In the end, he said, the prosecution exploited "the adverse myths about women" to convict Michelle. "They have used every single one of them," he said. "She's manipulating. She manipulated John Diamond to kill Marty. She's selfish. . . . She's loose sexually. You know, no matter what you believe about her behavior—and I think many of you very much disapprove of her, about her seeing other men—that's not what we're here about. We're here about her guilt or innocence in the murder of her husband."

And on that score, he said, "we've had seven incredible women"—from Dr. Moira Artigues to Captain Katie Martin—testify for the defense.

Osborn next sought to explain the disappearance of the gun that Diamond had borrowed from Peyton Donald, providing a sequence of events that prompted objections from the prosecution. When Osborn said that when John and Michelle had returned from Florida, John checked into his barracks, Russ and Butler snapped, "Objection." There was in fact no evidence of that.

"Sustained," said the judge.

"He's making it up as he goes along," complained Russ.

The last of many more objections came as Osborn—spent, losing the jury—wrapped up his case by telling a parable about a little boy who tries to outwit the village wise man by holding a canary in his hands and asking, "Is the bird alive or dead?" If the wise man said, "Dead," the boy would let the bird fly free; if he said, "Alive," the boy would crush it to death.

"And so he goes up to the wise man and he says, 'Wise man, I've got this bird in my hands. Is it alive or is it dead?' And the wise man says to the little boy, 'It's in your hand, my son.' "

At this point, Osborn began to cry again. "And so," he said through tears, "we hand you this case. I don't want to let it go. I don't."

"Objection," Russ grumbled.

The judge didn't even rule.

"When I sit down," Osborn continued, "I can't say anything more. But I hope that when you hear the state's arguments, that you will apply what I have told you and listen. . . . When you consider all the evidence in this case, you will find and we will ask you to find Michelle not guilty and set her free. Thank you."

It would be a lot to ask of the jury. After a break, the oft-objecting Buntie Russ stood before the jury and, now attracting all the attention that Osborn had lost, methodically went through the guts of the prosecution case: the circumstantial evidence. She spared the rhetoric that her colleague had provided earlier, telling the jury instead of the crime scene, of witnesses, of phone calls, of physical evidence that together painted a picture of guilt.

"You've heard the evidence," said Russ. "You can see that this defendant and John Diamond clearly set up a situation in which Marty Theer lost his life," she said. "Think about what you heard, and the state genuinely believes that the only reasonable verdict that you can return is guilty of first-degree murder by aiding and abetting theory and lying in wait."

The case went to the jury.

In three hours, there was a verdict.

42

On the afternoon of Friday, December 3, 2004, Judge Lynn Johnson called his court to order.

Michelle sat at the counsel table. She turned and caught the attention of her mother, Ann, and sister, Angela, in the audience.

"I love you," Michelle said.

In the front row sat Marty's mother, Linda Gettler. Behind her, the courtroom was packed with spectators.

The jury foreman stood and read the verdict.

Guilty on both counts: conspiracy to commit murder and murder.

Michelle never moved. She stared straight ahead, her back to the audience, her face—her expression—shielded from the audience.

She seemed frozen. She barely flinched when jurors, one by one, confirmed their votes of guilty.

When the proceeding moved to the sentencing phase, the judge asked if Michelle had anything to say.

She shook her head, no.

After hearing from Marty's mother, Judge Johnson handed down the sentence, and it was severe: life in prison for murder, another 16 1/2 years for conspiracy.

It was just days before Michelle's 34th birthday. She was still a young, healthy woman, with a long life ahead of her—a life that would be spent in the women's prison in Raleigh, North Carolina.

A bailiff handcuffed her and led her out of the courtroom.

43

Michelle Theer was sent to the North Carolina Correctional Institution for Women in Raleigh. Once a licensed psychologist with a promising practice, Michelle now stands for hours on end on arthritic hips in the prison's "clothes house," bundling and handing out clean garments to the dining room workers—a laundry lady with a doctorate.

John Diamond is serving his life sentence behind the twin rows of fourteen-foot fences in the US Disciplinary Barracks at Fort Leavenworth, Kansas, the military's only maximum-security prison. Once dreaming of attending medical school, he now spends his days as an amateur lawyer, helping other prisoners with their legal papers. His mother, Kris Diamond, has visited him once a year since his conviction. "It's hard for me to go over there and see him," she says. "I just can't handle it, and I know that he can't stand for me to cry, and it just puts more stuff on him." They talk on the phone, though, two or three times a week, she says, "in our own little language, so that nobody knows what we're talking about."

Michelle and John: once lovers, now prisoners. And though they will, in all likelihood, never see or speak to each other again, they continue from their distant cells to engage in a lovers' quarrel, each blaming the other for the bloody scene outside a Fayetteville office building that cold night in December 2000.

In late 2005, Michelle spoke to Edward T. Pound of the magazine *U.S. News & World Report*, which ran extensive excerpts from her jailhouse interview on the medium that had caused so much trouble for her, the Internet. In it, she filled in some of the gaps about her life history, portraying her childhood in darker terms than her sister had on the witness stand, a childhood traumatized by her parents' divorce and a Southern Baptist upbringing. She said that to this day she is plagued by father issues.

Still, after all that had happened, worried about her reputation, Michelle downplayed her amorous activities—painting herself as a lonely officer's wife looking for companionship. She said she'd only gone to a swingers' club twice, once with a male friend and once with John, and that time was a bust. John had gotten mad when a man made some "fairly innocuous comment about thongs" to Michelle, grabbed her by the arm and dragged her out. "And that was sort of it for the night," she told the magazine. She described the swingers' club as "a place where couples go to meet other couples to have fun, drink, dance, flirt." Asked if it involved sex, too, she answered, "Possibly, yes."

She did give more details of the night of the murder, saying that the phone call to John from the Fox and Hound was to ask his advice on the repair of her Corvette, that she'd let it ring three times, then hung up just before it clicked into voice mail after the fourth ring. She said she hadn't left a message because she didn't want John calling her back while she was with Marty.

She gave an account similar to the one she'd given police of the drive back to the office, the gas run and going up to her office to fetch her books, only to hear the gunshots. When she'd gotten outside and seen Marty on the ground with blood on his head, she thought he had fallen down the stairs. He was still breathing, but barely. He didn't look at her when she asked him, "Marty, Marty, Marty, are you OK?" Panic had driven her to run to the video store to get help.

As for the aftermath of the murder, Michelle denied that she'd continued to be intimate with John—she placed their last sexual encounter at the hotel on that weekend before the killing. The neighbors who'd seen him come and go at her house were either mistaken or misinterpreted what had happened. A lot of people visited her, she said. But she did acknowledge staying in touch with John, and worrying within days of the murder that he may have done it, which is why she'd confronted him. She'd believed him when he said he wasn't involved—believed him because that's what she'd wanted to believe. Or maybe it was because he was such a good liar, she said.

She said she knew nothing about John borrowing a gun. When he'd first told her that his military weapon had been stolen from his car after they'd been to Florida, she'd assumed it was his bayonet.

Throughout the interview, Michelle portrayed herself as a woman wronged—by police, by prosecutors, by the press, and, most of all, by John, who she says she now believes was the gunman. Somehow, she says, despite her psychological training, she'd missed the signs.

"I made a lot of mistakes," she told the magazine, "and ultimately, I may be responsible for Marty's death because, if it wasn't for me, John Diamond would never have come into our lives."

From Leavenworth, John Diamond's voice has also been heard, though not in a media interview, for he continues to turn down requests to talk to reporters.

John is expressing himself through his appeal.

Bent on not repeating what he sees as mistakes of the past, mistakes he feels resulted in a five-day trial and conviction for a crime he says he didn't commit, John has hired one of the nation's top military lawyers for his appeal, Donald Rehkopf Jr., a former military defense lawyer now in private practice in Rochester, New York. Rehkopf, who has traveled the world defending soldiers in trouble, on charges ranging from drugs to murder, has launched an aggressive appeals campaign, with a major surprise.

John's brief filed in the Army's Court of Criminal Appeals begins predictably enough, attacking a number of the court-martial judge's rulings, namely those allowing such damaging evidence as Michelle Theer's statements about calling John before the murder and about being in the office at the time of the attack.

"The end result was that a boatload of unreliable and suspect hearsay from the mouth of charged co-conspirator, Dr. Theer, was used to 'prove' uncharged, irrelevant and nonexistent conspiracies, all to the significant prejudice of SSG Diamond," the appeal said.

John's appeal also goes after his former civilian lawyer, Coy Brewer, alleging he failed to adequately investigate the crime, to make important objections, to file proper motions and to explore a plea deal that could have meant much less time in prison.

In the most serious allegation, John puts Brewer financially in bed with Michelle, claiming the lawyer accepted a $1,500 retainer fee from her that he never disclosed to John, the prosecution or the judge. (Michelle told *U.S. News* that she'd given some money to John's sister, but said her "memory about some of this stuff is very bad." Brewer says he never took a retainer from Michelle.)

But it was not just the 61 pages of history and legal arguments that make the appeal so remarkable. In it is new information, including an account of how one of the military prosecutors, Sean Summers, approached John's sister, hoping to get John's assistance in the prosecution of Michelle. Summers made his pitch in an email to Deborah Dvorak shortly after John's conviction.

> Mrs. Dvorak,
>
> I understand that we will never see eye to eye on the results of the trial. Having said that, I believe that we both know that Michelle Theer played a part in her husband's death. Your brother has a long life ahead of him. If he wants to get out of prison anytime for the rest of his life, now is the time to come clean. His court-martial takes approximately three months to be "officially approved." Anytime before it is approved, we can cut him some sort of deal in exchange for testimony. So now is the time to make a decision.
>
> I personally believe she manipulated your brother into doing something that wasn't his idea. I think he would have been happy if she divorced her husband and her and your brother went off where ever it was that they wanted to go.

> We intend to prosecute her with or without your brother's help. Our job is obviously easier if he helps and that is why we would compensate him for his co-operation. If we prosecute her without his help, he will never get out of jail for the rest of his life.
>
> Please discuss this with your parents and talk to your brother. She isn't worth spending the rest of his life in jail when he doesn't have to. I can assure you that she has had numerous boyfriends since your brother was put in jail.
>
> Nothing I did at court was personal toward anyone in your family. If it was your child who was killed, I'd assure that justice was administered in the same manner.
>
> If you'd like to talk, don't hesitate to call me and I thank you for your time.

It was signed, "All the Way! Captain Sean Summers."

The email stands out in a couple of respects, not the least of which is its tone. The same prosecution that, in trying to get a conviction, portrayed John Diamond as a cold-blooded killer thinking nasty thoughts as he watched Marty Theer die, now, in trying to get his sister's cooperation, paints him as something of a victim of Michelle's feminine wiles. Also, the appeal argues, Summers committed potential misconduct by approaching one of John's family members directly when John was still being represented by a lawyer.

At first, Deborah was skeptical, sending a return email saying that, yes, they will never see eye-to-eye, that she was certain her brother never shot Marty Theer, but that she was "willing to do whatever you ask" if it meant John would only serve the time that he really deserved.

"And you understand," she added, "just your word is not good enough for me. There will have to be something in writing signed by someone I know can't take it back."

Summers responded with a provocative question: "Other than the fact that he is your brother, how do you know that he didn't do it?"

But then he laid out two options:

- John keeps quiet and spends the rest of his life in prison.
- John tells what really happened and prosecutors "will negotiate a lower sentence" with the defense attorney, "probably talking life with parole," making him eligible for parole in 20 years.

"We will prosecute her with or without his help," Summers wrote. "It is a shame that she is out there partying it up when your brother is in jail. If we prosecute her without his help, he will never get out of jail. His only hope is to come clean and tell the truth. What I'm asking you to do is tell him that there is no sense in protecting Michelle Theer."

He added, "Any deal we do with your brother would be in writing and with his attorneys' recommendation."

John's sister took the deal to John and his military attorney, Katy Martin.

They huddled, and decided to play ball with the prosecutors.

Martin drafted a request for clemency. Submitted on January 11, 2002, the document says that in exchange for a reduction in John's sentence from life without parole to a maximum of 12 years in prison, he would agree to testify against Michelle in state court.

The document then presents everything he would say, and his and Michelle's actions up until the months after John's court-martial. Called a "proffer" in legal terms, the 13-page narrative of what John says he would tell a jury that he and Michelle had done and said is a compelling account, the detail so vivid that to read it means never looking at the murder of Marty Theer the same way again.

• • •

"Michelle Theer and Staff Sgt. Diamond met in a chat room on the Internet," the proffer begins, then explains that as they continued to chat online, John separated from his wife, Lourdes, and ultimately met Michelle in person at O'Charley's restaurant by the Wal-Mart Supercenter in Fayetteville.

According to the proffer, in January 2000 they then "commenced a physical relationship," meeting mostly at Michelle's house when Marty was away, with John parking away from the house and Michelle picking him up. In February or March 2000, Michelle invited John to travel with her to Alaska, where she was to run a marathon, but he couldn't go, which turned out fortuitous since Marty unexpectedly showed up. "She was very upset and agitated," the proffer said. "She said Marty intruded on her time, she said he had no right to invade her vacation."

Not long after that, when John returned from a month-long visit to Belgium for a commando course, Michelle expressed interest in his training, asking, "What does it feel like to kill somebody?" according to the proffer.

John and Michelle began seeing each other more often in the spring of 2000, up to five times a week. It was around this time, the proffer says, that Michelle began to speak of witchcraft and voodoo.

"She said the practices were part of her past," said the proffer. "Michelle explained that her great-great grandmother practiced root magic. . . . Prior to the court-martial, Michelle gave Staff Sgt. Diamond a small seashell. In a letter to him, she said 'a voodoo priestess blessed it' and he had to keep it with him for good luck."

Michelle's interest in John deepened, and she began speaking more of starting a family with him after divorcing Marty. When John and a friend talked about swingers' clubs, Michelle "expressed immediate interest," researched the clubs on the Internet and bought a one-year membership to one of them, Carolina Friends.

"Michelle and Staff Sgt. Diamond began attending events for swingers," the proffer says. "Michelle used cocaine and ecstasy on many occasions at the swingers' events. She said she was not addicted and could not become addicted because she knew how to control her use. She said she used the substances to relax."

Michelle couldn't get enough of John, meeting him late at night in her office after group therapy sessions, on weekends in the afternoons and evenings, getting away from Marty by saying she couldn't sleep and would use the late hours working, the proffer says.

Once, Michelle told John that she had two sets of keys to her office—she'd gotten a second set because she'd once locked herself out.

When John visited Michelle at the office, he always parked on the opposite side of Raeford Road because Michelle was afraid somebody would spot his car. He would then watch the building and await her signal that it was clear to come in: the lights in her office would go on. Michelle would meet John at the door, and John would go up to the attic for blankets and a small television set, which they used in Michelle's office, the proffer says.

Michelle made no secret of her hatred toward her husband, according to the proffer, complaining about Marty's nagging for her to get pregnant, his waffling on whether to stay in the military, his carelessness with money. Michelle spoke frequently about wanting to get a divorce, but then would say she might stay with Marty to reap the benefits of his military pay. She talked of retiring early, if Marty would just stop spending so much money.

As their physical relationship intensified, Michelle pushed John to open up emotionally, encouraging him to talk about his childhood and painful secrets from his life. She told him, "A relationship requires people to share. I want to share everything with you and I want you to share everything with me so we know what makes each other tick," according to the proffer. Michelle offered counseling to John and "administered computerized psychological evaluations" of him in her office to build his psychological profile. The results, she told him, "were what she would expect from somebody in Staff Sgt. Diamond's profession," the proffer says.

After serious knee problems and surgeries, John realized he could no longer serve as an active Ranger and would have to either change military jobs or leave the service. He spoke to Michelle about taking courses to become a physician's assistant. She told him that she was considering a college teaching job, and that if they were married, he could attend classes at the same school for free. Michelle spoke of her dreams of living in the tropics, and told John about a medical school in the Caribbean where she could work and where he could attend classes tuition-free, if they were married.

As spring turned to summer, Michelle characterized her marriage as increasingly troubled—and dangerous. Marty constantly criticized her and insulted her, saying she was getting fat. Twice, he'd hit her, she told John. She said that one day she had been taking a nap in the garage while Marty worked on a car; the next thing she knew, Marty was gone and paramedics were treating her. She'd been taken to the hospital for carbon monoxide poisoning. Marty claimed that he had forgotten he had left the car running, but Michelle didn't believe him. She later came across a letter from the insurance company showing that Marty had increased the life insurance policy on Michelle. She told John that she believed the letter and the garage incident were related.

In the summer of 2000, John and Michelle moved into an apartment together, with Michelle talking about divorce and how she would divide the marital assets. Once, John heard

Michelle on the phone yelling at Marty, but he didn't know what she was talking about. Michelle said it was money, always money. "He owes me a lot more than he thinks he owes me," she told John, according to the proffer. It was a divorce lawyer who recommended that Michelle move back in with her husband in the fall of 2000, according to the proffer. The lawyer said that if she were living with Marty, she'd get more money in a divorce settlement.

Moving back in with Marty didn't end Michelle's problems with men. She claimed to John that a lover from her past had threatened her. Michelle asked John to teach her martial arts moves in case the man came after her. She then suggested they go to Alabama so the man could see her with John—that would make him back off. When John asked her if she wanted him to fight the man, she said, "No, but if you did, I know you could handle yourself."

They never went to Alabama, but the threats continued, Michelle told John. She worried because she worked late and left by the back door of her office. She said she feared that if something happened, nobody would see it. She bought a Taser for protection.

Concerned that wouldn't be powerful enough, she said she wanted a gun.

Michelle and John went to Jim's Pawn Shop to look for guns. Michelle said she wanted a weapon that would protect her but that she wouldn't have to fire a lot of times. She had only handled M-16s when she was in the reserves, and wasn't trained in handguns. According to the proffer, she asked John if he would get a gun so she could try it out.

That's when John borrowed the 9mm from Army pal Peyton Donald.

John and Michelle went to a range and John showed her how to fire it. John's proffer said that after an hour at the range, Michelle was no expert, "but she hit the target."

John returned the gun to Peyton, but borrowed it again at

Michelle's request. They went back to the range, where Michelle fired it some more. She asked about buying the gun from Peyton or one at a gun show.

By now it was December 2000. In the weeks leading up to Marty's murder, Michelle told John that her divorce was nearly complete, and that all that had to be worked out was the property settlement. On the weekend of December 9–10, they went to Raleigh to celebrate her 30th birthday, hitting a club with her old friend Rafael Harris.

"Michelle commented to Staff Sgt. Diamond that she looked forward to a future where they could do things like this more often," says the proffer. "Michelle talked about Marty very little. When she mentioned him, the topic surrounded the divorce and what she wanted."

As soon as they returned from Raleigh, however, Michelle's demeanor changed. John met her at the office late after group therapy, just as he always had, but she was upset and wouldn't say what was bothering her. Then, the next day, Michelle called John at the barracks. In the call, overheard by his Army mates, Michelle told John that Marty had raped her when she returned from Raleigh.

"I am going to kill him," she told John, according to the proffer. "I swear I am going to kill him. He needs to pay for what he did, and I can do it."

She spoke of how she could do it. She said she could kill him at home and blame the death on an intruder. She asked John to get Peyton Donald's gun. When John refused, she became irate, accusing him of not caring for her. John tried to settle her down, suggesting she call Marty's superiors in the Air Force to handle the matter. John asked if he could see Michelle. She said yes, later that night.

When Michelle hung up, a worried John called Michelle's boss, Tom Harbin. But Harbin wasn't there. John asked the receptionist to tell Harbin that Michelle had been abused.

Michelle then called John, saying she was mad that he had called her boss. She said she didn't want people knowing her personal business and told him never to do it again.

That night, they met at Michelle's office around 9 p.m. Michelle had calmed down about Marty.

"I talked to him," she said, according to the proffer. "I scared him. I told him that I would ruin his career."

That pushed Marty's buttons, she told John. Hit him on the career. But she still was afraid of Marty—and still afraid of the former lover from Alabama. She said she would feel safer if she had a gun around, if only to scare these men if they ever tried to do anything.

John called Peyton Donald, but his wife said he was away. John told Michelle he'd get the gun, but they would have to wait a couple of days.

On either December 14 or 15, Peyton had returned. John borrowed the gun, then brought it to Michelle's office. It was unloaded and without an ammunition clip. Michelle placed the gun on her desk, and John left. He said he never knew where she'd put it after that, according to the proffer.

On Sunday, December 17, John met Michelle at Harbin & Associates. They went to Zorba's for lunch, then returned to her workplace. She told him about the office Christmas dinner that night, but not to worry. They could still see each other. She said she wouldn't be out too late. She asked John to meet her at the office around 11 p.m., just like they always did.

That night, John's proffer says, he watched a movie with wife Lourdes and her mother. When it ended, and the house was quiet, he left through a side door and drove to near Michelle's office, parking behind the buildings across the street as he always did. He kept the car idling and listened to the CD player.

Shortly after he arrived, he saw the Theers' Ford Explorer drive into the parking lot. John cut the engine, turned off the CD, got out of the car and started to walk across Raeford toward Michelle's office.

Suddenly, he heard shots. He hit the ground.

When he realized the gunfire was coming from Michelle's office, he ran across the street and headed toward the back of the building. As he ran, he heard another shot.

He approached the building on the side behind the shrubbery. When he rounded the corner, he saw a man on the ground lying in a pool of blood. He couldn't tell who he was, but knew from the amount of blood lost that the man was dead.

Michelle was standing over the man. She was pointing the gun at him. She had on latex gloves.

According to the proffer, Michelle didn't immediately recognize John. He told her it was him, and asked for the gun. She handed it to him. John told her to get away and call for help. John said he would take care of the gun.

Looking back, John couldn't recall exactly what Michelle had been wearing, but it wasn't the Santa-covered sweater that police found her in when they arrived at the scene.

John brought the gun back to his apartment and hid it in a duffel bag in the top of a closet, the proffer says.

The next day, John fired a gun at Jim's. He assumed that police would contact him and he wanted to account for the residue on his hands, according to the proffer.

When police contacted John on December 19, he called Michelle to find out what she knew. Michelle's mother answered, took a message and Michelle called back that night, saying she was using her father's cell phone because she was afraid police were tracking her calls. When she called him, John was in his apartment with Lourdes and her mother, who were watching TV. He went into another room and spoke to Michelle. She asked him to meet her at an empty house on English Saddle Road. John told Lourdes he was going out for coffee and met Michelle at the location. She had walked there with her dog. They drove to another neighborhood so they could talk in private.

"Michelle said she had to kill Marty because he was going to get away with all he did to her," according to the proffer.

She said that she would wrap up some of her own sweaters and put them under the Christmas tree so people would not think it odd that she had no presents there. She worried about police, and asked John about his interview with detectives. She told him in detail everything he should and shouldn't say from now on.

Still, she wasn't too concerned about the investigation. If anything, she thought police would have held her longer and spent more time at the scene. She was angry that police had kept Marty's commander away from her.

John returned the gun to Peyton on December 21 or 22. Michelle then asked to meet with him again in private. They drove to Rim Lake, a picnic spot just outside Fayetteville. The area was closed, but they hopped a fence, and Michelle talked about how to deal with police. As they walked around the lake, they got a shock: a police officer approached them, asking what they were doing. He said that somebody could break into their car because the cell phone was clearly visible.

After Marty's funeral in Colorado, Michelle returned to North Carolina earlier than she had told police, then went to Myrtle Beach with John for the weekend of January 10, staying at a Holiday Inn.

"She said she hated being at the funeral because she hated Marty," according to the proffer. "She said she was sick of everybody talking about him like he was perfect. She said if everybody knew him, there would be no sympathy. She was mad about having to act like the grieving widow. She said she hated him and he got what he deserved."

Saying she had bright attorneys, Michelle "became self-righteous," the proffer said. "She said she got justice when others could not. She acted impressed with her actions as though she accomplished a great feat."

But in the coming weeks, every time police interviewed somebody, Michelle became agitated. She craved information about the investigation, and insisted on dictating John's every move. She outlined various scenarios and responses. John told her that police had spoken to Lourdes, trying to make her say he wasn't home, scaring her and threatening her. Michelle wanted to talk to Lourdes herself, but didn't.

She told John that she had gone to Raleigh to take a polygraph, and though she'd been certain she could beat it because she had researched the process on the Internet and taken Xanax to relax, she still failed.

Michelle became increasingly nervous. She asked John about the gun. She wanted to get rid of it. John said he would do it, but Michelle insisted that she dispose of the gun herself. John suggested they both do it. John got the gun back from Peyton and brought it to Michelle's house. In the garage, they sat on an old carpet, dismantled the gun and filed off the serial numbers. Michelle packed the gun pieces in containers and took the carpet to a Dumpster.

Michelle then got an idea: she and John could marry. That way the law would protect them from testifying against each other.

"Michelle said they should go to the county courthouse and take care of it because it would be completed really quickly," the proffer says. "She said she did not want anyone to know."

The police, she told John, were incompetent, and the evidence wasn't there. She said that before the murder she had researched gunshot residue and knew that wearing latex gloves might not be sufficient to hide it.

"Don't worry, I'm not stupid," she said. "I knew to wear two pair."

The gloves, she said, had been taken care of.

That just left the gun pieces. According to the proffer, John and Michelle disposed of the dismantled gun during their February 2001 trip to Florida, stopping at exits along the way to dump a piece at a time in Dumpsters.

The trip served another purpose. Michelle told John that she wanted to see a former professor who could treat her for post-traumatic stress disorder by relaxing her, then talking her through the incident. Alarmed, John questioned the wisdom of telling all to the therapist, but Michelle assured John that she knew how the process worked and that she could control what she said.

In the end, she said, she could produce a record of psychological trauma from her husband's death if she were ever subpoenaed. If she ever had to go to trial, her attorneys would put a lot of women on the jury and they would have a "documented traumatized widow issue," according to the proffer.

When they returned from Florida, Peyton Donald called John asking about the gun. As Michelle listened to the conversation, she panicked. She told John to claim that the gun had been stolen. She said they could fake a break-in at the base and leave civilian police out of the investigation.

After John's arrest, Michelle told him that she had retained the best lawyers in Fayetteville, paying them with a money order. She said they golfed with the district attorney and John would never be convicted. During his confinement at Camp Lejeune, Michelle continued to contact him by mail and by phone. She used fake names on the letters—Lainey Smith and Wilma Sherman—and had other people write them for her. She talked to him at different phone numbers he was allowed to call.

"She said he needed to be calm, that her attorneys assured her there was no way he would ever be convicted based on the evidence," the proffer says. "She said she would stand by him and they would get out of this."

Her love, she said in her letters, endured.

"[She] missed him and loved him and . . . her life was empty without him," the proffer says. "She tossed and turned [at night] imagining his living situation."

When it was all over, they would live together, she said. She snuck him in a set of silver rings before the court-martial—she called them wedding rings, to prove her love for him. She implored him to be patient, in what she called "Secret Squirrel" mode. She loved him even more "because of the hardship he was enduring for her," the proffer says.

She even hinted at a double-suicide.

"She knew she would never survive in jail, and she said she had 'the method and the means to go to the next life,' and asked him to join her," says the proffer. "She said she had the means to make it happen and said she could sneak some pills to him if he wanted to go with her."

If need be, she said, she would take the stand in his court-martial, to "correct errors and clarify issues," the proffer says. She told him to be assertive with his defense attorneys and to remember to stick to the timeframe story that she had set up, according to the proffer.

After his conviction and transfer to Leavenworth, Michelle contacted him to say that she assumed she would soon be arrested. She said she wasn't scared, and was already building a "battered wife" defense. She had seen psychologists, whom she called idiots who bought everything she said. The therapy in Florida would also help in her defense, she told him.

"Michelle's contact with Staff Sgt. Diamond quickly decreased," the proffer says. "She became confident she would beat any charges the state would bring, and she talked to Staff Sgt. Diamond in shorter blocks and less frequently."

The proffer's narrative ends by saying why John was coming forward: "Staff Sgt. Diamond decided to talk about the incident as doubts about Michelle's sincerity came to light."

In summing up John's position, the proffer said that he'd helped Michelle cover up the murder because he'd believed her claims of abuse by Marty. John had loved Michelle and fallen under her spell, literally.

"She introduced him to religious ideas similar to Wicca," it says. "She prayed to goddesses and taught him about spells and magic. He bought into the idea that Michelle was his soul mate, and he had to protect her and goddesses would protect him. He considered himself bound to her by their beliefs and promises."

Once John helped destroy the gun, he felt he had gone too far to turn back, and that he would never be believed. He thought that at worst he would be found guilty of the cover-up, but not the actual murder. Only too late did he realize that his trust in Michelle was wrong.

"Staff Sgt. Diamond knows his actions on 17 December violated the law and he respects that he must serve time for covering up the incident," the proffer concludes. "But Staff Sgt. Diamond does not want to serve a sentence for the crimes he did not commit."

The proffer was provided to the military prosecutors, who provided it to the state prosecutors slowly building a case against Michelle. No deal was ever reached for John and he remains under a life-without-parole sentence. His attorney now claims on appeal that John was duped by the military, which only wanted to know what he knew and, it is claimed, never seriously considered his request for clemency. (Military prosecutors declined to comment.)

But is what John's proffer said the whole truth?

In her *U.S. News & World Report* interview, Michelle denied the most serious allegations, saying she hadn't murdered her husband, hadn't disposed of the gun, didn't practice witchcraft, hadn't conspired to cover up a murder, and, most assuredly, wasn't the manipulative cold-hearted beast portrayed in the proffer. Also, John never signed the proffer and he never testified about any of the allegations against Michelle under oath.

That could all change if John Diamond gets a new trial.